THE CINEMA OF RITHY PANH

GLOBAL FILM DIRECTORS

Edited by Homer B. Pettey, Professor of Film and Comparative Literature at University of Arizona, and R. Barton Palmer, Calhoun Lemon Professor Emeritus of English at Clemson University

Volumes in the Global Film Directors series explore cinematic innovations by prominent and emerging directors in major European, American, Asian, and African film movements. Each volume addresses the history of a director's *oeuvre* and its influence upon defining new cinematic genres, narratives, and techniques. Contributing scholars take a context-oriented approach to evaluating how these directors produced an identifiable style, paying due attention to those forces within the industry and national cultures that led to global recognition of these directors. These volumes address how directors functioned within national and global marketplaces, contributed to and expanded film movements, and transformed world cinema. By focusing on representative films that defined the directors' signatures, these volumes provide new critical focus upon international directors who are just emerging to prominence or whose work has been largely ignored in standard historical accounts. The series opens the field of *new auteurism* studies beyond film biographies by exploring directorial style as influencing global cinema aesthetics, theory, and economics.

Recent titles in the Global Film Directors series:

Leslie Barnes and Joseph Mai, eds., *The Cinema of Rithy Panh: Everything Has a Soul*
Nam Lee, *The Films of Bong Joon Ho*
Jim Leach, *The Films of Denys Arcand*

THE CINEMA OF RITHY PANH

Everything Has a Soul

EDITED BY
LESLIE BARNES AND JOSEPH MAI

RUTGERS UNIVERSITY PRESS
New Brunswick, Camden, and Newark, New Jersey, and London

Library of Congress Cataloging-in-Publication Data

Names: Barnes, Leslie, 1976- author. | Mai, Joseph, editor.
Title: The cinema of Rithy Panh : everything has a soul / edited by
Leslie Barnes and Joseph Mai.
Description: New Brunswick : Rutgers University Press, [2021] |
Series: Global film directors | Includes bibliographical references.
Identifiers: LCCN 2020044281 | ISBN 9781978809796 (paperback) |
ISBN 9781978809802 (cloth) | ISBN 9781978809819 (epub) |
ISBN 9781978809826 (mobi) | ISBN 9781978809833 (pdf)
Subjects: LCSH: Rithy Panh—Criticism and interpretation.
Classification: LCC PN1998.3.R5755 C56 2021 | DDC 791.4302/330922—dc23
LC record available at https://lccn.loc.gov/2020044281

A British Cataloging-in-Publication record for this book is available from the British Library.

♾ The paper used in this publication meets the requirements of the American National Standard for Information Sciences—Permanence of Paper for Printed Library Materials, ANSI Z39.48-1992.

www.rutgersuniversitypress.org

Manufactured in the United States of America

CONTENTS

CHRONOLOGY

1863–1953	Protectorate within French Indochina
March–October 1945	Japanese occupation
November 1953	Cambodia becomes independent from France under King Norodom Sihanouk
1949–1954	First Indochina War; the Vietnamese defeat the French at Điện Biên Phủ
1955–1970	Sihanouk abdicates the crown to found a political party, the Sangkum, and becomes prime minister
1955–1975	Second Indochina War/Vietnam War
April 1963	Rithy Panh is born in Phnom Penh
1967	Repression of the Samlaut uprising, a landmark of the early revolutionary movement
1967–1975	Cambodian Civil War between the Khmer Rouge and the Kingdom of Cambodia/Khmer Republic
1969	U.S. president Richard Nixon launches Operation Menu, an extensive bombing campaign in Cambodia; American bombing continues until 1973
March 1970	Sihanouk is deposed in a U.S.-backed coup; Lon Nol is self-proclaimed president
1970–1975	Khmer Republic period
April 1975	The Khmer Rouge enter Phnom Penh
1975–1979	Democratic Kampuchea period; Panh's family is evacuated to the countryside
January 1979	The Vietnamese invade and occupy the country, expelling the Khmer Rouge from Phnom Penh and establishing the People's Republic of Kampuchea (PRK); Panh leaves Cambodia for a refugee camp in Thailand
1980	Panh arrives in France, where he eventually studies at the Institut des Hautes Etudes Cinématographiques (IDHEC; today La Fémis)
1988	The Vietnamese withdraw from Cambodia

1989	Panh releases *Site 2*, his first documentary; PRK renamed the State of Cambodia
1991	Paris Peace Accords are signed
	Cambodia, Between War and Peace (*Cambodge, entre guerre et paix*)
1993	United Nations Transitional Authority in Cambodia monitors elections, resulting in a coalition government with Norodom Ranariddh (Funcinpec) and Hun Sen (Cambodian People's Party [CPP]) appointed as prime ministers
	"Souleymane Cissé," episode of "The cinema of our time" (*Souleymane Cissé. Cinéma, de notre temps*)
1994	Panh releases *Rice People* (*Neak Sre*), his first feature and the first Cambodian submission to the Academy Awards for Best Foreign Language Film
1995	*The Tan Family* (*La famille Tan*)
1996	*Bophana: A Cambodian Tragedy* (*Bophana, une tragédie cambodgienne*); "Prosthesis," episode of "Shedding light on a massacre" (*La prothèse. Lumière sur un massacre*)
1997	The Cambodian government requests assistance from the United Nations to begin prosecution of crimes committed between 1975 and 1979
1998	*One Night after the War* (*Un soir après la guerre*)
1999	Arrest of Kaing Guek Eav, alias Duch, the head of the S-21 interrogation center under the Khmer Rouge
2000	*The Land of the Wandering Souls* (*La terre des âmes errantes*)
2001	"Let the boat break its back, let the junk break open" (*Que la barque se brise, que la jonque s'entrouvre*)
	Publication of "Filmed speech: To vanquish terror" ("La parole filmée: Pour vaincre la terreur")
2003	The Cambodian government and the United Nations finalize an agreement to form the Extraordinary Chambers in the Courts of Cambodia (ECCC)
	S21: The Khmer Rouge Killing Machine (*S21, la machine de mort khmère rouge*)
	Publication of *La machine Khmère Rouge: Monti Santésok S-21* with Christine Chaumeau (Flammarion)

2004	*The People of Angkor* (*Les gens d'Angkor*)
2005	ECCC agreement enters into force
	The Burnt Theatre (*Les artistes du théâtre brûlé*)
2006	First staff members of the ECCC begin duty, national and international judges and coprosecutors sworn in
	Panh and Ieu Pannaker open the Bophana Audiovisual Resource Center, named for S-21 victim Hout Bophana, in Phnom Penh
2007	Arrest of Khieu Samphan, Ieng Sary, Nuon Chea, and Ieng Thirith; ECCC adopts Internal Rules
	Paper Cannot Wrap Ember (*Le papier ne peut pas envelopper la braise*)
	Publication of *Le papier ne peut pas envelopper la braise* with Louise Lorentz (Grasset)
2008	*The Sea Wall* (*Un barrage contre le Pacifique*)
2010	Duch found guilty of crimes against humanity in Case 001 and sentenced to thirty-five years' imprisonment
2011	*Duch, Master of the Forges of Hell* (*Duch, le maître des forges de l'enfer*)
	Shiiku, the Catch (*Gibier d'élevage*)
2012	Following appeals, the Supreme Court Chamber sentences Duch to life imprisonment
	Publication of *The Elimination: A Survivor of the Khmer Rouge Confronts His Past and the Commandant of the Killing Fields* with Christophe Bataille (*L'élimination*, Grasset)
2013	Death of Ieng Sary, Brother Number 3
	The Missing Picture (*L'image manquante*)
	Publication of *L'image manquante* with Christophe Bataille (Grasset)
2014	Nuon Chea and Khieu Samphan found guilty of crimes against humanity in Case 002/01 and sentenced to life imprisonment
2015	"France is our homeland" (*La France est notre patrie*), episode of "Forbidden docs" (*Docs interdits*)
2016	*Exile* (*Exil*)
2018	*Graves without a Name* (*Les tombeaux sans nom*)

2019 Death of Nuon Chea

2020 *Irradiated* (*Irradiés*)

Publication of "Peace with the dead" with Christophe Bataille (*La paix avec les morts*, Grasset)

NOTE

The following sources have been consulted in the compilation of this timeline: eccc.gov.kh; David P. Chandler, *A History of Cambodia*, 4th ed. (New York: Routledge, 2018); Alexander Laban Hinton, *Man or Monster: The Trial of a Khmer Rouge Torturer* (Durham, NC: Duke University Press, 2016); Khatharya Um, *From the Land of Shadows: War, Revolution and the Making of the Cambodian Diaspora* (New York: New York University Press, 2015). The release dates for Panh's films correspond throughout this volume to those listed on his IMDb.com filmography page.

THE CINEMA OF RITHY PANH

INTRODUCTION

Rithy Panh and the Cinematic Image

LESLIE BARNES AND JOSEPH MAI

A political film should unearth what it invented.

—Voice-over in *The Missing Picture*

Rithy Panh was born in 1964 in Phnom Penh. In 1975, after years of political instability (a coup d'état, war with Communists of both Khmer and Vietnamese origins, the massive carpet-bombing of Cambodia by American forces), the Khmer Rouge entered Phnom Penh, overthrowing the government and emptying the city. A reign of terror, forced labor, and starvation took hold of Cambodia for nearly four years and claimed the lives of much of Panh's family. Panh managed to survive and, after some time spent in a United Nations Border Relief Organization (UNBRO) refugee camp in Thailand, made his way to France at age sixteen, where he eventually attended the Institut des Hautes Etudes Cinématographiques (IDHEC, now La Fémis) film school in Paris.[1] After nearly a decade in France, he returned to a still volatile Cambodia to make his first film, the documentary *Site 2* (1989), in another UNBRO camp.

Growing out of this experience, Panh's cinema is rooted in the tumultuous history of Cambodia, especially the period of Democratic Kampuchea (DK), which he knew firsthand: like *Site 2*, many of his nearly twenty documentaries, feature films, and adaptations document the effects of war, genocide, displacement, dehumanization, and loss. They explore the enduring effects of the period on the individual and collective identities of survivors: their need to memorialize what has been lost, establish a functioning truth, assign responsibility, and seek justice for crimes against humanity. But this cinematic return to the DK period also involves repeatedly situating the Cambodian recent past and present in long-term historical structures and exploring broader themes that bring more depth to his portrayal of the Cambodian people. Panh frames many of his interrogations through the lenses of colonialism, independent nationalism, and imperialism, tracing, for example, the various historical contours of local and transnational regimes of economic exploitation. He is further committed to documenting Cambodia's transition from the DK period to democracy and the current global economy, and his films examine the effects of this transition on the urban environment, labor inequalities, and sexual exploitation, among other social issues. Panh is at once a Cambodian and a World filmmaker, and his work reflects a deep and ongoing engagement with human rights and the forces of dehumanization; with the often-overlapping categories of victim and perpetrator; with trauma and healing; and with the past, the present, and the future of Cambodia and its cinema.

This work has garnered great international acclaim and critical attention. Panh has been in competition for the Palme d'Or at the Cannes Film Festival and has taken home the festival's François Chalais Award for *S21: The Khmer Rouge Killing Machine* (2003), the France Culture Award for his commitment to Cambodian cinematographic memory (2007), and the Un Certain Regard award for innovative filmmaking for *The Missing Picture* (2013). *The Missing Picture* has also won, among others, a Lumière Award and a Cinema for Peace Award for Best Documentary. Panh's first feature, *Rice People* (1994), was the first Cambodian film submitted to the Academy of Motion Picture Arts and Sciences for Best Foreign Language Film (*The Missing Picture* became the first Cambodian film to make the list of nominees in 2013). When asked about his success, and in particular about his status as the first Cambodian filmmaker to win at Cannes, Panh is quick to share it with the Cambodian filmmakers who came before him—King Norodom Sihanouk, for example—and with the Cambodian people, for their resilience and artistic capacity to make award-winning films just over thirty years after such political and social devastation. "It means we're alive," he says, "creativity is here, imagination is here."[2] His films have also been recognized at film festivals in Vancouver, San Francisco, and Torino, and at the International Human Rights Festival in Nurenberg. In 2013, Panh was named the Asian filmmaker of the year at the Pusan International Film Festival, and in 2018, his work opened the Venice Film Festival.

In addition to his film work, Panh cofounded with Ieu Pannakar in 2006 the Bophana Audiovisual Resource Center, which not only offers free access for all to Cambodia's audiovisual documentary database but also provides vocational training for archivists as well as film, television, and multimedia technicians. In the same year, the first staff members took up their duties at the Extraordinary Chambers in the Courts of Cambodia (ECCC), otherwise known as the Khmer Rouge Tribunal, and the judges and coprosecutors were sworn in. One year later, Kaing Guek Eav, alias Duch, the director of the infamous S-21 interrogation center, was charged with crimes against humanity in Case 001, and in 2010, he was found guilty and sentenced to life imprisonment. The court has been subject to extreme domestic and international political pressure, however, and only two other Khmer Rouge leaders have been sentenced since. In 2018, Nuon Chea and

Khieu Samphan, already condemned for crimes against humanity in 2014, were found guilty of genocide against the Vietnamese and the Cambodian Chams (Cases 002/02 and 002/01, respectively). It was possibly the ECCC's final conviction, and it is not clear that the trials have brought a sense of justice or closure to victims.[3] The Bophana Center has been a chief collaborator in the cultural reparations initiatives that have emerged in response to Case 002 and pursues multiple projects that offer Cambodians the possibility of learning this history for themselves.[4] Bertrand Tavernier has written that the Bophana Center "questions memories, discloses and discovers them."[5] The archives disseminated by the center, along with its various production projects and the frequent cultural events it houses, are a complementary alternative to other institutional representations of Cambodian history. Uninhibited by legal procedures and, for the most part, political constraints, Bophana invites survivors, Cambodian and international scholars, students, and interested people from all classes and backgrounds to discover Cambodian history in all of its contradictory representations.

Panh is also a producer and mentor, contributing to the filmic endeavors of others in Cambodia, including the Franco-Cambodian filmmaker Davy Chou and Angelina Jolie, who directed an adaptation of Loung Ung's *First They Killed My Father: A Daughter of Cambodia Remembers* (2017). He has produced work by some of his mentees at the Bophana Center, such as Lida Chan and Guillaume Suon's documentary film, *Red Wedding* (*Noces rouges*, 2012), an intimate look at the experience of one woman who was coerced to marry under the Khmer Rouge and who later filed a civil complaint with the ECCC. The Bophana Center has more recently been working with Oxfam on a program called "Amplifying Voices," designed to provide two years of training in documentary filmmaking to twelve young people, especially women, from disenfranchized groups of the Mondulkiri and Ratanakiri regions in Cambodia. The center's "One Dollar Project" provides a platform for young activists worldwide who wish to use film and new media to create a "speaking space" for those living below the poverty level—not to speak for them, but to give them the chance to speak for themselves.[6] In these initiatives, Panh does not just contribute to building the infrastructure of the Cambodian film industry while facilitating the dissemination of Cambodian culture and memory across the globe; he encourages regional and transnational dialogue—through participatory cinema and multimedia—about access, discrimination, and injustice.

FILMED SPEECH, THE MISSING PICTURE, AND THE SOUL IN EVERYTHING

In his important early essay "La parole filmée" ("Filmed speech"), Panh refers to the Khmer Rouge, not for the last time, as a "machine," and precisely as a "memory erasing machine."[7] To become this machine, Khmer Rouge ideologues invented expressions designed to dehumanize, such as "reduction to dust" (*kamtech*), which they used in the place of "killing," or slogans like "to keep you is no benefit; to destroy you is no loss."[8] Their use of images and propaganda film, though less extensive, also screened out the starvation, exhaustion, and suffering by showing images of an agrarian utopia full of happy, enthusiastic laborers. The voice-over in *The Missing Picture* speaks of a "reality" that "Pol Pot forges conformant with his desire." The real bodies hidden behind this simulacrum were buried in unidentifiable graves—"graves without names"—lost to future generations. The Khmer Rouge permanently altered the Cambodian society and culture that had preceded them. They wiped out places of culture and memory, banned religious practice, repurposed schools into centers of torture and death, emptied cities, and drove their inhabitants into the countryside to become enslaved labor. The "imagined community"—the immense, modern independent nation-building projects of Prince Norodom Sihanouk[9]—disappeared into the three years, eight months, and twenty nights of the Khmer Rouge's paranoid utopia.

The erasure of the Cambodian people has extended beyond the period to include how media have represented its survivors after the wars. After the Khmer Rouge's failure and their eventual departure from the capital in 1979, thousands remained in the no-man's-land of the UNBRO camps on the Thai border—people like Rithy Panh himself, who spent some time there before migrating to France as a refugee. When he returned a decade later to Mairut to make *Site 2*, he was struck by the fact that contemporary discussions of the camp had little to do with the experiences of the people actually living in it. The ongoing Vietnamese occupation and the Khmer Rouge rebels dominated the talk of the day, "but nobody spoke about the kids who had never seen a paddy, who didn't even know where rice came from. In the Site 2 camp, none of the children under ten knew anything but barbed wire and thought rice came from trucks."[10] Documentaries and newsreels mediated the image of Cambodians through the analyses of non-Cambodian intellectuals, political commentators, and United Nations committees. Cambodians themselves were depicted as wordless victims, their image integrated into whatever conceptual logic the commentators had designed to explain their situation.

Panh has followed a different ethical and political path, one that has required a creative revision of cinematic technique. Panh was the first filmmaker in Cambodia to eliminate the voice-over by placing the camera and sound boom close enough to allow people to speak for themselves. He later developed such practices into the notion of *la parole filmée*, with which he names the art of restoring language to the body and its own attempts to make meaning rather than imposing a conceptual grid upon these attempts. Sometimes Yim Om, whose daily experience is at the core of *Site 2*, thinks out loud, repeats herself, stops speaking to take deep breaths. Panh does not edit these verbal wanderings into quotable sound bites. As he explained: "If I edited Yim Om's story, it would no longer be her words." Or: "I feel like I'm killing someone if I edit out their breathing. Now the editor knows that she has to respect the breath of the words. If you do not respect breathing, you don't respect anything."[11] Ambient sounds—tracking sound shots of chirping insects, the voices of children just on the other side of Yim Om's flimsy walls, the loudspeakers blaring out music, all recorded without accompanying images—similarly convey the life of a place experienced from within.[12] From here it is just a step on a continuum toward the use of music. Panh's longtime composer, Marc Marder, is first asked to "listen to people speak, the sounds of the neighborhood, the sounds of the rice fields."[13] Thus Panh creates a cinematic image with two functions. On the one hand, the image testifies to Cambodia's history and to the fate of its people through silent, though legible, signs inscribed on landscapes and bodies, in words and sounds. On the other, it remains silent in its raw, untranslatable presence, in the slowness of the exhale, for example, which carries no message other than the existence of a life.

This innovative cinema has a profound effect on the viewer precisely because it questions the grounding of our own epistemological positions and commitments. Instead of imparting knowledge about Yim Om's reality, Panh's conception of documentary forces us to encounter the reversibility of sensorial experience and that which bears meaning, neither of which is privileged, and in relation to which we have no special capacity based on who we are or what we know. It is no surprise, then, that Panh's cinema has attracted the interest of Jacques Rancière, whose notion of "mute speech" (*parole muette*), much like Panh's *parole filmée*, figures the image as "a way in which things themselves speak and are silent."[14] Much of Rancière's project is concerned with distinguishing between forms of visibility (e.g., in a film, in a work of literature) and the epistemological and social frameworks in which we receive and interpret them. These frameworks determine who and what is to be seen, heard, and represented within the social distribution of meanings, but for Rancière, they rarely line up with experience or with the expressions individuals develop in response to their position or situation. Panh's filming enacts a shift, opening a new perspective onto the world, wherein those who have previously been ignored take their place center stage, but in a way that is not always immediately comprehensible.[15] Panh's first film, *Site 2*, testifies to the experience of genocide and its aftermath, not through Yim Om's speech but through her breath, through the cries of children playing, through the watchful gaze of the camp's weary inhabitants. To understand this testimony—to understand how the camp "speaks and is silent"—demands a shift in the viewer's approach to the cinematic image. And in this shift, the well-ordered community in which we think we live and acquire knowledge is undermined, its "sensory fabric" torn and woven anew.[16]

Panh takes a similar approach in documentary films about those who did not survive the Khmer Rouge years, such as *Bophana: A Cambodian Tragedy* (1996), centered on the identification photograph made of Hout Bophana just after her arrest at the S-21 interrogation center, where the Khmer Rouge tortured and killed thousands.[17] This photograph, like those of Panh's loved ones, has an indexical connection between the present and those who have been lost and has attained a kind of sacred status in Panh's work, a bit like a Roman imago. It contains a striking juxtaposition of, on one hand, the macabre bureaucratic control implied in Bophana's Khmer Rouge–issued black clothes and the prisoner number pinned to her collar and, on the other hand, her handsome face and an intense gaze that suggests both fear and determined resistance. Panh combines this photograph and other "evidence" collected by her Khmer Rouge torturers (love letters she wrote in French to her husband, Sitha, some of the details of her "confession") with family recollections and other testimony to reconstitute something of a presence and distinguish Bophana from some of the 6,000 or so other photographs found at S-21. This "use" of the photograph differs profoundly from the description Lindsay French gives of the S-21 photographs displayed in a Museum of Modern Art exhibit in 1997, in which some twenty photographs were reproduced with no individual or cultural context beyond the simple confrontation with the viewer.[18] In Panh's film, Bophana's own language accompanies the index, in an ethical displacement of other uses and abuses of the victim's image.

The ethical dimension of filmed speech has remained at the heart of this cinema, but Panh's images have grown in complexity, as is illustrated by his genre-defying poetic essay film, *The Missing Picture*. Near its beginning, the "missing picture" of the title seems to refer to a photograph that would give visible proof of the crimes of the Khmer Rouge, something that might be useful to the ECCC. As Leshu Torchin has pointed out, however, the notion quickly widens to include "the recollection of all missing images: the Cambodia that once was, the stories of the victim, and the childhood of Panh himself." [19] In this recollection, Panh creates some of the most complex images in contemporary documentary, combining autobiographical testimony, paper archives, film reels, scenes from Panh's previous films, models and clay figurines standing in for the disappeared, diorama, voice-over, animation, painting, and old family photos. Encountering these images, the viewer repeatedly confronts the lack at their core. There is a brilliant example of Panh's creativity in the clay figurines representing his family that were carved for the film and play various roles in the mise-en-scène. They evoke the Cambodian earth, the rice fields and the killing fields, traditional artforms and autobiography, even artistic creation itself, since we see not only the figurines but also their fabrication and the invention of characters through them. Through editing, camera movement, animation, and voice-over, Panh's cinema, as we often say of cinema in general, comes close to bringing these figures to life. At the same time, they remain noticeably immobile figurines. They seem to be in an agonizing state between life and death: earth aspiring toward life, life blocked by stasis. This "missing picture" also evokes complex and important debates about the ethics, ontology, and aesthetics of images and their use in films evoking horrific events and their effect on the present. There are many reasons, practical and moral, to conclude that images are "missing," or inadequate to the suffering of the DK period. At the end of *The Missing Picture,* Panh acknowledges that he "has not found the missing image" that seemed to be at the origin of the film. At the same time, he avoids complex debates over the status of the image by recognizing the importance (and limits) of artistic creation. The image he has made, "invented" in the film, provides him with a fragile but palpable presence: he can "look at it"; he can "hold it in [his] hand." The image does not restitute what has been lost, but it is still, "like a beloved face," combining the proximity and distance at the heart of film images. Though Panh's cinema is deeply rooted in the loss and suffering he and so many Cambodians experienced during the tragic period, this continued act of creating stands as a form of resistance to whatever forces seek to silence the survivors and others who have no voice in contemporary society. A political film is a film of invention, as Panh claims in the epigraph that opens this introduction. Rancière, who believes that Panh's work helps displace and renew discussions of documentary and "the intolerable," does not hesitate to call Panh's films "a fiction."[20]

The political film is also a film that "unearths," since it gives form to experiences that had no previous place in the distribution of the sensible and invites us to acknowledge their power. At the very end of *The Missing Picture,* Panh offers the image as a kind of insistent gift eliciting a continuous response from the viewer: "And this missing picture, I now give it to you, so that it never ceases to seek us." The viewer who accepts such a gift, and the responsibility it entails, joins the filmmaker for the first time in a community, an "us," cemented in the way the image reorients our senses. For in Panh's cinematic image, the senses are not ontological absolutes but modes of relating with the diversity of vitalities surrounding us, with the soul in everything. Indeed, in Rithy Panh's work, "everything has a soul. Trees have a soul. Rice has a soul."[21] Clay has a soul. Even monsters have a soul. "Soul" is not to be understood here as a mystic or transcendent energy that names one kind of being; on the contrary, following Buddhist and animist worldviews in Cambodia, "soul," like "spirit," names the interrelatedness of all persons—human and other-than-human—within "a richly diverse community of life."[22] And in this ongoing reorientation of the senses, Panh's films often render a deep and ritualized communion with these persons—the people, places, and objects of Cambodia, past and present—each of which is embedded in a relationship of dignity and mutual respect.

To take but one example, in *Graves without a Name* (2018), Panh's most intensely personal film, in which he attempts to locate the resting places of his family members, the filmmaker looks to trees, ponds, and fields as witnesses to the deaths of thousands of Cambodians. Reflecting the animist worldview according to which life is not separated from death or inanimation, but instead intertwined with both,[23] the camera repeatedly approaches these landscapes with deference, lingering with them in long takes, communicating with them as other-than-human persons. Having lived through these moments of death and suffering, their other-than-human lives contain the memory of and were themselves transformed by the violent encounters unfolding within and around them, on their surface. An unconventional, (in)animate archive, today they share their embodied knowledge with those who "see through different eyes or know by a different sense."[24] The trees rustling in the afternoon breeze do not point to the unmarked graves of his missing family, though traces of the dead—visual and material, imagined and encountered—remain throughout these landscapes; they nevertheless testify as "active and relational beings, participants" in the traumatic past and "in the wider ecology of life" in its wake,[25] including as witnesses to one man's efforts to honor the dead. Though the attempt to locate his family would suggest a quest for closure, such scenes of communion—with the living, the inanimate, the dead—abound in Panh's cinema and point to a broader effort to create and sustain peaceful cohabitation in the absence of answers, of justice, of resolution.

AFTERMATH, TRANSITION, JUSTICE, CINEMA: GOALS AND ORGANIZATION OF THE CURRENT VOLUME

While curating this collection, we were guided by the idea of both deepening and broadening the perspective on Panh's work, which is best known for his lifelong quest to make meaning of the genocidal period in Cambodia and preserve memory for its victims and survivors. The contributors who write here about such influential documentaries as *The Missing Picture* and *S21* respond to and expand the existing scholarship, bringing novel approaches to bear and thus taking the conversation in new directions. We have also taken Panh's work as a catalyst for exploring themes that are occasioned by, but surpass, the brutal Khmer Rouge years. Thus, a number of chapters focus on themes such as empire and colonialism, global capitalism and labor, gender, diaspora, and human rights. These chapters also often include analyses of Panh's earlier or less frequently discussed films. To pursue this broad range, we have wanted the volume to be as interdisciplinary as possible: the reader will find essays by scholars of history, anthropology, genocide studies, diaspora studies, art history, literature, film studies, and philosophy. We have also sought a diversity of approaches in another way. Throughout the volume there are references to Western intellectuals who have shaped discourses about Cambodian history (Benedict Anderson, Elizabeth Becker, and David Chandler, for example), the ethical and artistic implications of genocide (Jean Améry, Jacques Rancière, Marianne Hirsch), as well as artists who have already visited similar terrain (Marguerite Duras, Claude Lanzmann).[26] But we have also endeavored to integrate explorations of Cambodian ways of remembering, coping with trauma, and seeking justice and spiritual healing. This work, spearheaded by Cambodian or diasporic scholars with first-hand experience, has contributed to a growing body of concepts and practices that are increasingly in dialogue with more familiar Western ones. These multiple approaches reflect not only the richness of Cambodia's history and cultural beliefs but also the complexity of Panh's personal history as a survivor, refugee, returnee, filmmaker, activist, and writer on the global stage.

To guide the reader, we have organized the volume around four distinct, though imbricated, lines of inquiry in Panh's oeuvre. These general themes, which center on questions of survival, (neo)imperialisms, justice, and filmmaking, respond to the filmmaker's ongoing engagement with Cambodia's past, present, and future; they also highlight a keen attention to the complex and shifting intersections among the personal, the political, the archival, and the aesthetic in the wake of conflict.

In the first part, "Aftermath: A Cinema of Postwar Survival," the contributors examine Panh's depiction of the grave humanitarian crises that took shape in the 1970s, and whose effects continued through subsequent transitions in power in the 1980s and 1990s. Focused on survival in spite of the exceptionally harsh conditions created during the DK period, this part highlights the equally mundane and profound transformations of the lives of Cambodian people in the wake of genocide: their family structures, their built environment, and their intimate lives in exile. Boreth Ly analyzes the debilitating psychological effects of the country's fractured social structures on women, drawing out the figure of the "mad mother" in *Rice People, One Night after the War* (1998), and *The Burnt Theatre* (2005). With a focus on gender discrimination and mental illness as a source of cultural shame, Ly argues for this figure as the embodiment of the morally incapacitated Cambodian nation in the post–Khmer Rouge period. Joseph Mai turns to the built environment, especially the monumental nation-building project of New Khmer architecture, and its depiction in *The Burnt Theatre*. This film, which explores national architecture and national identity as sites "of loss *and* reclamation," studies the return to life and the regenerative force of creative work within the postconflict ruins of Phnom Penh. For Mai, the stubborn pursuit of the arts despite the difficult circumstances in which the artists find themselves does not merely attest to their capacity to create anew; it serves as a model for Panh's own work. Khatharya Um examines states of physical and psychic displacement in her study of *Exile* (2016) and the French telefilm *Que la barque se brise, que la jonque s'entrouvre* (Let the boat break its back, let the junk break open, 2001), asking us to consider the effects of genocidal violence on the individual, the family, and the diasporic community. Um offers these films as two poles of "an experiential continuum" that together reveal the paradoxical postgenocidal condition within which both remembering and forgetting torment.

The second part, "From Colonial to Global Cambodia," examines the ways in which Panh's cinema acknowledges a number of supranational cultural, political, and economic contexts. Though the part is organized according to seemingly distinct historical stages—colonialism, imperialism, and capitalism—the chapters, like the films they study, point to the interrelatedness of these contexts. Through an emphasis on cinematic techniques such as point of view, adaptation, and the use of archives, they demonstrate how Panh's films encourage an active, almost archaeological, means of viewing Cambodia's place in the world. Jack A. Yeager and Rachel Harrison study Panh's 2008 adaptation of Marguerite Duras's most explicitly anticolonial novel, *The Sea Wall*, focusing on how both imagine the characters' struggle in relation to the land, colonizing powers, and their cultural identities. They argue that by concentrating on the rural space as a site of (potential) resistance and exploring local agents of exploitation, Panh's film reasserts the political critique delivered in Duras's novel and largely sidelined in its reception. In her essay on Panh's silent film, *La France est notre patrie* (France is our homeland, 2015), Jennifer Cazenave interrogates the filmmaker's return to the colonial past one year after releasing *The Missing Picture*. Cazenave presents Panh as a *chasseur d'images* whose excavation of archival footage from the colonies not only "reconstruct[s] a violent history *through* cinema but reveals the missing pictures of imperialism in "a seldom shown history *of* cinema." Cathy J. Schlund-Vials's essay juxtaposes the impersonal and the intimate, the view from above and the view from below, to describe *Shiiku, the Catch* (2011) as an instance of narrative reckoning. In his loose remake of Nagisa Oshima's film about a captured foreign fighter pilot in Japan, who becomes an American captured in Cambodia during the American War in Vietnam, Panh incorporates archival footage taken by American forces as they carpet-bombed Cambodia, which he contrasts with an "on-the-ground" narrative about the rise of the Khmer Rouge in a local village. In the final essay of this part, Leslie Barnes considers the relationship between the free flow of global capital and the limited mobility of the working poor in *The Land of the Wandering Souls* (2000). Developing the metaphors of connectivity and collectivity suggested by the film's focus on the project of laying Cambodia's first fiber-optic cables, Barnes underscores Panh's insistence not only on the thread of labor exploitation running throughout modern Cambodian history but also on the pursuit of dignity and mutual aid within such regimes.

The aims of the ECCC, which charged its first defendant in 2007, have been to establish the truth of the Khmer Rouge regime, punish its top cadres, and provide reparations for those targeted by its violence. Working before and alongside these institutional efforts, Panh's films have crafted encounters with the Khmer Rouge and its survivors and, remarkably, *between* the two. The chapters in the third part, "The Question of Justice," explore how Panh frames both within the context of the ECCC and indicate why his work is at the forefront of debates about how film represents crimes against humanity. Stéphanie Benzaquen-Gautier and John Kleinen seek to establish the specificity of Panh's approach to filming perpetrators by comparing it to that of other filmmakers, in Cambodia and elsewhere, including Joshua Oppenheimer's *The Act of Killing* (2012). In their analyses, the authors emphasize the signal importance of gesture in relation to word and image, memory and archive, noting Panh's interest in both the documentary and the ethical dimensions of filming the gestures of killing. In his study of Kaing Guek Eav, alias Duch, Donald Reid compares Panh's account of the head of the Tuol Sleng prison with that of the French anthropologist, François Bizot, who met Duch prior to his time at Tuol Sleng. Where the latter sees the universality of evil in Duch, coming to grips with his own capacity for cruelty in the confrontation, Panh uncovers a particular spirit motivating the ideologue's killings and laments that Duch failed to confront himself during their encounter. Raya Morag rounds out this part with a sustained reading of reconciliation and resentment in Panh's cinema. Beginning with a critique of the temporality of a politically motivated forgiveness, which involves the intervention of a third-party nonvictim and is associated with reconciliation, Morag draws out the strategies with which Panh develops a "nonvindictive moral resentment." These strategies, which she identifies in *Duch, Master of the Forges of Hell* (2011) and to a lesser extent, *S21: The Khmer Rouge Killing Machine* and *Graves without a Name*, resist the reconciliatory imperative to "move on" and point to "a way to distinguish how evil might be experienced, symbolized, judged, and finally incorporated into a system of ethics."

The essays in the volume's final part, "Memory, Voice, and Cinematic Practice," pose a series of interrelated questions: How does a filmmaker make images of events whose transmission is in doubt? What is the proper ethical framework within which one films the personal experience of genocide? How do archiving and remembering differ? What is the role or limit of the photographic index? Filming his own experience of history has pushed Rithy Panh to the forefront of formal investigations into the function of the cinema to represent, commemorate, and explore personal subjectivity. The chapters in the final part of the volume account for the ethical depth and cinematic richness of Panh's cinema while approaching broader formal considerations in new ways. Lindsay French opens the part with a consideration of Panh's ethical, political, and aesthetic approach to *Site 2*, his first feature-length film, which she places into dialogue with her own experience of conducting ethnographic research in the camp for more than twenty months at nearly the same moment in time. Reflecting on questions of resistance and privilege, both within and without the camp, and on the quest for a framework that could make its dangers and dehumanizing monotony intelligible both to the filmmaker/ethnographer and to the outside world, French presents the film as the beginning of a "work in progress." This work is not just a cinematic one, and not just one in which cinema speaks of and in response to its time—though it is and does both of these things; it is one in which cinema "make[s] and remake[s] the human world." In a similar vein, Vicente Sánchez-Biosca explores how Panh's cinema produces images that seek not just to represent reality but to create it. His focus is the regular presence in Panh's films of Hout Bophana, a young woman who was executed for the love letters she wrote her husband, conjugal love having been forbidden under Pol Pot. Tracing this presence—which is sometimes fleeting, sometimes only a suggestion—through his study of a number of filmmaking techniques, including composition, montage, and sound, Sánchez-Biosca offers a reading of Bophana as a force driving Panh's cinema forward. David LaRocca contributes to debates on the typology of images used in documentary about war, violence, and genocide, especially around the so-called indexical nature of the mechanically recorded image. Situating Panh within a broad range of documentary filmmakers, this chapter explores the heuristic effect that *The Missing Picture*'s complex style has had on the ontological, epistemological, and ethical principles involved. LaRocca argues that Panh's approach to the "essay film" does not "forestall the act of judgment" as some other films do, but sustains it continuously. Closing the volume is Soko Phay's essay on Panh as a "storyteller of the extreme." In her discussion of *Exile* and *Graves without a Name*, Phay reflects on the possibility of conveying extreme experiences such as the one Panh survived and on the signal importance of art in his interrogations of "the strange ways in which those who have survived relate to memory and to the fact of their own survival." Art and creativity, she argues, encourage us to remember, to think the unthinkable, to live on.

NOTES

1. For an autobiographical account of this period, see Rithy Panh with Christophe Bataille, *The Elimination: A Survivor of the Khmer Rouge Confronts His Past and the Commandant of the Killing Fields*, trans. John Cullen (New York: Other Press, 2013).
2. See "7 Questions with Rithy Panh," *Phnom Penh Post*, May 30, 2013, https://www.youtube.com/watch?v–QOzBvOtvtys.
3. The ECCC's decision to include civil parties in the proceedings marks an important development in victims' rights in the context of mass atrocities, and there were nearly 4,000 civil party applicants in Case 002. Victim participation in the trials has not been without its challenges, however, procedural and other; managing victims' expectations regarding justice and compensation, for example—expectations which were not met with Case 001—has led some to raise questions about other meaningful forms of victim participation. See Elisa Hoven, Mareike Feiler, and Saskia Scheibel, "Victims in Trials of Mass Crimes: A Multi-perspective Study of Civil Party Participation at the Extraordinary Chambers in the Courts of Cambodia." *Cologne Occasional Papers on International Peace and Security Law,* no. 3. Cologne: Cologne University Press, 2013; Elisa Hoven, "Civil Party Participation in Trials of Mass Crimes: A Qualitative Study at the Extraordinary Chambers in the Courts of Cambodia," *Journal of International Criminal Justice* 12, no. 1 (2014): 81–107.
4. Among the many projects with which Bophana is involved, see, for example, the 2018 exhibit on forced marriage under the Khmer Rouge, which brought together five young visual artists

(https://www.phnompenhpost.com/post-life-arts-culture/young-artists-explore-lasting-suffering-forced-marriages), and the *Phka Sla Krom Angkar* dance performance, which premiered in 2017 and represents a collaboration with the Sophiline Arts Ensemble, the Transcultural Psychosocial Organization, and Kdei Karuna, a national peace-building and reconciliation NGO. Bophana has also developed a multimedia education project called "App-learning on Khmer Rouge History," which combines an audiovisual app and classroom integration training with Cambodian high schools.

5. This quote is taken from the Bophana Center website opening page: see https://bophana.org/.

6. See http://onedollar.bophana.org/en/about.

7. Rithy Panh, "La parole filmée: Pour vaincre la terreur," *Communications* 71 (2001): 373. Unless otherwise noted, all translations are our own.

8. See Henri Locard, *Le "Petit Livre Rouge" de Pol Pot ou les paroles de l'Angkar entendues dans le Cambodge des Khmers rouges du 17 avril 1975 au 7 janvier 1979* (Paris: L'Harmattan, 1997).

9. The postindependence nation-building project is a key example through which Benedict Anderson defines this notion. See Benedict Anderson, *Imagined Communities: Reflections on the Origin and Spread of Nationalism*, rev. ed. (London: Verso, 2006).

10. Panh, "La parole filmée," 374.

11. Panh, 391.

12. See more on the use of everyday sounds in Panivong Norindr, "The Sounds of Everyday Life in Rithy Panh's Documentaries," *French Forum* 35, no. 2–3 (2010): 181–190.

13. Panh "La parole filmée," 390.

14. Jacques Rancière, *The Future of the Image*, trans. Gregory Elliott (London: Verso, 2007), 13. See also Jacques Rancière, *Mute Speech*, trans. James Swenson (New York: Columbia University Press, 2011).

15. Other films, some more difficult to access, such as *Cambodia between War and Peace* (1991), *People of Angkor* (2004), or *Paper Cannot Wrap* (2007), follow similar imperatives, rejecting preconceived interpretive frameworks and immersing the viewer in the daily lives of people. The first describes the daily struggles of a number of returnees to Phnom Penh at the moment of the United Nations Transitional Authority in Cambodia (UNTAC); the second focuses on the difficulties of laborers at the Angkor temples, going so far as to present their own, alternative interpretations to temple carvings; the last immerses the viewer in the daily lives and conversations of Phnom Penh sex workers without recourse to moral judgment. Each of the films establishes a relation of empathy and curiosity between the films' subjects and the viewer. For more on this immersion and its effects, see Leslie Barnes, "Objects of Pleasure: Epistephilia and the Sex Worker in Rithy Panh's *Le papier ne peut pas envelopper la braise*," *French Cultural Studies* 5, no. 2 (2015): 56–65; and Joseph Mai, "*Site 2*: Style and Encounter in Rithy Panh's Cinéma-monde," in *Cinéma-monde: Decentred Perspectives on Global Filmmaking in French*, ed. Michael Gott and Thibaut Schilt (Edinburgh: Edinburgh University Press, 2018), 25–44.

16. Jacques Rancière, *The Emancipated Spectator*, trans. Gregory Elliott (London: Verso, 2009), 56.

17. Panh was inspired by Elizabeth Becker, who first discussed Hout Bophana's story in *When the War Was Over: Cambodia and the Khmer Rouge Revolution* (New York: Simon and Schuster, 1986). See also Vicente Sánchez-Biosca's chapter in this volume.

18. Lindsay French, "Exhibiting Terror," in *Truth Claims: Representation and Human Rights*, ed. Mark Philip Bradley and Patrice Petro (New Brunswick, NJ: Rutgers University Press, 2002), 131–155.

19. Leshu Torchin, "Mediation and Remediation: La parole filmée in Rithy Panh's *The Missing Picture (L'image manquante)*," *Film Quarterly* 68, no. 1 (2014): 34.

20. Rancière, *Emancipated Spectator*, 102.

21. Rithy Panh, "Un barrage contre le Pacifique (The Sea Wall)—Interview with Rithy Panh," interview by Michael Guillen, *ScreenAnarchy*, September 25, 2008, https://screenanarchy.com/2008/09/tiff08-un-barrage-contre-le-pacifique-the-sea-wallinterview-with-rithy-panh.html.

22. Graham Harvey, *Animism: Respecting the Living World* (London: Hurst, 2005, 2017 edition), 119. In response to a question about the spiritual aspect of his work in recent years, Panh notes: "It's part of daily life in Cambodia, where Buddhism is enriched by animism. Living souls that we can pray to exist in the rivers, trees, rice fields and in the wind. Everything possesses an essence linked to spirits and rituals." "Rithy Panh Revisits the Horrors of the Khmer Rouge," interview by Frédéric Burnand, *Swissinfo*, March 16, 2019, https://www.swissinfo.ch/eng/graves-without-a-name_rithy-panh-revisits-the-horrors-of-the-khmer-rouge/44827132.

23. Harvey, *Animism*, 54.

24. Harvey, xx. Rather than reproduce a distinction between animate and inanimate, Harvey's discussion insists on the animist tradition of cultivating and respecting relations between human and other-than-human persons, for example, trees, stones, and ancestral spirits.

25. Harvey, 107.

26. Panh has credited his encounter with one such artist, the late filmmaker and Holocaust survivor Marceline Loridan-Ivens, for giving him the strength to pursue his most recent film, *Irradiated* (2020), unfortunately released after the completion of this project.

PART 1

AFTERMATH

A Cinema of Postwar Survival

1 • THE "MAD MOTHER" IN RITHY PANH'S FILMS

BORETH LY

> The mother is mad due to lack of solidarity,
> she is mad because of the war and poverty,
> she is mad because poor people fight to survive, but nobody takes care of them,
> she is mad because our generation is corrupt,
> she is mad like I am,
> she is mad but maybe she is free...
>
> —E-mail exchange with Rithy Panh, October 6, 2012

Mothers feature prominently in the history of Cambodian cinema. For example, in Hem Yvon's 1963 film, *Jet Mdai* (Mother's heart), we see a mother who dies of a broken heart after being abandoned by her husband. Chhay Bora's 2014 film, *Lost Loves*, presents a Khmer mother who makes great sacrifices in order to keep her children alive under the Khmer Rouge regime (1975–1979). It seems that the ideal Khmer mother is one who not only nurtures but also sacrifices herself for her children and family. This chapter considers a different representation of the mother in Cambodian films: the mad mother in Rithy Panh's *Rice People* (1994), *One Night after the War* (1998), and *The Burnt Theatre* (2005). I define madness here as mental incapacitation that transforms the mother into a menace—not only to her children and society but also to herself. I would like to state at the outset that I am not interested in the moral binary of the good versus the bad mother because in this case, the mother's failure to care for her children is attributed to her mental illness, and thus she has no rational control over her life. Moreover, her suffering invokes compassion and not judgment.

To the best of my knowledge, representation of the mad mother in Cambodian film and literature is scarce. This rarity might be attributed to the nurturing role that women are expected to play in society, especially in the arguably matrilineal culture of Cambodia, where the mother forms the main pillar of support for the nuclear family.[1] One rare exception comes from a folktale called "Kaun Lok" ("Child of the world"), which describes a widowed mother who plans to remarry; her new husband is a "good-for-nothing" man. The young widow cannot support her children, so she abandons her three young daughters in the forest. She provides them with uncooked rice and dry corn, hoping that they will either die from hunger or be eaten by animals. Fortunately, Varuna, the god of water, intervenes by looking after them.[2]

The heart of the story has to do with the mother's desperate desire for her daughters to be independent, despite their youth and vulnerability. She leaves them with uncooked rice and corn, which they are able to grow by a pond. The tale concludes with the mother returning to the forest in search of her daughters, but it is too late; they no longer need her. They have been transformed into magpie-like birds called *kaun lok*, which in Khmer literally means "child of the world." Indeed, in answer to her hopes, they have become independent children of the world: in the world and with the world. One cannot claim that the act of abandonment defines this mother as mad. However, considering Cambodian cultural expectations that a mother must nurture her children, this abandonment of her children is a decisive act of gender and cultural transgression. In brief, one might interpret the character of the widowed mother in the story of "Kaun Lok" as a predecessor to the mad mothers in Panh's films. More significantly, a haunting message returns: a single mother is not possible in this patriarchal society; she alone cannot support her children. As a single mother, she is a burden to society.[3]

This chapter examines the role the mother plays in the nuclear family in Cambodian culture and considers what happens when the mother is incapacitated. My argument is twofold. First, I explore the significant role of the mother in these films. I discuss how the portrayal of mad mothers in Panh's films provides us with a window on representations of the social world of gender inequality. Moreover, I demonstrate how symptoms of the mad mother mirror the morally broken Cambodian nation in the aftermath of the Khmer Rouge period. I argue that the mother is mad because the violence and ostracizations of shifting political regimes have displaced and dispossessed her. Second, I point out that mental illness is considered a source of cultural shame in Cambodian society and in Southeast Asian culture at large. A mentally ill person risks being contained and chained up in order to protect him or her from self-harm and from bringing shame to the family. To this end, I suggest that Panh's films help to call attention to the social taboo of mental illness.

THE MAD MOTHER IN *RICE PEOPLE*

Rice People is based on two sources. First, the fictional narrative of the film is based on a 1966 novel, *Ranjau Sepanjang Jalan* (*No Harvest but a Thorn*) by the Malaysian writer Shahnon Ahmad.[4] The Malay story takes place in a Muslim village in Malaysia, but Panh and his cowriter, Eve Deboise, changed the time and setting of

Shahnon's story to the post–Khmer Rouge genocide period in Cambodia.[5] *Rice People* tells the story of a couple who are rice farmers. They have seven daughters, but no son to help out with the farming. The film shows how farmers have to endure and struggle with nature, mirroring the harsh living conditions in many rice-farming communities in Cambodia. The father, Vong Poeuv (Mom Soth), is the patriarch. One day he steps on a poison thorn and dies from the ensuing infection. The mother, Yim Om (Peng Phan), has to carry on with the farming as well as looking after her seven young daughters. As a widow, she commits gender and moral transgression in her village and is subsequently ostracized by the patriarchal community. The ensuing stress and alienation eventually drive her to alcoholism and madness. She becomes disillusioned and incapacitated. The men in the village decide to lock her up inside a cage made of bamboo. Naturally, it is the oldest daughter, Sokha (Chhim Naline), who shoulders the responsibilities of raising her six siblings, taking care of her mentally ill mother, and tilling the land.

The second inspiration for the story of *Rice People* harkens back to Panh's 1989 film, *Site 2*, in that the names of the two main characters, Vong Poeuv and Yim Om, in *Rice People* are the same as the couple in *Site 2*.[6] *Site 2* is a documentary film about a Khmer couple who lived in a refugee camp located in Thailand after the Khmer Rouge genocide, during the Vietnamese occupation of Cambodia (1979–1990). In *Site 2*, Yim Om speaks poignantly about her despair and her dreams of returning to her home village in Cambodia, where she can grow her own rice on her own land. Although I analyze and compare the plot in Shahnon's novel to describe how it differs from the plot in Panh's film, I suggest that the metanarrative in *Rice People* is about Yim Om, the mother in *Site 2*, and her feelings of dispossession and longing for her homeland.

At the outset, the film focuses on the issues of gender difference and inequality in a patriarchal village and the conflict that needs to be resolved at the end of the film: namely, the fate of Om and her seven daughters. More important, it asks how a mad mother and her daughters are to survive in an agrarian society in which men dominate and thus hold control over social behaviors and determine the fate of women's lives. Moreover, it is about preserving the traditional family structures in a rice-growing culture where grain is not simply nourishment and sustenance, but also defines cultural identity, a way of life. Within the heteronormative gender binary, opposites complement each other on many levels: from fertility and procreation to the division of labor, analogous to a person's right and left hand. In the original Malay novel, Shahnon writes: "Lahuma said, Jeha is his right hand and he cannot live without her."[7] These pressure, responsibilities, and expectations ultimately drive Om, the mother, to madness. Poeuv and Om farm the land together; they are interdependent, forming an inseparable pair. Unfortunately, Om is attacked by a male cobra while working on her rice field. Although Poeuv and the men in the village manage to kill the snake, they fear that the female cobra is hiding somewhere and will come find her mate. The death of the male serpent foreshadows the inevitable separation of the human couple. Indeed, Poeuv steps on a thorn while plowing their rice paddy, and his right foot becomes infected. He subsequently dies from the infection, leaving Om a widow to look after their seven daughters.

According to Buddhist ritual, it is an obligation for the eldest son to shave his head to make merit for the deceased parent. In this family, however, there are only daughters. Sokha, the eldest daughter, thus shaves her head to make merit for her late father at his funeral. It is worth noting here that Panh's altering of the Muslim faith in Shahnon's novel to Theravada Buddhism in his filmic adaptation clearly gives gender flexibility and thus makes it culturally compatible for the Cambodian context. On his deathbed, Poeuv asks one of his daughters to bring seven sticks, and he bunches them together. Subsequently, he asks his daughter to break the sticks, but she cannot. The moral of the story is that they must stay together as a family and support one another. In effect, it underscores that they will be invincible when he is no longer there to protect them.

After her husband's cremation, Om lives with great emotional anxiety, prays in front of her late husband's funerary urn, and says: "The children help me but they're worn out now. We don't have your strength. Why do you abandon us, leave us alone and sad, without help like this?" As viewers, it is disheartening to hear Om's conversation with the ghost of her late husband, but she believes the strength of eight females collectively combined does not equal the strength of one man. Clearly, Om is lamenting the loss of a patriarchal moral strength and not physical strength. Indeed, the gender difference in this traditional society is not measured by physical strength because it is evident in the film that these eight women can perform the required labor on the rice field, but the real difference is confined to how social behavior and spaces are gendered in this village.

As viewers, we are to assume that Poeuv, the father, knows the lay of the land better than all the other members of his family. In one scene, Sophoeun (Pen Sopheary), one of the daughters, looks out of a window in their humble village home, while the bedridden Poeuv asks her to tell him what she sees. She describes life through the opened window: "Mother is trying to plow the paddy but the oxen refuse to move. Sokha [her eldest sister] is in the front trying to pull the oxen. What about Sokeoun? Oh, yeah, I see her under a tree trying to start a fire."

POEUV: What about the sky?

SOPHOEUN: There are lots of slow-moving clouds, black and white ones. Dad, so what is there beyond our rice paddies?

POEUV: Beyond our rice paddies, is Phnom Bok Koh [literally, "ox hump mountain"]. It is very cold on top of this mountain. Visitors can see their breath when they speak because it is so cold. There is a spring that provides very clear and cold water. It is a very high mountain. You can actually catch the cloud when you are on top of this mountain.

FIGURE 1.1. Sophoeun describing the world outside the window

Panh's use of an open window as a framing device, "a window into the world" for this particular scene, harkens back to the Renaissance perspective system invented by the fifteenth-century Italian artist Filippo Brunelleschi. Subsequently, artists began to follow this gridded window to render events and social lives in the outer world as if one were viewing objects and events through an open window.[8] Interestingly, in Panh's film, the viewer does not have direct access to seeing the images of the landscape on-screen, but simply through Sophoeun's and Poeuv's descriptions of them (figure 1.1). This "art of describing" filmic strategy helps to spark the viewer's imagination powerfully.[9] Moreover, Poeuv's knowledge of the landscape suggests that he is the only member of his family who knows what lies beyond the boundaries of their village. Indeed, the access to social space and place is gendered in this traditional society. Men are given access to a world beyond the confines of their village while women are restricted to their village and to domestic spaces, especially the kitchen.

Another example of gender transgression occurs after Om and her family fence off invasive crabs that threaten to consume the young rice stalks. In a moment of great anxiety and fear, Om is participating in a gambling and drinking party, a pastime that is traditionally reserved for men in this patriarchal society. To add salt to Om's wound, Amoy, the wife of the Khmer Chinese shop owner, scolds her for crossing the line: "Enough drinking, Om! Aren't you ashamed? What mother behaves like this?" The men at the party tell Om that they find her daughter Sokha sexually attractive. She starts to joke with them (though this is very painful for her): "I am equally attractive as my daughter Sokha." This sexual overture by the men coupled with the children's teasing her with their song "The Widow

FIGURE 1.2. Om looking into the cracked mirror

with Many Daughters" remind her of her destitute and vulnerable status, a widow with seven daughters and no man to look after them. It is this patriarchal and communal ostracization that drives her to a mental breakdown and subsequent madness.

She returns home drunk that evening. The next morning Om opens up her old trunk and pulls out her precious ikat-patterned silk skirt. Then she takes out her old cosmetics and starts to paint her face with the white powder in front of a cracked mirror (figure 1.2). In addition, she puts on bright red lipstick, trying desperately to recapture the beauty of her youth. Perhaps she is hoping to remarry for economic reasons. Subsequently, the dolled-up widow runs to take refuge in her rice field. There, she sees her painted face in the reflection of the water and is horrified by her own image and washes the makeup from her face. The children from the village hiding in the emerald green rice field throw rocks at her and continue to tease her with their chant, "the widow with many daughters," a communal song of ostracization. In the original novel, the harassment and marginalization of the character Jeha are even more violent: "The village children began to follow her around and aim little stones at her. Jeha moved away quickly but went on walking around. And the title 'bold widow-with-many-children' became 'bold-widow-of-swollen-Lahuma-with-many-children.' The title later became a children's song. They learnt it by heart and chanted it loudly whenever they saw Jeha scurrying around the village of Banggul Derdap."[10]

Om's hallucination becomes worse, and she sees her late husband's ghost calling her. She runs to the rice field to find him and works with him in the middle of the night. Finally, she reaches a stage of mental breakdown in which she is no longer able to make a distinction between her hallucinations and reality. Tong Somnang, the village chief, and other men come to inform Sokha, the eldest daughter, that her mother is mad. She needs to be locked up to prevent her from harming Sokha and her siblings. More important, to prevent the mother from harming herself, the men build a cage made of bamboo to confine her.

In short, it is this struggle to fit into this patriarchal community and her fear of failing as a mother to support her seven daughters, in addition to the harassment from her fellow villagers, that ultimately drive Om to insanity. The need to fit into the traditional family in order to survive in an agrarian village and patriarchal ideology is reinforced by the appearance of a young man who comes to help Sokha with her daily chores. As viewers, we are supposed to be comforted by the prospect and assurance that this young man will marry her, suggesting a better future. The mad widow and her daughters will again be safe, at least from the daily harassment in this patriarchal culture and community. However, she will be forever marginalized as the mad and "irrational other" and is likely to live her remaining days in the realm of madness.

Because the fictional story of *Rice People* is based on the nightmares and dreams of Yim Om from *Site 2* and thus she is arguably the prototype for the mad mother in *Rice People*, there are several explanations for why the mother is mad. I would like to suggest that comparable to the filmic device of the window into the social world, here we see a metanarrative embedded within a narrative. As mentioned earlier, we first saw Yim Om in Panh's "documentary" film, but interestingly, Panh has chosen to convey this metanarrative of the mother's madness in fiction, a narrative strategy and filmic enlargement that echo what Michel Foucault points out in his radio talk "Mad Language" (1963): "Words, their arbitrary encounter, their confusion, all their protoplasmic transformations are sufficient in themselves to bring into being a world that is both true and fantastic."[11] Thus, for Foucault, literature is madness, and I would argue that film magnifies further this monstrosity of the mother's madness. Madness and the mad mother, a trope that Panh often revisits, seem essential to an understanding of the lasting trauma of Khmer history, how the burden of trauma is gendered, and what is left unsaid and undone.

On one level, in Shahnon's novel the mother's madness is attributed to grief. The villagers in the novel claim, "Jeha had gone mad because her husband was dead."[12] Indeed, grief coupled with ostracization from her community drive the mother to madness in both the novel and the film, *Rice People*. The violent message of this ostracization is embedded in the lyrics of the children's song, which reflect the adults' opinions about Om's and her seven daughters' social status in their village. I would like to suggest another reason that accounts for the mother's madness in *Rice People*. In the film, we see that Om and her daughters do everything they can to kill the invasive crabs; they crush and boil them, but to no avail. It is the lost battle against these invasive crabs that sends Om into a state of despair and ultimately breaks her resilience.[13] I argue that these invasive crabs are metaphors that stand for the political regimes that came to occupy and to rule Cambodia in the post–Democratic Kampuchea (1975–1979) period. My e-mail interview with Panh reinforces this interpretation:

BORETH LY: The invasive crabs in your film, *Rice People,* are they metaphors? If so, what do they stand for?

RITHY PANH: The crabs are metaphors for what arrived later to our country. . . .

BL: You mean, after the Vietnamese invasion in 1979?

RP: Yes, but it could also be the new capitalists.[14]

It was thus the Vietnamese occupation and the subsequent capitalist regime that drove the character of Yim Om, the mother in *Rice People* and *Site 2,* and her family away from their community and homeland. In fact, Om from *Site 2* shares with us:

> I left Cambodia with my family. There were many problems in the village. It was harder and harder to make a living. In addition, we were under the Vietnamese control, and we had to work collectively in the rice fields, like before. Under Pol Pot, we'd already worked like that. Everything was shared except our bodies. Instead of giving us our liberty, we were forced once again to work collectively. So I said to my husband, let's go live at the refugee camp, where they hand out rice, let's go live there! Otherwise, we had to work collectively, without knowing what happened to the fruits of our work. It wasn't worth staying, everything became difficult, so we decided to go live in the land of others.

Moreover, she worries that her displaced family, especially her young children, has become so dependent on the welfare provided by international organizations in the refugee camps that they have lost their agrarian roots. Om tells us in *Site 2,* "If all the children continued to live in this camp, they won't know how to sow rice, or how to replant it. In Cambodia, they would have learned." To this end, she can only dream from the location of this suffocating refugee camp. Perhaps these multiple ostracizations from a narrative within a narrative drive these Khmer mothers to madness. Consider the seemingly inexplicable scene in *Rice People* that captures Poeuv's nightmare of soldiers burning down houses in his village, thus compelling him and his family to flee into the jungle. This scene only makes sense when one considers it as a metanarrative that connects the horrorscape of the two films. In short, civil wars, the ensuing genocide, and subsequent shifts in political regimes are the haunting events that contributed to the displacement and dispossession of each of these mothers from her community and homeland. The line between fact and fictions is thus blurred; the mothers in both *Rice*

People and *Site 2* shoulder the same burden of having to care for their families and ultimately to find ways to survive.

ONE NIGHT AFTER THE WAR

Another one of Panh's films that features the mad mother is *One Night after the War* (1998), which was one of the first films to address the legacy of trauma and memory in the post–Khmer Rouge genocide period. The film narrates the tragic death of Savannah (Narith Roeun), a twenty-eight-year-old ex-soldier who falls in love with a nineteen-year-old "bar girl" (i.e., a prostitute) named Srei Peouv (Chea Lyda Chan). The story is told from the perspective of Srei Peouv, who is working as a waitress and who has a daughter, Bophana, with Savannah. Srei Peouv, who is a victim of oppression in this patriarchal society, interrupts and interrogates the narrative of the film in a voice-over whenever social injustice comes to the fore. We are told in the beginning that the film is set in August 1992, and that the "King Father" (i.e., King Norodom Sihanouk), the nation's patriarch, has just returned to Cambodia after years of living in exile. On that night curfew has been lifted, and nightlife returns to the streets of Phnom Penh. That is, the film takes place in a period after the collapse of Pol Pot's communist regime (1975–1979), during this reemergent capitalist period in Cambodian history.[15]

We find the theme of the mad mother once again in *One Night after the War*. A scene from the film shows Srei Poeuv's nightmare and how she is forever haunted by the death of her father, who was a farmer but was compelled to join the army. She was merely a young girl when the army brought her father's dead body back to the village. Srei Peouv's mother (played again by the same actress, Peng Phan) was so traumatized by the death of her husband and his subsequent absence from the family that she became mad. She was self-destructive and thus incapacitated; her children were compelled to put a chain on one of her ankles and attach her to one of the pillars that support their humble family home (figure 1.3).

Another scene depicts the mad mother's recollection of what happened to her late husband. She holds Savannah's hands (thinking that he is her son) as she narrates her memory:

MOTHER: Then one day they took him [her son] away to war. His father asks if he can take his son's place. Subsequently, he died. Now they are coming to ask my son to join the army.

The wounds . . .

The wars . . .

The tears . . .

You promise me that you won't join the army like your late father, you promise me!

FIGURE 1.3. Srey Poeuv unlocking her mother's chains

It seems clear that the female characters in these two films are conditioned by patriarchal society to fear that the absence of a male figure in the household means they not only will have to shoulder the economic burden but also will lose the respect of their fellow villagers. This anxiety contributes to the mother's madness. Again, the daughter must shoulder the family's financial burdens. Like the oldest daughter, Sokha, in *Rice People*, in *One Night after the War*, Srei Peouv must work; she finds a job as a "bar girl" in Phnom Penh City so that she can send money home to support her mad mother and her siblings, who remain in the village.

THE BURNT THEATRE

Four of the female characters in Panh's *The Burnt Theatre* (2005) are relevant to my discussion of the theme of the mad mother, especially the character named Penh Phan (interestingly, the actress Peng Phan played the mad mothers in both *Rice People* and *One Night after the War*). The film's title refers to the Bassac Theater, designed by Cambodian architect Vann Molyvann in 1966.[16] The National Theater survived the Khmer Rouge era but burned down on February 11, 1994. This burned theater sets the stage for Panh's film. *The Burnt Theatre* is a memorial and homage to the history of the National Theater; the date of the fire is marked on a half-burned calendar and is uttered and repeated by one of the actors in the film. Many stories are narrated within this film, but I would like to look specifically at four female characters who are relevant to the topic at hand: the mad mother. A journalist named Bopha Chheang interviews all the actors in this film, including Peng Phan, who plays both herself and a Khmer Rouge survivor who suffers from psychosomatic illness. Moreover, we are told that she was engaged to a medical doctor before the war. They separated, and he subsequently died during the Khmer Rouge genocide. She suffers from survivor's guilt. The recurring nightmares she experiences contribute to her sleep deprivation. She is plagued by mental illness that has no easy cure and reports symptoms ranging from eyesight problems to insomnia.[17] She goes to the hospital, where she receives more medications, but none of these medicines cures her psychosomatic illness. She ends up collecting many kinds of ineffective medications. More frustratingly, no one understands her or believes she is ill. One particular scene, which takes place in the corridor of a hospital where Phan's character waits to see a doctor, captures the shared traumatic experiences that Khmer mothers suffered in the post–Khmer Rouge period. While waiting, she has a conversation with two Khmer mothers who are her age and who also suffer from psychosomatic illness:

PHAN (asking a Khmer mother sitting next to her): Sister, why are you here?[18]

MOTHER 1: I don't feel well. I think I have a lot on my mind that keeps me from sleeping at night. If in the middle of the night, my neighbor screams, I get frightened and I wake up. Subsequently, I cannot go back to sleep.

PHAN: At night when I have a headache, I have nightmares of the violence that I experienced under the Khmer Rouge period.

MOTHER 2 (joins in the conversation): For me, when I saw a documentary film that they showed on television about the Khmer Rouge, I said to my children, you have been killed by them and you are reborn today into my family. That is what I told them, but some of the children don't believe us. They won't believe that we suffered so much back then. They don't believe that we had nothing to eat. They were born yesterday. They have it all and they are confused. Some of them listened to their mothers. And when they don't anymore, they go smoke marijuana and do other bad things. They won't listen to their parents. In 1975, my father was separated from us and has been so until today. I never saw him again.

PAN: (to her journalist friend, Chheang Bopha): Bopha, the patients say the doctors ask a lot of questions. I don't know what to tell him. I am scared.

BOPHA: You tell him how much you suffered. You have insomnia and nightmares.

PAN: So I tell the doctor the whole story of my life?

BOPHA: Yes, medicine alone won't cure this illness. If you tell the doctor the truth, he'll help solve your problems.

PAN (she turns her head and looks around the waiting room): Look at each patient's face. What kind of traumatic experiences haunt them?

The conversation between the four women in this scene provides insights into the gravity of this mental illness and the pressure that Khmer mothers have to bear in the post–Khmer Rouge period.[19] First, these mothers survived the brutal regime that killed 1.7 million of the population in Cambodia.[20] They survived death camps, and now they believe they are the progenitors of the Khmer people. They believe the children they gave birth to are the ghosts of those who were killed under the regime and have decided to be reborn in their wombs. Second, it is both frustrating and painful for the women to know that their children do not believe their stories of how much they suffered under the Khmer Rouge regime. These traumatic histories and memories contribute to their psychosomatic illnesses. Sadly, there are almost no professional psychiatric hospitals in Cambodia, nor do these women know how to articulate their mental illness. A case in point is when Phan's character shares her fear with Bopha: How should she convey her symptoms to the doctor, since she feels both physical and mental pain? This sharing of stories and symptoms of illnesses as a collective experience among these Khmer mothers in Panh's film suggests that trauma and treatment of mental illness are culturally specific.[21] Western medication alone does not help; the women also need communal therapy. As a result, the three Khmer women characters in Panh's film became collectors of medications due to the lack of culturally sensitive and holistic approaches to the treatment of trauma and mental illness. Like the chained-up and caged mad mothers discussed earlier, these mothers are reduced to silence through medication.

In his 2012 memoir, translated as *The Elimination*, Panh shares another tragic story about a mother's plight. During the Khmer Rouge era, a mother learned that all of her children were killed and the whereabouts of their corpses was not known. In a state of despair, the destitute mother committed suicide by drowning in a river.[22] Had the mother chosen to go on living, how might she have coped with her trauma? Of course, she could have turned to Khmer Buddhist teachings that attribute her sufferings to *kam* (Sanskrit, *karma*), the law of cause and effect in Buddhist teaching. She suffered during her lifetime because of her *kam*, in order to terminate the endless cycle of rebirth. In theory, there is no God in Theravada Buddhist teaching. There are only the laws of *kamma*; these laws determine and punish the perpetrators' actions and consequences. Alternatively, she might have sought psychotherapy. Of course, there is always the problem of availability and cost: Would she have been able to afford this expensive treatment? At any rate, chances are she would have succumbed to madness.[23] Furthermore, death is not an option for the widowed mothers in Panh's fictional films discussed in this chapter because Cambodian cultural expectations demand that the mother play the role of a nurturer. Suicide is possible only if her children are dead and she is thus free of the responsibility to care for them.

This might explain Panh's proclivity to portray these destitute mothers as mad. In an e-mail exchange with the filmmaker, I asked why many of the mothers in his films are mad, Panh replied with a poem:

The mother is mad due to lack of solidarity,
she is mad because of the war and poverty,
she is mad because poor people fight to survive, but nobody takes care of them,
she is mad because our generation is corrupt,
she is mad like I am,
she is mad but maybe she is free . . .[24]

Madness is perhaps one of the desperate ways for these mothers in Panh's films to survive and, paradoxically, to sustain their sanity. I would further argue that the mad mother is a symbolic embodiment of Cambodia, a land that has been ravaged and plundered by different political regimes that cause her displacement and dispossession. Like Yim Om in *Site 2*, she can only dream about her former self before being dispossessed. Perhaps it is this ineffable loss and the impossibility of reclaiming her homeland and former self that drove her to live in a state of madness. Furthermore, it explains why the mad mother in Cambodian films has emerged only in the post–Khmer Rouge genocide period of Cambodian history. To this end, Panh's films help to give verbal and visual representations to alternative ways of being, albeit highly marginalized ways of existence. Indeed, due to cultural shame, there is no acknowledgment for individuals living with mental illness in many Southeast Asian cultures and societies.[25] In Cambodia, the mentally ill are kept out of the public to prevent them from shaming their families, as well as to allow mad individuals to save face and prevent them from harming themselves.[26] Moreover, psychiatric hospitals are few, and psychotherapy is not yet a cultural norm.[27]

Over the years, Panh has been concerned with the dearth of psychiatric hospitals for survivors of the Khmer Rouge regime in Cambodia. The filmmaker stated: "At Preah Sihanouk Hospital in Phnom Penh, the only department that provides psychiatric treatment takes patients from all over the country. Sometimes there are 250 of them waiting in the corridor. You only have to see how many are depressive and destitute to realize something must be done. There is a massive collective wound."[28] In her 1995 book, *Primitive Passions*, Rey Chow has put forward a persuasive argument that what is seemingly perceived as self-Orientalizing in Zhang Yimou's films such *Ju Dou* (1990) and *Raise the Red Lantern* (1991) is actually an exposé of the feudalistic oppression of women in Chinese history and society.[29] In a similar filmic strategy, Panh's portrayal of the mad mother in postgenocide Cambodian society is a filmic magnification of this repressed and hidden cultural shame. His films are windows into the social world of gender inequality and family trauma—a cracked mirror. In short, Panh draws the attention of both local and international viewers to the mental illness wrought by the legacy of Khmer Rouge trauma, how it is gendered in discourse, and how it needs urgent psychiatric and medical attention.

NOTES

1. Judy Ledgerwood, "Khmer Kinship: The Matriliny/Matriarchy Myth," *Journal of Anthropological Research* 53, no. 1 (Autumn 1995): 247–261.
2. David Chandler, "Songs at the Edge of the Forest: Perceptions of Order in Three Cambodian Texts," in *At the Edge of the Forest: Essays on Cambodia, History and Narrative in Honor of David Chandler*, ed. Anne Ruth Hansen and Judy Ledgerwood (Ithaca, NY: Cornell University Press, 2008), 31–46.
3. The late Adrienne Rich addresses this patriarchal control of the female womb and critiques this unfair societal and cultural expectation of women as nurturers. See Adrienne Rich, *Of Woman Born: Motherhood as Experience and Institution* (New York: W. W. Norton, 1995).
4. Shahnon Ahmad, *No Harvest but a Thorn* (London: Oxford University Press, 1972).
5. Sylvie Blum-Reid, *East-West Encounters: Franco-Asian Cinema and Literature* (New York: Wallflower Press, 2003), 107–110.
6. I would like to thank Joseph Mai and Leslie Barnes for pointing out the connection between the main characters in Rithy Panh's films *Site 2* and *Rice People*. An additional thank-you to Rithy Panh for giving me access to viewing his film *Site 2*.
7. Shahnon, *No Harvest but a Thorn*, 114.
8. Filippo Brunelleschi illustrated his optical understanding of one-point perspective way of rendering the world, using a mirror. Subsequently, in 1435, Leon Battista Alberti, a mathematician, used geometry and numbers to codify Brunelleschi's mirror into a gridded window. See Samuel E. Edgerton, *The Mirror, the Window and the Telescope: How Renaissance Perspective Changed Our Vision of the Universe* (Ithaca, NY: Cornell University Press, 2009), 1–10, 44–53.
9. Svetlana Alpers, *The Art of Describing: Dutch Art in the Seventeenth Century* (Chicago: University of Chicago Press, 1984).
10. Shahnon, *No Harvest but a Thorn*, 114.
11. Michel Foucault, *Language, Madness, and Desire: On Literature*, ed. Philippe Artières, Jean-François Bert, Mathieu Potte-Bonneville, and Judith Revel, trans. Robert Bononno (Minneapolis: University of Minnesota Press, 2015), 28.
12. Shahnon, *No Harvest but a Thorn*, 114.
13. Though she is white and her madness is not as extreme, a similar fate awaits the French mother in *The Sea Wall* (2008), where the invasion of crabs, burrowing through the ill-fated walls, leads to the mother's financial, psychological, and ultimately physical demise.
14. E-mail exchange with Rithy Panh, January 9, 2020.
15. Boreth Ly, "Screening the Crisis of Monetary Masculinity in Rithy Panh's *One Night after the War* and *Burnt Theatre*," in *Film in Contemporary Southeast Asia: Cultural Interpretation and Social Intervention*, ed. David C. L. Lim and Hiroyuki Yamamoto (London: Routledge, 2012), 66–67.
16. Robert Turnbull, "A Burned-Out Theater: The State of Cambodia's Performing Arts," in *Expressions of Cambodia: The Politics of Tradition, Identity and Change*, ed. Leakthina Chau-Pech Ollier and Tim Winter (New York: Routledge, 2006), 133–149.
17. See Joseph Mai's chapter in this volume for an understanding of trauma and architecture in the Khmer context. See also my examination of the Khmer concept of *baksbat* (broken courage) in Boreth Ly, *Traces of Trauma: Cambodian Visual Culture and National Identity in the Aftermath of Genocide* (Honolulu: University of Hawai'i Press, 2020), chap. 1.
18. I have changed and edited some of the English subtitles to reflect a more accurate translation of the original Khmer.
19. See *Khmer Rouge Victims Struggle with Trauma*, https://www.youtube.com/watch?v=qUKA1xJkh1g.

20. David Chandler, *Voices from S-21: Terror and History in Pol Pot's Secret Prison* (Berkeley: University of California Press, 1999), vii.

21. Steven V. Jensen, "Mental Illness: Walking above the Earth," *Globe_Lines of Thought across Southeast Asia*, July 29, 2019, https://southeastasiaglobe.com/cambodias-hidden-mental-health-problem/.

22. Rithy Panh with Christophe Bataille, *The Elimination: A Survivor of the Khmer Rouge Confronts His Past and the Commandant of the Killing Fields*, trans. John Cullen (New York: Other Press, 2013), 246.

23. Ly, *Traces of Trauma*, 123.

24. E-mail exchange with Rithy Panh, October 6, 2012.

25. See *Bali's Shame*, a documentary on the mistreatment of the mentally ill in Bali, https://www.youtube.com/watch?v=zdUrrlRgMFw.

26. See *Caged and Chained: Cambodia's Mentally Ill*, https://www.youtube.com/watch?v=dxq-busFi8M.

27. Jensen, "Mental Illness."

28. Rithy Panh, "Cambodia: A Wound That Will Not Heal," *UNESCO Courier* 52 (December 12, 1999): 30. See also Denis Hruby, "Cambodia Suffers from an Appalling Mental Health Crisis," *Global Post*, June 17, 2014, http://www.globalpost.com/dispatch/news/regions/asia-pacific/cambodia/140616/cambodia-suffers-appalling-mental-health-crisis.

29. Rey Chow, *Primitive Passions: Visuality, Sexuality, Ethnography, and Contemporary Chinese Cinema* (New York: Columbia University Press, 1995), 142–172.

2 • RESILIENCE IN THE RUINS

Artistic Practice in Rithy Panh's *The Burnt Theatre*

JOSEPH MAI

> We must think of something else; we must think of living, and also of the future.
>
> —Rithy Panh, "Ce sont les petits gestes qui éclairent les grandes causes," interview by Marie Ingouf

At the beginning of Rithy Panh's *The Burnt Theatre* (2005), viewers must work through some disturbing and all-too-familiar images. The film opens in medias res: a shabbily dressed woman in medium full shot crawls through thick vegetation and over rocks, seemingly deep in a jungle, while another woman's voice cries out, "The house is on fire! Hide our children!" A chorus of other voices laments inarticulately. The woman hurries past some plantings (are we near a village?) while others carry a wounded man on a stretcher. A corpse lies at her feet; the dead man's wife, crying hysterically, scurries by, calling for help for the baby in her arms. For more than a full minute we are caught in this horrifying drama, and the film will be a difficult one to endure if it continues like this. Dead bodies, a mother's grief, bombs, indignities heaped upon victims: the depressing cinematic tropes of dehumanization one expects, according to our present distribution of images, in a film about war in Southeast Asia, genocide, and the Khmer Rouge.

But all is not as it seems. Some may already be distracted by the setting, which, as the camera draws slightly out, looks less like a village and more like the outskirts of a town, or a demolition zone. Despite the smoke, we do not see explosions or falling bombs, and the percussive sounds, produced on musical instruments, are not quite realistic. There is a cutaway to a group shot of four people (the litter-bearers carrying the injured man) now watching the action. A return to a full shot shows the two women in a stagelike space. The young woman exits the frame, and the first actress speaks, her gestures more theatrical. "Why do Khmers kill each other? What future will our children have?" A cut back to the group, and one man, the director, grows impatient: Why is she going off script? Why is she moaning like that? He comes onstage to admonish her (her name is Peng Phan). While they squabble over the text, the corpse stands up, and the woman walks by holding her baby, a dummy, upside down by the feet. We have moved from the territory of "realistic" fictional representation of an action from the past—a traumatic scene of dead bodies and falling bombs—to an exploration of the nature of representation, of the meaning-making process. Phan is not reliving the destiny of the victim, but reliving and rethinking experience (with her director, Rotha, and others). The fiction plays out in a setting that is both theater and film set. The image we see is mediated, ruminated, criticized; or, as Panh has written, "The image in a film is an interpreted image. Interpreted by me."[1]

But once understood to be a space of performance and critique, the built environment becomes problematic again. This is no ordinary film set, nor is it recognizably a theater. Immediately afterward, we see Doeun, an actor, sauntering through a corridor in shambles, populated by stray dogs, with rubble and a roofless auditorium planted with vegetables. We understand that the film is set in ruins, those of the Preah Suramarit National Theater, one of the greatest architectural symbols of Cambodian independence. The ruins are therefore a metonymy of a wrecked national identity and the broken courage (*baksbat*) of many Cambodians: the first half of this chapter will explore the symbolism of the theater and the context (the postwar turn toward global capitalism) and significance of its loss.

At the same time, these "ruins" are not depicted in typical fashion, as Diderot theorized them in the "poetics of ruins" in the eighteenth century—that is, melancholic, abandoned, and finally interchangeable reminders of the ephemeral existence of all civilizations.[2] On the contrary, they are still inhabited (even providing food by the crops the artists have planted there), still animated with creative energy. They are a site of loss *and* reclamation, and we will be concerned with this tension. The second half of the chapter considers the wide-ranging work of the artists—comprising music, puppetry, theater, and cinema—as a form of resistance against forgetting, dehumanization, and the tropes of victimization. These artists serve as partners in collaboration and models of resilience to Rithy Panh himself, whose films can be interpreted as a meditation on the power of creative work to construct new images in the ruins of a nation.

FROM NATION TO RUIN: THE BASSAC THEATER

The setting in the Preah Suramarit National Theater (shortened to the Bassac Theater or National Theater) immediately puts us onto the symbolic map of the

Cambodian nation. In *Cultures of Independence*, Ly Daravuth and Ingrid Muan describe five domains of the new national cultural identity, fostered by Prince Norodom Sihanouk, after independence (1953), the founding of the Sangkum Party (1955), and his ascension to head of state (1963): New Khmer architecture, the speaking (or French-inspired) theater, the Cambodian cinema, modern music, and modern painting. Some of the arts were modern: jazz and pop music, or "talking theater"; some were new twists on classical arts, such as Apsara dancing.[3] Of these fields, architecture was perhaps the dearest to Sihanouk. Previously, of course, the Angkor temples were a source of pride. But, as Benedict Anderson has pointed out, the French colonial archaeologists, inspired perhaps by Diderot's poetics, disconnected the temples from contemporary Cambodians by framing them as "disinterred, unjungled, measured, photographed, reconstructed, fenced off, analysed, and displayed."[4] According to colonialist discourses, contemporary Cambodians were incapable of caring for such artifacts. Sihanouk sought to reclaim the Angkorian heritage and undertook a proliferating number of new building projects that would, like the other arts of the time, combine tradition and modernity to forge a new Khmer national identity. He emphasized this architecture in public events, in his own films, and in *Kambuja*, the glossy cultural magazine he edited (and mostly wrote). Architecture meant freedom and identity.

Sihanouk's evocations of Angkor could be heavy-handed and kitschy, but the New Khmer architects had goals of a more practical, human sort: managing water flow and population growth, adapting to the climate, and, especially, providing appropriate living and cultural spaces for a modern citizenry. Among them was Vann Molyvann, a crucial figure in education, public works, and cultural administration, and above all, the greatest of the new architects. He was responsible for the National Monument, the Bassac riverfront development, the design of the port city Sihanoukville, the massive Olympic stadium, many other landmarks, and of course the National Theater. Ashley Thompson describes Molyvann in this way: "His is not a miserly or narrowly nationalistic love; in its most general expression it takes the form of a double exigency: at once infinitely respectful of the past, and moved by an indefatigable hope for—and investment in—the future; an unusually deep knowledge of the cultural heritage and an extraordinarily modern creative force; a pride in and concern for things uniquely Cambodian and yet a deep commitment to a certain internationalist, and I would even say universalist perspective."[5]

One of Molyvann's most ambitious projects was the Bassac riverfront development, with its crown jewel, the National Theater. Led by Molyvann, the architects of this project needed to manage the specific landscape of a rapidly growing, tropical city prone to flooding, heat, and poverty. Using silt from the river, they shored up the Bassac River area. They built a number of rent-controlled housing projects (of which the White Building is the most important example). In this,

Molyvann was influenced by Le Corbusier's internationalist style, including his "Modulor" human-sized scaling system: Le Corbusier had famously called the home a "machine for living," and Molyvann wanted to integrate livability into his own designs.[6] The Bassac area integrated water (moats and pools to accommodate flooding and add vegetation) and an east-west orientation for cool ventilation. Molyvann built the National Theater on stilts and in reinforced concrete to reduce moisture, while using orientation and design elements to organize light and air flow. The theater was also modular, with different sections serving different purposes: the lobby could be a practice space, there was an outdoor performance area, and families would picnic near its fish pond. The theater was a proud and thriving space in which all of the other arts of independence could be practiced, by artists who themselves lived in the nearby apartments, especially the White Building. Its overall shape famously evoked a ship setting a course toward the sea; more symbolically, one might see it plotting its course toward a grand, idealistic, and more democratic Khmer future.

Sihanouk's own devotion to this democratic vision had important limits. According to Milton Osborne, pursuing filmmaking and architectural projects had distracted Sihanouk from the daily grind of proper governance, and his luxurious life—in *Crépuscule* (1969), he tools around the temples in Mustangs and Corvettes—caused resentment.[7] He was also authoritarian: Ben Kiernen points to Sihanouk's brutal repression of the 1967 Samlaut uprising as an important moment of the early revolutionary movement in Cambodia.[8] The tumult of the coup d'état and then the arrival of the Khmer Rouge put a full stop to this vision of a unified citizenry with thriving, dignified, and cultured lives. The more than 300 artists of the theater were among the earliest sent to be "reeducated," and few survived the wars. The Khmer Rouge used the National Theater for a small number of state ceremonies, where ideological songs were sung. But the building still stood. After the wars, the Ministry of Culture made efforts to draw the remaining artists back to the city and train new artists, some of whom are in Panh's film. Panh does not delve deeply into the political and economic situation during the period that followed.[9] But the fire that ravaged the building took place during what Panh, in his suggestive way, has called a "climate of unbridled capitalism."[10] This was 1994, during an uninsured French-led renovation, ten years before Panh filmed in its rubble, and when it was becoming clear that the theater would not survive. The film is a final tribute to this building and what it represented.

BROKEN COURAGE

The deterioration of the building had severe implications for the artists. For Hoeun and Doeun, the two central male artists in Panh's film, it represents a disappearance of national union. Doeun saunters through the theater in the first scene, happily whistling, because he has found a briefcase containing props and photos salvaged from a production of *Cyrano* from that period and which he will share with the other artists. The choice of play is significant: Edmond Rostand wrote it at a moment of French difficulties, hoping to combine romanticism and flamboyance to bring a collective sense of pride. The men reminisce nostalgically over the old hat and the prosthetic nose. There is also a cast photo taken of the production, in which we see much younger Doeun and Hoeun, barely recognizable even to themselves.[11] But their desire to remember turns bitter. The nostalgia associated with the photograph is undermined by Hoeun's commentary as he identifies faces in the photo through their absence: this one left for America, this other one was his friend who died of AIDS. Nostalgia seems absurd in this space: the scene ends with Hoeun borrowing Cyrano's hat and sword and comically jabbing it into the plants that have overgrown the stage, without an audience.

Many ghosts of the past haunt the film, some emerging directly from the Cultures of Independence era, such as the actor Ta Loto. Loto was a well-known comic actor from the Sangkum period who used his physical form, affected by dwarfism, to explore themes of virility in a comic vein. He is now diminished by age and perhaps senility. He has also lost his voice and can only mumble incoherently, a decline his son attributes to punishment for having neglected to make a sacrifice to the spirit of the theater. Nor is Ta Loto the only artist from the 1960s whose presence haunts the film. Later, Doeun calls in to a radio karaoke program, where he and Hoeun will sing a song to be played to the station's public. The song, "Tender Love," evokes the heyday of popular Cambodian music and its biggest star, Sin Sisamouth. But Sisamouth is also infamous because of his mysterious disappearance and death during the Khmer Rouge regime. Again, nostalgia is frustrated. Sisamouth has not survived; Loto has not survived intact.

Along with troubling nostalgia, Ta Loto's character illustrates a breakdown in transmission toward the future common in Panh's work. Loto's story is told through the perspective of Chheang Bopha, a young journalist writing an exposé about the "lives of artists today." She tracks Loto down first by locating his young children, who spend days at a garbage dump, collecting metal cans; the shots of the dump are awful images of poverty, of dirty people, old and young, scrambling over heaps made by bulldozers (echoing the construction machinery), their faces covered with grimy kramas to lessen the stench. Later she helps his children cut their fingernails and avoid infections. In one of these scenes, Panh's frame composition emphasizes the difficulties of transmission in a shot organized along an axis in a way developed in earlier films. The son, sitting on the floor, speaks to Bopha while his father sits on a slightly higher platform behind him and to the left. Both are in the frame, but the boy is not looking at the father and the father is separated from him and in the background, as if the frame were divided in two. One finds similar composition in *Site 2* (1989), when Yim Om worries about her son's future while he stands in the background, framed by a doorway to another room, over her shoulder. "What future will our children have?" asks Peng Phan at the film's beginning: both frames pose the same question visually.

Starting from the influential figure of Hanuman, the monkey warrior character of the *Reamker*, Boreth Ly has argued that the postwar economic context of ultraliberal capitalism has produced diminished figures of masculinity in Panh's films. If Hanuman (and other monkeys in folktales) is powerful, humorous, and sexually attractive, the men here are poor (they complain about friends who have become rich politicians) and have no romantic prospects (Hoeun, for instance, is too ashamed of his poverty to return to his wife and children).[12]

To Ly's analysis, one could add that—as in the case of Ta Loto and his children—economic hardships are inscribed in the physical body of these men. Generally, they are tired and have grown flabby; but even when some of them lift weights in the auditorium, they seem like a parody of masculinity, with no context in which to show off their muscles. Doeun, used to playing romantic leads, is growing older and softer, and lacking in roles. When Hoeun gives moto rides to make a little money, the film emphasizes his sweat in the heat or his soaked clothing in the flooding rains. He shares his food with dogs. Panh concentrates meticulously on how the men feed these bodies, in what he has called a "culture of survival."[13] In one scene, for instance, one of the young artists gathers bats from a fallen ceiling and the men chop their wings off and fry them for food; the camera films the skinning and cooking in close-up. Filming their bodies and their food in this way echoes previous indignities of people reduced to sheer survival under the Khmer Rouge. The bats, for example, foreshadow a story told by Peng Phan about having to eat rotten snake while she was their prisoner. Some viewers may divert their eyes from such images of the fragility of the body, but trusting Panh's direction leads also to images of human dignity despite this reduction: the men themselves, though they joke about their hunger, are thankful for eating bats when all one has is bats to eat.

The physical and mental wounds of memory are constantly reopened by these present circumstances. In one scene, Hoeun is working the leather from which he makes complex moving puppets for the puppet theater, when Doeun arrives, reading the newspaper. For Doeun, this daily exposure to drug deals, tuk-tuk holdups, strangulations, prison cell suicides, and acid attacks exacerbates his personal experience of trauma. As the camera pans up from the image of the dead man on the page toward Doeun's face, he explains that he has been intensely afraid since the time of the Khmer Rouge, during which he lost dozens of family members. Hoeun defines his friend's fear with the Khmer word *baksbat*, a term most often translated as "broken courage." *Baksbat* has a clinical history that has been studied most comprehensively by the psychologist Sotheara Chhim, who places the notion under the broader category of "idioms of distress," or culturally specific or "interpersonally effective ways of expressing and coping with distress."[14]

Baksbat covers some of the semantic territory occupied by the clinical language of post-traumatic stress disorder, though it lends itself to a more flexible usage. According to Chhim, *baksbat* has both individual and collective implications: ranging from fatigue, headache, and poor sleep to the avoidance of action, a loss of courage, the inability to confront or help others, and mistrust in general. In this scene, Hoeun defines *baksbat* in language very similar to that of Chhim: a "sickness caused by your having undergone injustices, oppressed and crushed by the Khmer Rouge regime, a suffering that subsists today." The fear Doeun feels when reading about a knife attack triggers previous fears he experienced under the Khmer Rouge, making his daily living more difficult.

Nor is Doeun the only character suffering from broken courage. Peng Phan's experience under the Khmer Rouge was dehumanizing. In 1973, she tells Bopha, Phan was presenting the news on the television. When the Khmer Rouge learned that she had been on television, they put her in prison, where she was tortured and witnessed the killing of others. She tells one revealing story about catching a snake, asking a "base person" to cook it for her, and keeping the small piece that the villager returned to her in her pocket for weeks; she ate small bits at night until it soaked her clothes in oil and rotted. She also tells the story of her fiancé, a doctor, who tried to find her but was killed instead. Phan's past weighs upon her: she suffers from a fear that continually returns, as she says, "like for the first time," giving her headaches and preventing her from sleep and work.[15]

But the trap of broken courage widens to enmesh the entire nation. The film links deeply with Benedict Anderson's analysis of two themes essential to the formation of national identities. The first is journalism. According to Anderson, the mechanical reproduction of the printing press helped create the conditions for a sense of national identification.[16] Newspapers and magazines, radio and television, build common experiences and a sense of national belonging among people who have never met. In the early seventies, Peng Phan was a news anchor: her imprisonment was an act against that nation. In the present, Bopha chooses to expose the fragility of national solidarity and the loss of culture, regretting that she herself was not born at a different moment in which these things mattered. But most media in the film passively reflect a stark erosion in solidarity, printing only the stories and photos that exacerbate Doeun's fear. The second way, of course, is through the bond between architecture and museification. The rubble of Sihanouk's nation-building program and the daily news unveil a shared message: the nation is broken.

WHITE BUILDING, RESILIENCE, AND ARTISTIC PRACTICE

To understand the determination of the artists to persevere under these conditions, it is helpful to consider closely the second architectural icon of the Sangkum era in which the film is set, the White Building. In one shot, Bopha stands on a roof and looks at the construction site of the casino, which dominates the more traditional Buddhist Institute next to it. The camera turns with her as she turns to gaze upon the White Building, a movement that links the theater and the building in complementarity, both stubborn holdouts in the changing cityscape. The White Building was designed not by Molyvann but by Lu Ban Hap and Vladimir Bodiansky, within Molyvann's general development plan and in harmony with his democratic spirit. It was designed to provide accommodations to low-income residents, functionaries, and especially the artists themselves. Over the years, the building had stopped being a symbol of national pride and took on a physical form of its own, becoming a kind of urban artwork, as residents added components here and there to increase capacity. After the war, it was extensively squatted and inhabited by sex trade workers who lived alongside the other residents. In its later years, before its demolition in 2017, the apartments had been so neglected that many saw them as "noisome squatter camps."[17]

Panh has filmed the White Building on a number of occasions, most notably in *Paper Cannot Wrap Ember* (2007), which documents a community of sex workers who lived there. Here is what he writes about the building in an accompanying book: "For me these spaces represent the struggle for dignity par excellence. Against all expectations, the building stands despite the whims of history; even in ruin, it remains an architectural jewel where, despite the most oppressing heat, the wind circulates pleasantly through the corridors and refreshes moist skin. Artists resist within her. . . . The decomposing building gives off an incredible energy, its inhabitants seek to preserve their identity."[18] He insists that the "words" of the artists and sex workers who live there "rise up against the negation of the human." Complementing the theater, the White Building reflects the resistance, creativity, and resilience of the nation's artists and most vulnerable citizens.

Cutting into the building, Panh examines more closely how Peng Phan begins to face the "negation" of her own humanity at the hands of the Khmer Rouge. Initially, she relies only on one of the treatments Chhim suggests in his clinical work—medical intervention—and the film reflects negatively on the mountain of drugs that doctors have prescribed for her. One shot shows Phan looking toward the camera from outside a dispensary window, surrounded by the window's bars, while the pharmacist fires off a litany of absurdly complex directions: take the pink one in the morning, the blue one at night, never the yellow with the blue, if you have severe side effects take the white one, and so on. This would be funny, except for the severity of the side effects and the image of the bars that evoke her imprisonment in both the past and medicine.[19]

But there are other approaches. First of all, Chhim suggests simply an "understanding of the context underlying [the] problem."[20] A part of this involves coming to a recognition that is important to all of Panh's work. Chhim explains *baksbat* through the image of an elephant that has sat on the thatch (*sbat-sbov*) from which the roofs of some houses are made. Similarly, he suggests, broken courage is not something that can just be repaired; it is a "permanent breaking of the spirit." Toward the end of *The Missing Picture*, Panh says that it would be better to die than to experience and witness certain events and survive.[21] Here, too, there is a sense of no return that makes words like "healing" or "solution" or "recovery" seem out of place. If medical intervention aspires to repair something, here there is no such pretension. At the same time, something new needs to be constructed. Hoeun tells Doeun that he will fail if he tries not think about fear, but he can learn to stand with courage in other ways.

This construction of new forms of courage is a vast project and is essential to all of Rithy Panh's cinema. In this film, it is forged in artistic practice itself. When Ta Loto's son reminisces about his father's performances, we sense the healing of joy and laughter. Sin Sisamouth's song gives voice to the melancholy of love. When Hoeun plays the traditional stringed instrument, the *trô*, he sets a mood of serenity and establishes continuity in the midst of the ruins. Hoeun and Doeun's short performances of puppet theater, very reminiscent of the cinema in the use of light, shadow, and framing, provide examples of the pedagogical elements of narrative. Apsara dancers rehearse in the theater's vast lobby and bring visions of beauty to Hoeun's dreams. Even if the theater now lacks an audience, Hoeun and Doeun and the other artists give these arts a fragile but real continued existence. Singing along to Sin Sisamouth's song is a form of repetition different from the traumatic repetition found in the newspaper. Art and media are opposed; art offers comfort, beauty, and dignity, a slow apprenticeship of the complexities of living after the "negation of the human." Panh's cinema itself, often echoing the techniques of these artists so closely that the border is blurred between their work and his own (figure 2.1), archives the artists, songs, and films of the past, builds upon their model, and establishes continuity with them.

The work of the artists expresses critical thinking and autonomy. Some scenes, such as the opening sequence, in which Phan casts off the clichés of representations of war, have an almost Brechtian sense of self-awareness. In another, Phan and two other women are preparing food while Hoeun, the director, and some of the other men watch television. Doeun arrives with a case of Angkor beer and some food; he is wearing a new jacket, paid for with money he has earned from filming a bogus political campaign spot, a project for which none of the actors has respect. He brags, talking about going off to the United States with his money; the other characters describe ways in which people are tricked into going abroad, only to work menial jobs or, for women, to be sold into prostitution. Offended, Doeun storms out. But then he turns around and returns, and they all discuss how the scene has been performed. Instead of objects of the whims of history, they have become active, able to assume a critical distance in order to explore and criticize the choices they might make in such a situation.

FIGURE 2.1. Cinematic shot of the hand-cut leather puppet theater

A similar creative approach gives Peng Phan ownership over her past at the individual level. With Bopha, she returns to the village where she was imprisoned by the Khmer Rouge. She relives the past, reciting the simplistically ideological text of a song she was forced to sing at that time, and cautiously approaching a stupa where she was interrogated. As in Panh's previous film, *S21*, putting Peng Phan in the spaces of her trauma brings out deeply embodied memories.[22] But what is important here is not so much that the memories return to haunt her but how she struggles for agency over them. A second technique announces an element of *The Missing Picture*. Phan tells her story to Bopha while the two women sit around a scale model of the village, including stupas, houses, ponds, and at least one empty grave, on which she can move various pieces (figure 2.2). In close-up, the camera shows her hands as she shapes the arrangement of houses and stupas around the village, telling Bopha her own story, writing history from her point of view.

At one moment, Bopha is surprised because Phan seems to contradict something she had previously told her. But rather than casting doubt on Phan's story, this rectification of a detail offers a reminder of the goals of testimony and memory. The goal after courage has been broken is not to access or recount an absolute truth, nor to repair the irreparable, but to construct an image of the past. Art is about producing representations—in the cinema this means visual and sound images. This does not mean that "l'idée fait le monde" (the idea creates the world) as it did for the Khmer Rouge, with their utopian ideology and refusal to acknowledge reality.[23] But images are always "interpretations," are always *for* someone. In the case of this model village, the image is Phan's, controlled by her, manipulated and brought into language by her. The village is a physical archive

FIGURE 2.2. Peng Phan arranging the miniature village

she now controls. Here again the artist provides a model for the filmmaker who hopes to leave on the screen images that are not missing, but which take the missing into account.[24] Sometimes the camera pans over the image like a landscape, insisting on its power to fill the screen and stand in for reality. But it does not contain any human figures, and it remains an image haunted by ghosts—an image that is there, and that one can, using a word that again appears in *The Missing Image*, "possess," if incompletely. To overcome broken courage and "think of living," as Panh says in the epigraph that opens this essay, requires not medication but this recuperative work on the site of the past, performed through a creative gesture, an approach that has inspired Panh throughout his career.

Such memory work, which depends on Bopha as an interlocuter, is also a resistance against social death in the present. One could insist on a stylistic attentiveness to the placement and movement of the camera. Already, there is a contrast between an off-screen space, conveyed by the constant jackhammering of the casino's construction (figuring the unbridled global capitalist development), and a separate, frequently interior space (the theater, the White Building, the house where Bopha and Phan speak), where characters converse. These latter spaces retain the human scale of Molyvann's machines for living: Phan's apartment is quiet, lit with soft natural light (a result of the architect's design), with white tiles and sky-blue walls. Through attention, commonplace details become essential to Panh's style. While speaking, in the apartment or in the village, the women sit on the ground. The handheld camera, always slightly moving, embodies the viewing experience. It is also low, at the level of the women as they speak, framing them in medium close-up, so that we feel a proximity to them (figure 2.3). Instead of cutting, the camera pans from one face to the other. In these ways,

FIGURE 2.3. Phan and Bopha in Phan's apartment, White Building

Phan's dignity and sociability are reemphasized through lighting and framing. Analogous camera and sound techniques are used when filming Doeun and Hoeun, and really cut across Panh's work, especially the documentaries like *Site 2*, *The Land of the Wandering Souls* (2000), and *Paper Cannot Wrap Ember*.

HOMELESSNESS AND RESILIENCE

These burgeoning hints of trust in others and confidence in the future make the ending of the film all the more anguishing and ambiguous. For Hoeun, fear involves returning to his home: he is ashamed to tell his wife and his children that he has nothing to show for the last few years and fears she will reject him. But Doeun convinces him and even takes him to the village in a motorcycle side-car. A cut later, however, we know that the visit has not gone well: Hoeun is alone in the auditorium, ripping up the plants he has grown and burning them in a bonfire. If artistic practice is, as Hoeun has claimed, about freedom, beauty, and love—in short, about trust in the world—this is a bitter failure, an impossible future with his family, perhaps an end to his dream of the performing arts. The moment matches an earlier scene in which Doeun, also on the edge of despair, hangs an effigy of himself, in a way that makes the viewer think, at first, that he is committing suicide.

At the end of this scene, the camera cranes up, following the smoke of the bonfire, leaving Hoeun in the auditorium, and points outward, over the theater, toward the northern half of Phnom Penh (the last shot of the film). Here we leave the world of the friends to gaze at a more hostile exterior, where the built environment is structured by rampant construction, unhinged capitalism, and social disintegration. There is the suggestion that the artists will, like this smoke, wander out into this city, and of course we know that the theater was demolished in 2008, and that the White Building, which survived until 2017, has also been torn down. This long shot establishes nothing for the artists. Like many of Panh's long shots, it conveys something homeless and errant. And yet, the shot does not negate what we have learned from the artists: perhaps Hoeun and Rithy Panh are creating a role (like Doeun's with his papier-mâché effigy or Phan at the film's beginning), provoking a debate, presenting a cautionary tale. It does not erase the stubborn persistence of these artists to build a different future.[25] Here the camera points to the unknown: Where, if anywhere, will the artists find a home?

Since the camera has shown us this worried view over Phnom Penh, I suggest that our interpretation might be informed by Panh's own place in, and contribution to, the arts of his city; for Panh's tireless work over the years to construct spaces for artistic practices follows in the footsteps of Vann Molyvann and these other artists. An exhaustive list of his efforts in this sense would be too long, but would include his cofounding of the Bophana Center and its diverse mission providing historical pedagogy, exposition and screening space, and training and production support. It would also include his artistic mentoring and collaborations, public engagement, and, of course, his commitment as an artist to creating images in and about Cambodia, past and present. In this light, *The Burnt Theatre* is neither a simple lament for a lost building nor a poignant reminder of the passing of a civilization. It is a living homage to the creative and resilient spirit of the artists who worked at the theater and lived in the White Building, whose example is preserved for the present and future.

NOTES

Rithy Panh, "Ce sont les petits gestes qui éclairent les grandes causes," interview by Marie Ingouf, *Les Ecrans Terribles*, November 28, 2017, http://www.lesecransterribles.com/petits-gestes-eclairent-grandes-causes-rencontre-rithy-panh/46720. Translations are mine unless otherwise noted.

1. Panh, "Petits Gestes."
2. See Diderot on Hubert Robert in the Salons of 1767 in Denis Diderot, *Diderot on Art II*, ed. and trans. John Goodman (New Haven, CT: Yale University Press, 1995), 190–220.
3. Ly Daravuth and Ingrid Muan, *Cultures of Independence* (Phnom Penh: Reyum, 2001).
4. Benedict Anderson, *Imagined Communities: Reflections on the Origins and Spread of Nationalism*, rev. ed. (London: Verso, 2006), 179.
5. Ashley Thompson, "Preface," in Vann Molyvann, *Modern Khmer Cities* (Phnom Penh: Reyum, 2003), iv.
6. Le Corbusier, *Toward an Architecture (Texts and Documents)*, trans. John Goodman (Los Angeles: Getty Research Institute, 2008). See also Le Corbusier, *The Modulor*, trans. Peter de Francia and Anna Bostock (Basel: Birkhäuser, 2000).
7. See Milton Osborne, *Sihanouk: Prince of Light, Prince of Darkness* (Honolulu: University of Hawaii Press, 1994), 177–186.

8. Ben Kiernan, *How Pol Pot Came to Power: Colonialism, Nationalism, and Communism in Cambodia, 1930–1975* (New Haven, CT: Yale University Press, 2004), chap. 7.
9. For an informed and polemical discussion of patronage, politics, and land development, see Sebastian Strangio, *Hun Sen's Cambodia* (New Haven, CT: Yale University Press, 2014).
10. Rithy Panh, "Rithy Panh's Comment," https://filmex.jp/2005/burnt_win-e.htm.
11. For the use of photos in postgenocide texts, see Marianne Hirsch, *The Generation of Postmemory: Writing and Visual Culture after the Holocaust* (New York: Columbia University Press, 2012), pt. 2.
12. Boreth Ly, "Screening the Crisis in Monetary Masculinity: Rithy Panh's *One Night after the War* and *Burnt Theatre*," in *Film in Contemporary Southeast Asia: Cultural Interpretation and Social Intervention*, ed. David C. L. Lim and Hiroyuki Yamamoto (London: Routledge, 2012), 53–72.
13. Panh, "Rithy Panh's Comment."
14. Sotheara Chhim, "*Baksbat* (Broken Courage): A Trauma-Based Syndrome in Cambodia," *Medical Anthropology* 32 (2013): 161.
15. See Boreth Ly's chapter in this volume for a compelling analysis of the "mad mother" figure in Panh's films, several of whom are played by the actress Peng Phan herself. Ly has also authored a major recent monograph exploring artistic practices in the wake of the Cambodian genocide through Khmer concepts and practices. Notions like *snarm* (the trace) and *baksbat* are important elements of his framework. Boreth Ly, *Traces of Trauma: Cambodian Visual Culture and National Identity in the Aftermath of Genocide* (Honolulu: University of Hawai'i Press, 2020).
16. Anderson, *Imagined Communities*, 24–36.
17. Milton Osborne, *Phnom Penh: A Cultural History* (Oxford: Oxford University Press, 2008), 133.
18. Rithy Panh with Louise Lorentz, *Le papier ne peut pas envelopper la braise* (Paris: Grasset, 2007), 16.
19. Ly, in her chapter in this volume, emphasizes the imprisonment of the mad mother figure in Panh's cinema.
20. Chhim, "*Baksbat* (Broken Courage)," 166.
21. "There are many things that man should not see or know; and should he see them he'd be better off dying." Official translation of the original French text that served as voice-over to *The Missing Picture*. See Rithy Panh with Christophe Bataille, *L'image manquante* (Paris: Grasset, 2013), 68.
22. On reenactment and memory, see Deirdre Boyle, "Shattering Silence: Traumatic Memory and Reenactment in Rithy Panh's *S21: The Khmer Rouge Killing Machine*," *Framework* 50, no. 1/2 (Spring and Fall 2009): 95–106.
23. Panh, *L'image manquante*, 59.
24. "This missing picture I now hand over to you: let it never cease to seek us out." Panh, 69.
25. It is worth mentioning that Hoeun still participates in a small but thriving artistic community of Phnom Penh.

3 • THE WOUNDS OF MEMORY

Poetics, Pain, and Possibilities in Rithy Panh's *Exile* and *Que la barque se brise*

KHATHARYA UM

In this age of displacement, where mobility in its plurality has become a key facet of modernity, exile has acquired added importance as an intellectual concern. Long a part of the human vocabulary, the scale and complexity of displacement in form, cause, and consequence have made this century an "age of anxiety and estrangement" that is "spiritually orphaned and alienated,"[1] with its swells of refugees, the stateless, and the unauthorized urging critical reflections about the human condition and the moral crisis of our time. Drawing upon two of Rithy Panh's films, *Exile* (2016) and *Que la barque se brise, que la jonque s'entrouve* ("Let the boat break its back, let the junk break open," 2001), this chapter looks at the effects of genocidal violence on the individual survivor, the family, and the diasporic community, and at their internal and external negotiations of the exilic conditions that it engenders. It addresses the notion of exile, not one of cosmopolitan nomadism and liberating flexible citizenry,[2] but of dislocation and uprootedness, of the "anguish," as Edward Said describes it, of the "mass exiles with broken lives."[3] Approaching the two films as an experiential continuum, though in reversed temporality, the chapter traces the trajectory of trauma through multiple registers, from the private and personal to the social realms, as inflected by time, generational distance, and diasporic remove. The internal struggle of an individual to remember in *Exile* and, in so doing, to cling to his humanity in the destructive grip of a regime insistent on historical erasure, is juxtaposed in *Que la barque se brise* with the struggle of a survivor in the diaspora to forget. In essence, both remembering and forgetting torment in the genocidal aftermath.

Tracing the contours and turns of memory, this chapter is about movement—across time, space, and generations, and between past, present, and future—

straddling problematic binaries and juxtapositions of life and death, real and imagined, bare life and artistry, remembering and forgetting, survival and resistance, Cambodia and the diaspora. While survivors' public testimonies abound in the genocidal wake, and visuals of atrocities at times tread the slippery slopes of ethics and poetics, we are not often offered the opportunity to witness the inner turmoil—the nonpublic, nonarticulated experiences—of those who endured these historical traumas. *Exile* allows us glimpses into that private realm, the solitary journey of survivors through and after genocide. In exposing the genocidal world of Democratic Kampuchea in its contradictions and falsehood and the rendering bare of life in this state of exception, to evoke Giorgio Agamben, it is a searing interrogation of the disconcerting conditions of our time, of soul-injuring state violence, alienation, solitude, and rupturing aftereffects. It is also a reminder of the possibilities that remain under the genocidal debris.

The small bare hut, devoid of any furnishing save for a water jar in the corner, that is the principal backdrop of *Exile* epitomizes the materiality of bare life in Democratic Kampuchea, where, as the narrator comments, a metal spoon was prized more than life itself. Introduced in the opening scene with the visual of a young man slicing off and chewing a piece of hide from a cow's tether, the permeating sense of deprivation is underscored by the imagery of hunger so extreme that it makes one "grow fond of roots, rats, soil," as images of watery porridge, grilled snails from muddy ponds, insects, and a metal tree that bore no fruit move across the screen. All-consuming, hunger was intentionally deployed as an instrument of the terroristic state that sought to annihilate all that is human and render the individual into an unquestioning, disposable labor implement. As for many who lived under the Khmer Rouge, the monotony and barrenness of life in *Exile* were punctuated only by the constant quest for food. In the bleak conditions of the Khmer Rouge work camps, of merciless toiling to produce food that disappeared as soon as it was harvested, living registered only in the search for life itself.

In this state of exception, a prison *sans barreaux* to which most Cambodians and virtually all urban residents were exiled, it was not just quotidian life, disciplined by surveillance, terror, starvation, and life-sapping, seemingly absurd tasks, that was made barren, but the human condition itself, which was voided of meaning, purpose, and peoplehood. The boulders that materialized in the hut did not merely roll back in Sisyphean futility; they were swallowed up by sand and, like the many Khmer Rouge projects for which thousands of lives were sacrificed, ultimately relegated to oblivion.

A system that dispensed of human life with banal disregard rests upon its ability to divest people of their humanity. It is only through their dehumanization that people could be used and disposed of at Angkar's despotic will as mere objects and tools of the revolution, lives so devalued that a worker could be killed for breaking a farm implement. This process of dehumanization, systematically enacted, began at the moment of evacuation as people were herded out of their homes and histories in inhumane conditions. Along the way, with each conscious and unconscious submission to the basal instinct for survival—the decision to abandon a loved one, to be deaf to the cry of an orphaned child stricken with thirst, to come to see an aging parent as nothing more than a burden—they had discarded a piece of their humanity. This process continued in the new settlements, where, as the narrator in Panh's *The Missing Picture* recalls, "there are no individuals—only numbers. They cut our hair. They take our watches, glasses, toys, books. They dye our clothes black. They change our first names." There, ravaged by hunger and fear, their former selves diminished further with every self-implicating act of survival. What was left upon death was swallowed up in mass graves, a final annihilation of identity, history, and personhood so complete that "not even your relatives, not even your ancestors can find you."[4]

Systematic dehumanization was reinforced by the stalking fear that compelled individuals to adopt new names and new biographies, to bury their past—photos, identity, memory wrapped in the black cord of mourning—as the narrator in *Exile* has had to do in order to survive the present. What he later retrieves—perhaps could only retrieve—in essence are the material remains of the past, for his own face that stares back at him reflects a sense of estrangement, the broken mirror a metaphor for the fractured self, for the life fragments that survivors have had to pick up and reassemble, often in despairing futility. This act of unrelenting excavation for things buried or lost "as if the filmmaker is exhuming himself as a boy" is, for many survivors, a lifelong performance of trauma that is as insistent as it is in vain.[5] In the end, the narrator moves through his hut, looking at the imaginary wall of photos not with relived endearment but seemingly with detachment, as if he is moving through a gallery, looking impassively at object remains of someone else's history.

Totalitarian systems like that of the Khmer Rouge strip people not only of their material wellbeing, but also of their self. In this exilic condition, as Rithy Panh reflects, "one's self is lost, one suffers, one fades away."[6] Ultimately, the narrator is left with nothing more than a self-loathing recognition of his insignificance: "I despise the dust I am made of which now speaks to you." Dehumanization and the destruction of the self reinforced the material bareness of life under the Khmer Rouge, the contrast with the revolutionary rhetoric provoking an ontological crisis, prompting the narrator to muse: "Can the powerful life we live in be called life? I am a buffalo, I am a spoon, I am a tool with no name." Wrapped in paralyzing fear and hunger, like scurrying rodents in unrelenting search for food (*Exile*), "watched, counted" under Angkar's panoptic gaze, the individual was bereft of all that gives meaning to life, atomized and fearful not only of resisting but even of the thought of resistance.

ALONENESS, LOSS OF SOCIALITY, LOSS OF SELF

Regimes such as Democratic Kampuchea, however, are not content with mere subjugation and killing; they need to sever human connections and to destroy sociality. As Rithy Panh reflects, "Genocide is not only killings; it is not only deaths. It is much more than that. It is the complete destruction and deprivation of our culture and our identity."[7] The destructive force wielded to dehumanize was also directed at the social bonds that envelop an individual in a larger collective, that inform his identity and provide coherence, meaning, and purpose to his world. The loss of social vitality, as Claudia Card contends, is in effect a loss of identity, hence of coherence and meaning in one's existence.[8] By assigning every individual, including children, to a work team with whom they lived and worked with virtually no contact with their families, and in constant displacement, the Khmer Rouge effectively unraveled those ties that are at the core of the Cambodian identity. In so doing, they divested the individual of the source of solace, support, strength, and purpose and undercut the potential for personal and collective resistance. They also dismantled the family institution, a core underpinning of Khmer identity, replacing it with the Party, which now commanded the authority and loyalty once reserved for kin. It was in this totalitarian logic that Angkar usurped the tradition-sanctioned parental right to "arrange" marriage.

Terror further eroded sociality as institutionalized denunciation and guilt by association fostered distrust, undercutting the formation of new relationships and compelling the disavowal of existing ones, including familial ties, for the sake of survival. In essence, what differentiates genocide from other forms of mass atrocities is this intentional assault on sociality, the injuring effects of which extend beyond physical death. As Card points out, "Seeing social death at the center of genocide takes our focus off body counts and loss of individual talents, directing us instead to mourn losses of relationships that create community and give meaning to the development of talents."[9] Images of the young man, curled into himself in sleep, wrapped in a child's longing for maternal love made manifest through the ghostly hand of caress and a haunting lullaby, or moving restlessly in his house of poetic imagining, all evoke a feeling of utter aloneness; "It used to rain voices . . . now no more. Words are cold."

While physical death may have been forestalled, what replaced it was social death,[10] marked by a plurality of losses, including the loss of the sense of moral entitlement to personhood through degradation and systematic alienation of the individual from his family, his community, himself. What results is the rendering of the individual into a nonperson, a "man who feels no more," who treasures his metal spoon more than his life, for "who do you love when there is no one left?" (*Exile*). These are losses, numbing in their normalization, for which "mourning is difficult; [for] there is no end to the burial," as the photos disappear one by one from the wall of memory in *Exile*. For many survivors, it is this haunting presence of absence—the unfillable emptiness of an upturned palm (*Exile*)—that shadows them in the genocide afterlife. Against images suggestive of post-genocide mobility—possibly of return to natal homes, possibly of yet another relocation/dislocation to the border camps—the narrator in *Exile* speaks of stasis: "I counted the days, I counted the dead, the moons. I was lost."

Forced removal from one's home and relational web engenders an exilic condition that is both external and internal. Defined by an orientation elsewhere to a different time and a different place, exile is, in essence, a way of "dwelling in space with a constant awareness that one is not at home."[11] It is thus that Panh describes exile as "an abandonment, a terrifying solitude."[12] A liminal state of indefinite waiting without certainty or foreseeable end, sustained by unrequited anticipation of change, it is a metaphor for hope equally insistent in its possibility as it is elusive: "I loved the moon. I sent her wishes. Promises I couldn't keep. But the night lets you down. Nothing ever happens. Except for the return of morning." The imagery of birds in flight that is often associated with mobility and freedom is depicted in *Exile* as circling in the air, an entanglement of departure and return from which they seem unable to break free.

REMEMBERING AS RESISTANCE

For Rithy Panh, exile presents an answer onto itself, for like death, "exile is a sheet of paper," its pristine blankness evoking void and, simultaneously, a sense of renewed possibility. As he puts it, when "one is face to face with oneself as well as the gigantic totalitarian machine that is the Khmer Rouge, one must find that which makes them human, gives them dignity, and what makes them capable of creativity, learning languages and seeing the world in color."[13] As the narrator in *Exile* instructs, "In this night of ignorance, you need to steal fire. Lock your gaze on a face. Cling on to a magic word, to a poem." Resistance and self-preservation are found in the willful retreat to that inner space where "one can find one's self in the land of words, of image, in reverie."[14] In the "last exile" of sleep or dream, symbolized by the bright moon, the only light in the bleak world of Democratic Kampuchea, self, identity, history, and human dignity are reclaimed. In that space where the presence of absence is summoned, bare existence is replenished not simply with materiality of the past (photos on the wall, books, colorful clothing, a guitar, a clock that works, endless rows of bowls brimming with white rice) but, more important, the missing texture of life—color, sound, the handful of buttons signifying not just quotidian objects but the solace of wearing a shirt, of normalcy. Imagination thus makes possible the reemplacement of an uprooted life, through which home becomes, at once, "a memory and a hope."[15]

In their work on trauma narration, Kay Schaffer and Sidonie Smith contend that, through acts of remembering otherwise, "individuals and communities narrate alternative or counter-histories coming from the margins, voiced by other kinds of subjects—the tortured, the displaced and overlooked, the silenced and unacknowledged—among them."[16] In the otherworldliness of Democratic Kampuchea, where life was governed by a different reality, survivors were left only with a recognition of the absurd. Survival, for Panh, thus hinged upon the ability to accept this condition of absurdity, not in passive submission but as active embracing of the struggle in its futility, and in so doing transcend it, for, as Camus puts it, "There is no fate that cannot be surmounted by scorn."[17] Through imagination, the narrator in *Exile* creatively remakes his world, filling it with presence, color, and life, thereby ensuring the preservation of his self, his dignity, and his humanity; even the boulders, signifying both the trauma and the absurdity of his existence, can be lightened, made to spin in the air. Of living with trauma, Panh notes: "When you have gone through a history like mine, you cannot really be assuaged. There is something broken in us forever. We can just try to be less angry with these criminals."[18] Elsewhere, he further reflects, "I cannot forget, even if I wanted to. You have to learn to live with this pain."[19] A gesture toward transcendence, itself a very Buddhist stance, the final scene in *Exile* is one of shadowy movements suggestive of the Buddhist walking meditation that evoke and supplant the earlier image of the labored motion of the enslaved in the Khmer Rouge work camps.

THE CONDITIONS OF EXILE

If *Exile* is about the struggle of an individual to resist and survive state terror, *Que la barque se brise* unveils the challenges facing survivors in the genocide afterlife. Through the personal struggles of Bopha, a single mother, a restaurateur, a refugee, and a genocide survivor, it provides a glimpse into diasporic life, haunted by loss and unsettled by forced displacement and reemplacement, making legible that which is often obscured by the overemphasis on refugee resilience. As Jean Langford reminds us, "The violence registered by nightmares and hauntings is not only remembered and embodied violence of war or state terror but also the structural violence of minoritization and poverty."[20] If Panh's *La France est notre patrie* ("France is our homeland," 2015) is a postcolonial interrogation of the relationships between the colonized and the colonizer, *Que la barque se brise* places the Southeast Asian refugee diaspora in a country of resettlement tinged with coloniality, where references to separateness and difference are conveyed in veiled response, in Vietnamese, about the misery of interracial union.

For many refugees, resettlement has not meant reintegration in the full sense of the term, beyond what is commonly uttered in policy discourse and essentially reduced to employment. Instead, what is engendered by forced migration is a sense of double estrangement—of the alienation that comes from the physical and psychical deracination from home and land, and the alienation of nonbelonging and incompleteness in the place of resettlement. It is this acute and unabated sense of marginalization and nonbelonging that defines what I have referred to elsewhere as "refugitude"—the state and consciousness of dislocation, of being a refugee, that remain long after the expiration of the label.[21] For Minh, a protagonist in *Que la barque se brise,* as for many refugees, that alienation began in the refugee camp where he arrived denuded of his identity, without an age or a name—neither his nor of his family. In this state of disavowal, encoded in the designation of *apatrides* (stateless), the refugee figure is recast without roots, history, or identity, save that of the rescued.

Refugees, as Edward Said contends, as such, live in a metaphoric exile where "habits of life, expression or activity in the new environment inevitably occur against the memory of these things in another environment," where "the new and the old environments are vivid, actual, occurring together contrapuntally."[22] In contrast to the bare life and silent monologue of *Exile, Que la barque se brise* is a gathering of life debris in the genocidal aftermath, marked by the return of laughter in work, chatter, sound, movement, and the cacophony of the diaspora. Though fuller with diasporic reassemblage of family and community, the fraying of exilic life poignantly captured in *Exile* persists in the aftermath of historical trauma. Survival is shadowed by guilt and laden by obligations to both the living and the dead. For Minh, an orphan, honoring his parents means not only shouldering responsibilities for his siblings left behind in Vietnam but also having to achieve the kind of success that is expected of him and for which his mother had made unrepayable sacrifices, but one that is not of his choosing such as inheriting the family business and submitting to an arranged marriage. Like many Cambodian genocide widows who constitute a significant part of the diaspora, Bopha, in turn, has to be both mother and father to her daughter, a dutiful daughter to her widowed mother, and a breadwinner for her all-female household. Remarkable as her accomplishments may be, they are muted by the constant recall of her inability to conduct the appropriate funeral rites for her father. It is this sense of unfulfilled and unfulfillable obligation and the despair that it engenders that torment many survivors; for Bopha, the chronic leg pain that plagues her, a metaphor for the emotional paralysis that impedes her ability to move forward, could not be alleviated with Western medicine, for what she sought was not cure, but forgiveness.

The "normal" functioning self, often lauded uncritically as refugee resilience, thus coexists with the deeply anguished one. Evoking Jankelevitch's reference to the sensation of being "drowned again and again," Rithy Panh speaks to the temporality of genocidal violence, noting that "for us, genocide is continuous, you get it for all your life. . . . It is like you are drowning and you cannot breathe."[23] Amid the cacophony of life forced into a new messy order of normalcy, loneli ness prevails as survivors work to straddle their renewed existence and the "other life," one deeply internal, unarticulated, wrenchingly private, solitary, that cannot be shared. Of the injurious encounter that renders even the ordinary extraordinary, Panh notes: "Daily reality cannot be said or told in its totality unless it is lived."[24]

That which is suppressed, hidden away, nonetheless resurfaces if only as flashes and statics, nocturnal torments, self-destructive behaviors, unspoken tensions, and photos on the family altar without frames or contexts. It is in essence the ever presence of absence, echoed through the prewar music constantly playing in the background, that thwarts the movement toward normalcy. Like the Sisyphean boulders in *Exile*, the traumatic past places itself in the way of the survivors' struggles to "rebuild their capacity to be a human being again."[25] In this interstice where the past bleeds into the present, survivors confront the infusibility of "the life before" and "the life after," for exile, as Said reflects "is life led outside habitual order . . . no sooner does one gets accustomed to it than its unsettling force erupts anew."[26] Whereas in *Exile* the past is invited in as an existential compass and a lifeline for survival, the past in *Que la barque se brise* is intrusive, disorienting, an anchor connoting not emplacement but immobility. Even in their seaside escapade, the ocean for Minh does not conjure romance but memories of rape and murder on the high seas. Similarly, for Bopha, the romanticism of an evening stroll, tango music, and lipstick that marks an attempted recovery of her feminine self is rendered ephemeral by the resurfacing of memory, for "just as you begin to think of something else, to live . . . it comes back." If what survivors are looking for are life and living, what is afforded to most is mere survival.

The unveiling of private struggles, frailties, and the many places and traces of trauma destabilizes the notion of effective resettlement and interrogates the meaning of success. Bopha's forays into Paris's gambling dens, her paralyzing affliction from what Veena Das terms "poisonous memories,"[27] the refugees' pained response to Khmer Rouge leader Khieu Samphan's failure to acknowledge responsibility for the genocide, the long-suppressed unadulterated pain that Panh describes as "douleur brute" expressed by the grandmother whom he encountered during the casting for *Que la barque se brise*—all index the surfacing of trauma at an unpredictable time and place, like the memory flickers in the water bowl in *Exile*. These eruptions are the transmutations of trauma that preclude speech: "You cannot recount horror. You can only recount moments" (*Que la barque se brise*). Such disarticulation, however, does not reflect the unrepresentability of the experience but, rather, the desubjectification of those whose traumatic experiences have engendered an inability to speak; as Bopha puts it, "I cannot recount it. I can't seem to do it. It stays inside."

Whereas in *Exile* it is the system that denies them life and living, in *Que la barque se brise*, it is the survivors, spiritually broken (*baksbat*) by state violence, who seem unable to allow themselves happiness in the genocidal aftermath; like

Sisyphus, they have cheated death, only to be cast into a tormented existence. Haunted by loss and feeling as if they have no right to life, happiness seems to only magnify the suffering, the ordinariness of quotidian life making even more unreal the extraordinariness of their experiences. This inner torment that plagues survivors provokes a fundamental question about life claims, about the possibility of insisting on their moral entitlement to living after social death, one in which they have been made to feel implicated. As Panh points out: "If there is a duty to remember, there is also the duty to forget, for life to resume. But before forgetting, the work of memory and mourning must be done."[28] Mourning for the disappeared, for unmet obligations, and for all the intangible losses, however, is an interminable process, an engagement with liminality that can never bring an end to itself.

With life and death inhabiting the same plane, trauma in *Que la barque se brise*, as in many Cambodian families, trails across generations. Both Bopha and her daughter, Leaksmey, survived because their fathers gave up their lives for their families. Whereas for Bopha the trauma is in knowing, Leaksmey's pain is rooted in not knowing. Her query "What is this scar on my back?" references not only the cicatrix, but the burden of embodied history that she carries. Secrets, aimed to protect, instead widen relational fissures. Secrets are then buried under other secrets. The self-destructive resort to gambling is "both a leap into the void, and a solitary adventure" in search of hope afforded through the anticipation of a winning hand.[29] As Panh puts it, "For people who have been crushed by a fate they did not control, it is a vertigo that gives the illusion of relying on the almost magical instances of Chance,"[30] a sensation that is, perhaps, also a much-needed reminder that they are still alive. As Panh reflects, "When you have survived a genocide, it is as if you were already dead, then reborn. But the difference is that you are reborn with this death in you."[31] Under the Khmer Rouge, whether one lived or died seemed like a matter of chance; here, they could at least feel that they could walk away. Accustomed to living for and in the moment, survivors can escape Time, even if only momentarily, for in gambling, where "there is no past, no future," it is "this instance that matters."

Like gambling, the romance between Minh and Bopha is similarly dangerous, defiant, hopeful. As in *Exile* where the void is also a site of possibility, exile in *Que la barque se brise* also pries open the space for a romance that may otherwise not be possible given "the racial tension that has lasted for centuries and centuries and brings nothing good for either community."[32] It gestures toward the potentiality of a new beginning in the erasure and anonymity of displacement: "You, like him, on your identity cards, it's written 'stateless.'" The film, nonetheless, acknowledges the tenacious grip of the past, for while Bopha and Minh seek comfort in each other, they remain entrapped in their isolated life. The optimism is reserved for the end, conveyed in a postcard from Cambodia that reiterates the hopeful message of the film's title, a poetic nod to the power of human agency. Despite their self-eroding experiences, survivors can still dictate how they live their lives, at least what remains of them.

THE WORKINGS OF TEMPORALITY

In its interrogation of genocidal violence and memory, *Exile* is a meditation on loss and temporality. What is captured in the laid-out table of half-eaten food, left to gather dust over time, a childhood so ephemeral that the narrator feels having experienced it less intensely than exile, in essence, is life interrupted in motion, captured in a still frame. What it evokes is temporal rupture, a silent clock frozen in time that demarcates the "before" and the "after" in what survivors have referred to as inhabiting "one body, two lives."[33] Speaking of his own journey, Panh recalled: "I left Cambodia when I was 15 with a spiritual wound I knew would never heal. . . . As soon as I reached the camp at Mairut, in Thailand, I stopped fearing for my life, but I felt a profound sadness, whereas I should have been happy. I felt my whole life was already behind me, that it belonged to those years of struggle for survival."[34] Such reflection, echoed by many survivors, calls for a different imagining of time. A regime that rooted its revolutionary future in a paradoxical turn to a past of greater purity and glory was radical in its reversal of movement, none more so than in its forced emptying of cities back into the countryside. With its new chronology, beginning in what has been termed "Year Zero," all that predated this new temporality, including memory, was considered corrupt and irredeemable, to be "crushed" (*kamtech*) into oblivion. In this universe of temporal reverse, nighttime is when living begins—hunting for food, dreaming, and imagining "real life."

REFUGEE TEMPORALITY

As it is for Minh and Bopha, the living present for survivors in the diaspora is constantly punctuated by the past, an interruption not only of the resumption of normalcy but of living. In the lived simultaneity of diasporas' afterlife, time moves forward and backward, a simultaneous and divergent movement that, I argue, characterizes refugee temporality whereby, as time marches on, survivor-refugees are forced back to the traumatic past;[35] as the narrator in Panh's *The Missing Picture* muses, "In the middle of life, childhood returns." Made fifteen years apart, *Que la barque se brise* and *Exile* can be read as an experiential continuum but chronotopically in reversed order, with the examination of the collective, geospatial exile of the diaspora paving the way for the confrontation with what Panh describes as "not just my physical exile but also the internal exile—the building of an emotional island."[36] It took Panh forty-five years to arrive at that moment. That a certain temporal distance is necessary for self-reflection and confrontation with personal trauma may account for the resurgence of post-traumatic stress disorder in many aging survivors in the diaspora.

ART AND RETRIEVAL: THE POLITICS BEHIND THE POETICS AND THE PERSONAL

A "meditation on time, memory, resistance, and revolution," *Exile* is an unflinching critique of the political system that created the Khmer Rouge state of exception. With "L'Internationale" playing in the background and the Maoist Red Book in stark contrast to the black-and-white archival footage, the bare life of Democratic Kampuchea is placed in sharp relief against the glorious rhetoric of a revolutionary regime that came to power on utopian promises only to implode in self-inflicted violence. By strategically placing scenes of lived moments against Khmer Rouge propaganda footage, Panh shows how the archive is also implicated in state violence. In exposing the contradictions, the film delivers a searing indictment less of revolution, which the narrator describes as "always a blatant crime that destroys another crime," an "evil that is the price to pay for the common good," than of "the attempt at destruction, false purity that has seen so many false disciples." With piercing directness, the narrator addresses the "armchair revolutionaries" whose engagement with the world's proletariats is merely through "visits" amounting to nothing more than "landscapes, experiences, theater" with the question "Have you ever been set straight as I was in Cambodia?" It is a demand for critical self-reflexivity that remains elusive, and with moral impunity, among Western intellectuals. The film also forces viewers to interrogate their moral selves by challenging them to reconcile the instinctual gasp registered at the sight of skinned rats and live insects being grilled and consumed, a live chicken being strangled with bare hands, with the muted, if not outrightly absent, revulsion at the system that created the abjection that made those acts necessary.

In their examination of haunting and erasure, Panh's works also raise important questions about film as counterhistory and, ultimately, about the possibility of a "return to poetry" that is simultaneously of commemoration, resistance, and repair in the genocide afterlife. Film mediates against what Jean-François Lyotard describes as the destruction of the ability to speak or to keep quiet that plagues survivors.[37] As a medium for those without language or words, it offers survivors an expression for the unsayable, "words to erase death that erases them." Overcoming the neutering of speech and the evacuation of meaning in words, film makes it possible to "enter history though images."[38] Of *S21*, Panh reflects: "Making films is how I've learned to *live* with my pain. . . . If I didn't make films, I don't know how I would talk about S-21. How?"[39] If it is as Theodor Adorno remarks that writing is a place to live for a man with no homeland, then recounting is also a way to bring an end to the physical and existential voiding that constitutes exile. As Panh notes, "The dignity that you lost under the Khmer Rouge can be recovered by this act," one that, for Panh, is a necessary, albeit Sisyphean, endeavor: "I don't feel better after making a film but making it is a necessity,"[40] for "to resist you need to have this poetic imagination."[41] It is, in that sense, a reclaiming of the right to live—with memories, imagination, hope, and investment in futurity and the potentiality for change. Exposing gaps, contradictions, paradoxes, and possibilities, *Exile* and *Que la barque se brise* are poignant renderings of the ravages of genocide and the indomitability of the human spirit that convey the message not necessarily of hope, but of the imperative of hoping in times of despair.

NOTES

1. Edward Said, "Reflections on Exile," *Granta* 13 (1984): 159.
2. Aihwa Ong, *Flexible Citizenship: The Cultural Logics of Transnationality* (Durham, NC: Duke University Press, 1999).
3. Said, "Reflections on Exile," 163.
4. Personal conversation with Vuthy Sok (alias), Stockton, California, 2019.
5. Deirdre Boyle, "Exile within and Without: New Work in Two Modes from Rithy Panh," *Film Quarterly* 71, no. 1 (2017): 11.
6. Boyle, 11.
7. Rithy Panh, "Rithy Panh on Film Preservation and the Importance of Memory," interview by Frako Loden, International Documentary Association, November 19, 2014, https://www.documentary.org/feature/rithy-panh-film-preservation-and-importance-memory.
8. Claudia Card, "Genocide and Social Death," *Hypatia* 18, no. 1 (2003): 63.
9. Card, 63.
10. See Lisa Marie Camacho, *Social Death* (New York: New York University Press, 2012).
11. John Barbour, "Edward Said and the Space of Exile," *Literature and Theology* 21, no. 3 (2007): 293.
12. Boyle, "Exile within and Without,"11.
13. "Rithy Panh on Exile and Dignity," interview by Alessandro Marazzi Sassoon, *Phnom Penh Post*, March 4, 2017, https://www.phnompenhpost.com/post-weekend/qa-rithy-panh-exile-and-dignity.
14. Boyle, "Exile within and Without," 11.
15. Marco Gemignani, "The Past If Past: The Use of Memories and Self-Healing Narratives in Refugees from the Former Yugoslavia," *Journal of Refugee Studies* 24, no. 1 (2011): 148.
16. Kay Schaffer and Sidonie Smith, *Human Rights and Narrated Lives* (New York: Palgrave, 2004), 16–17.
17. Albert Camus, *The Myth of Sisyphus*, trans. Justin O'Brien (New York: Vintage, e1959), 90.
18. Rithy Panh, "Rithy Panh: 'Je travaille comme un archeologue,'" interview by Marcos Uzal, *Liberation*, June 20, 2019, https://next.liberation.fr/cinema/2019/06/20/rithy-panh-je-travaille-comme-un-archeologue_1735109.
19. Florence Morin, "L'image manquante, le chef d'oeuvre de Rithy Panh," *Le Petit Journal*, August 28, 2014, https://lepetitjournal.com/sortie-cinema-limage-manquante-le-chef-doeuvre-de-rithy-panh-208607.
20. Jean M. Langford, *Consoling Ghosts: Stories of Medicine and Mourning from Southeast Asians in Exile* (Minneapolis: University of Minnesota Press, 2013), 4.

21. Khatharya Um, *From the Land of Shadows: War, Revolution and the Making of the Cambodian Diaspora* (New York: New York University Press, 2015).
22. Said, "Reflections on Exile," 148.
23. Rithy Panh, "On a Morality of Filming: A Conversation between Rithy Panh and Deirdre Boyle," *CineAction* 39 (2016).
24. Cited in Sylvie E. Blum-Reid, "Khmer Memories or Filming with Cambodia," *Inter-Asia Cultural Studies* 4, no.1 (2003): 132.
25. Panh, "On a Morality of Filming," 39.
26. Said, "Reflections on Exile," 149.
27. Veena Das, *Life and Words: Violence and the Descent into the Ordinary* (Berkeley: University of California Press, 2007), 54.
28. Christine Chartier, "Que la barque se brise, que le jonque s'entrouve," *Arte France*, October 2001, http://download.pro.arte.tv/archives/fichiers/01676247.pdf.
29. Chartier.
30. Chartier.
31. Morin, "L'image manquante."
32. Personal communication with Rithy Panh, May 31, 2019.
33. Um, *From the Land of Shadows*.
34. Rithy Panh, "Cambodia: A Wound That Will Not Heal," *UNESCO Courier* 52 (December 12, 1999): 31.
35. The commemorative exhibit *Re/Membering: Meditation on War, Hope, and Home* (2015) that I curated was arranged counterclockwise both in the Buddhist gesture of mourning and to reflect this temporal reverse. My usage of the term "refugee temporality" is different from Eric Tang's, which refers to the continuous stage of "captivity" that marks refugee migration and resettlement journey.
36. "Rithy Panh on Exile and Dignity."
37. Jean-François Lyotard, *The Differend*, trans. George Van den Abbeele (Minneapolis: University of Minnesota Press, 1989), 11.
38. Rithy Panh, "Rithy Panh: J'entre dans l'histoire par les images," interview by Marie-Noelle Tranchant, *Le Figaro*, November 19, 2018, https://www.lefigaro.fr/cinema/2018/11/19/03002-20181119ARTFIG00251-rithy-panh-j-entre-dans-l-histoire-par-les-images.php.
39. "Rithy Panh on the Remembrance of Times Past," *Phnom Penh Post*, December 15, 2006. https://www.phnompenhpost.com/national/rithy-panh-remembrance-times-past.
40. Panh, "On a Morality of Filming," 39.
41. Panh, "Rithy Panh on Exile and Dignity."

PART 2 FROM COLONIAL TO GLOBAL CAMBODIA

4 • RITHY PANH'S *THE SEA WALL*

Reinventing Duras in Cambodia

JACK A. YEAGER AND RACHEL HARRISON

In 1950, midway through the First Indochina War, Marguerite Duras's novel *The Sea Wall* appeared in France, her third publication. It was also the first installment of what Panivong Norindr in his landmark *Phantasmatic Indochina* (1996) called her Indochinese Trilogy that would include *The Lover* (*L'amant*) (1984) and *The North China Lover* (*L'amant de la Chine du nord*) (1991).[1] Many readers justifiably favor the first of the three for its compelling condemnation of French colonialism in Southeast Asia, told here through the story of a mother and her son, Joseph, and daughter, Suzanne, fighting to create, through the construction of a levee, arable land from a flood plain annually inundated by the sea. The rich, multilayered text combines trenchant political critique with a family story, the obsessional struggle of a single parent and her complicated relationship with her children; their coming of age; and, finally, the discovery of sex and desire as well as exploitation in the context of the family's fraught interactions with a character named M. Jo.

In 2008, Rithy Panh made a film version of *The Sea Wall* in Cambodia, reinforcing the setting that inspired Duras's novel based on her own family history. Like Duras, he brought to this story a personal perspective, one that is linked to his experience of growing up in Cambodia and engaging with the country's, and implicitly his own, relationship with France.[2] In this sense, both novel and film speak to a theme of how the characters relate to the land on which they struggle to survive and how, in the process, they straddle differing cultural identities, caught in a space of ambivalence between colonizing powers and more localized affiliations.

In relation to this, two important aspects of *The Sea Wall* stand out in an examination of Rithy Panh's adaptation of Duras's famous text: the city and the portrait of M. Jo.[3] Through an exploration of his transformations of Duras in depth, we highlight in this chapter how Panh reasserts Duras's political critique, one largely de-emphasized in the reception of the novel.[4] Panh achieves this, we argue, in two key ways. One is by altogether excluding the city from the cinematic narrative and instead privileging rural space as a site of potential resistance as Duras indicates, fully realized in Panh's portrayal of a peasant revolt. The other is through the characterization of M. Jo as an ethnically Chinese entrepreneur who stands in as the new embodiment of exploitation from whom both Khmer peasants and impoverished French colonials are at risk.

THE CITY

The description of the colonial city in the opening pages of the second part of *The Sea Wall* is one of the most famous passages from the pen of the writer born in the Saigon suburb of Gia Dinh.[5] The city in her novel is depicted as the largest in the region, with about 100,000 inhabitants dispersed "on either side of a wide and beautiful river." But like all colonial cities, this city is actually two cities, "the white town—and the other."[6] The white city has its own distinct neighborhoods with spacious, immaculate villas in a residential ring surrounding an urban center with its multistory buildings, the seat of political and financial power in the colony.[7]

Key ideas of Duras's critique of colonialism emerge in this justifiably well-known depiction, interpreted as Saigon, but as we read, any colonial city: race and class divisions and attendant power captured in the physical separation of "two towns," populated by the colonizing individuals and the colonized masses.[8] Space, elevation, and lush plantings signify the luxury of the white town. "The sidewalks in the fashionable district were immensely wide. An orgiastic space, quite uselessly wide, was provided for the heedless steps of the powerful-in-repose," obliviously wasteful.[9] The avenues were "wide, bordered with exotic trees and divided in two by lawns and flowerbeds . . . [s]prinkled several times a day, green and flowering."[10] Obsessive and "impeccable cleanliness" characterize the colonizers: "As soon as the whites arrived in the Colonies, they learned to take a bath every day. . . . They also learned to wear the Colonial uniform, suits of spotless white, the color of immunity and innocence."[11] On the "immense terraces of their cafés," under the tamarind trees in the evenings, "the inhabitants enjoyed themselves in their own congenial company. . . . And until late at night, seated in rattan armchairs, behind the potted palms and the jacketed waiters, you could see the whites sipping Pernods, whisky and soda or brandy, acquiring a Colonial liver, in harmony with all the rest," a powerful evocation of their leisure time and stereotypical alcohol abuse.[12] Around them, "Only the café waiters were natives, and they were disguised as whites, having put on dinner jackets. Similarly, the palm trees of the terraces had been put into earthenware pots," a comparison demonstrating what Aimé Césaire famously termed the "thingification" ("chosification") of the colonized.[13] In this schema, the latex flowing from the rubber trees is more precious than the spilled blood of the forced laborers on the plantations, encapsulating the economic exploitation of the land and its people. In an extraordinarily resonant moment, Duras's memorable passage drips with sarcasm.

For Joseph and Suzanne, marooned and isolated on the Kam plain on the coast of what is now Cambodia, the far-off city nourishes their dreams of escape, captured in the teenage girl's time spent waiting by the bridge near the house.[14] The occasional car passes on the single dirt road leading to the city some 800 kilometers away; perhaps, one day, "a man would stop because he had seen her sitting near the bridge. Why not? Possibly he would like her looks and would offer to take her to the city."[15] The luxury, chaos, and promise of the city attract Joseph and Suzanne, as does the possibility of sexual pleasure, as Duras suggests with words like "orgiastic" and "brothel."[16] This pleasure is encapsulated in later sections in the darkened space of the cinema where Joseph will meet the woman who will eventually come to take him away from the plain and where Suzanne hopes for her own encounter.[17] The errant elbow of a man brushes her own during a film, and "after that, she was surer than ever that where you met them [men] was in the palpitating gloom of the movies. . . . It was only there, in front of the screen, that everything became simple. To be an unknown person in front of the same image gave you a desire for the unknown. The impossible became attainable, obstacles flattened out or became imaginary. There, at least, you felt an equality with the city, whereas in the streets it eluded you and you escaped it."[18] Finally, it is during one last ride in M. Jo's Léon-Bollée limousine, through the "chaotic brilliance and darkness" of the city, that Suzanne, "intoxicated with the city," becomes aware of her own sexual power: "And above the terrifying city, Suzanne saw her breasts, saw the erection of her breasts higher than anything that stood up in the city. Her breasts, then, would be justified. . . . She, while looking at the city, was really only regarding herself. She was regarding in solitude her empire, over which reigned her waist, her legs, her breasts."[19]

In sharp contrast to Duras's *The Sea Wall*, Rithy Panh's cinematographic transformation of the novel renders the city entirely absent, with certain aspects of the urban center telescoped into the small town of Ram with its canteen, some sixty kilometers from the family house.[20] This elision shifts the emphasis in the film away from the city's potentials and Suzanne's moments of self-discovery and prepares the ground of a reorienting of Duras's story as told by screenwriters Michel Fessler and the director himself. Joseph will meet the elegant woman in the Ram canteen, and they will furtively make love in the space below the building raised on stilts. He will leave with her for a brief stay in the unseen city, then return home, only to leave again after the mother's death, effectively echoing the novel's presentation of the longing of the children to leave. In fact, they frequently threaten to abandon the "concession" in arguments with their mother.

The novel's crucial scene of Suzanne's sexual apotheosis riding through the city at night survives, but highly truncated and muted, in a different part of the narrative and on the road from Ram to the house by day. While in the car with M. Jo in a driving rain, he declares his love for her, then touches her knee and slides his hand up her leg. She invites him to feel her breasts through her dress, then, in a radical mood shift, rudely rejects him, getting out of the car and running away in the rain. In de-emphasizing Suzanne's sexuality and the city, Panh highlights nonurban space and the land itself with its rice paddies, a gesture that suggests why the city has diminished thematic importance in his retelling of this narrative. While the unseen city remains powerful in the imaginary as a draw to Suzanne and Joseph, Panh shifts the emphasis to rural space to underline the exploitation of indigenous populations, here to some extent aligned with the mother and her children, and focus on the revolutionary potential of the land.

M. JO

The portrait of M. Jo in *The Sea Wall* also draws our attention in the context of Rithy Panh's film adaptation. According to the novel, he is a rich "rubber planter from the North," "just back from Paris."[21] At the Ram canteen, the mother and her children look at him:

> He was alone at his table: a young man, about twenty-five years old, dressed in a beige suit of tussore silk. On the table in front of him he had put his felt hat which was the same color, beige. When he lifted his glass of Pernot, they could see a magnificent diamond on one of his fingers. Ma gazed in silence, open-mouthed. . . .
>
> The diamond was enormous, the silk suit was well tailored. Never had Joseph worn a silk suit. The soft hat looked like something in the movies. . . . It was true, his face was certainly not handsome, nor was his figure. His shoulders were narrow, his arms were short, he must be much shorter than the average man. His small hands were well cared for, thin, rather good-looking. And that diamond gave his hand a royal, almost an ethereal quality. He was alone. He was a planter, he was young, and he was looking at Suzanne.[22]

This initial description sets the tone for M. Jo's treatment by the family; in effect, his physical presence is reduced to his "rather good-looking" hands and especially the diamond ring.

When he stands up to approach Suzanne and ask her to dance, "his ugliness became apparent." Everyone looks at his diamond as he crosses the room. His dancing is qualified as "not bad" although "academic," as if trying to impress Suzanne, self-consciously imitative, perhaps a reference to "aping" the behavior of others.[23] In an allusion to his imprecise origins, his voice is different from those of the planters and big-game hunters who frequent Ram: "It came from somewhere else, it was soft and distinguished," influenced perhaps by his stay in Paris.[24] Identified with his possessions, he is "the only son of a very rich speculator whose fortune was typical of those made in the Colony," a suggestion that he may be from Europe.[25] Several paragraphs later, we read: "Monsieur Jo was the ridiculously incompetent son of his ingenious father, whose big fortune had but one heir and that heir without a trace of imagination. He represented the one failure in this father's life. For you cannot speculate on your offspring."[26] So far, he has failed at everything: his studies in Europe and a career in business, and he has not lived up to the weight of his wealth and expectations of his class.[27]

The negative portrait seems to open the door to M. Jo's exploitation by the mother and her children and their blatant mistreatment of him. They ask for gifts, and he complies. At the moment he offers Suzanne a new phonograph, "he had ceased . . . to exist. And really, deprived of his limousine, his tussore silk suit, his chauffeur, maybe he would become completely insubstantial, as empty of interest as an empty suitcase."[28] In fact, Suzanne "extract[s]" the phonograph from M. Jo,[29] as if mining the land itself, a parallel with colonialism that seems to unveil who M. Jo is, if only by suggestion. The family treats him with condescension, rudeness, and disdain, in a way similar to their behavior toward their Malay domestic servant (presented in chapter 11 of the novel),[30] "their only property" who works for nothing,[31] as well as the English businessman Barner. M. Jo thus adheres to a group of characters who are outsiders to the family with direct ties to France, the mother and her husband seduced decades ago by the dream of striking it rich in the colonies.[32] Though hopelessly lovesick, M. Jo does finally conclude that Suzanne and her family have used him, that they are only interested in his wealth and how it might help them. In a conversation with Suzanne at the end of part one, he accuses: "You are [all] profoundly immoral,"[33] then leaves the house for the last time. That particular accusation adds crucial and problematic overtones to the presence of the family in the colony, a family of white colons who do not belong there.

In his film Panh chose to cast Randal Douc, a Franco-Cambodian actor, as M. Jo, thereby removing much of the ambiguity around this character as presented in the novel. One might say Panh has simply acted on the suggestions in Duras's text and confirmed them. Or he has read *The Sea Wall* retrospectively in light of *The Lover* and *The North China Lover* in which Duras portrays the lover as Chinese. As it happens, however, Panh explained his choice in an interview he gave to *Allociné*, indicating that despite many readers thinking that M. Jo is white and that Duras never specifies his nationality or ethnic background, he reads M. Jo as a Westernized Sino-Cambodian like many from well-to-do families who could afford to send their sons to study in France and who upon their return would work for the colonial administration and in turn exploit their compatriots.[34] Panh's casting then indicates a more complex choice. Strikingly handsome, M. Jo becomes a different kind of presence on-screen from the M. Jo in the novel and provides a bridge to other changes in Rithy Panh's reinvention of Duras's work.

The lines describing M. Jo initially are given to Carmen, the proprietor of the hotel in the city where the family stays in the novel, now a manager/waitress at the Ram canteen Chez Bart. He is watching the family, and the mother smiles at him, telling her daughter to do the same. Confident, he approaches the table to invite Suzanne to dance. The apparent awkwardness from the novel is gone in the scene of M. Jo's first encounter with the mother and her children (Joseph notices the car with envy). Only Joseph replicates the rudeness we see in the novel, refusing to say hello when M. Jo comes to the house, revealing his racism when he declares: "We are not monkeys here, right?" as the "ape" comment from the novel reemerges here.[35] The well-known scene from the novel of M. Jo knocking at the door of the enclosed shower stall where Suzanne is washing off before going to Ram reappears here.[36] When she complies with his request and opens the door, then shows him her breasts, he promises her the phonograph, as Duras writes. Suzanne then slams the door, shouting, "You're trash," running him out of the house.[37]

Rithy Panh's reinvention of the Durassian M. Jo, however, extends far beyond his portrayal and his relationship with Suzanne and her family. Identified openly as Chinese in the last half of the film, he becomes, himself, a colonizer in this Khmer setting. With the help of the French, he expropriates the peasants living on the plain near the family house so that he can use the land to cultivate Kampot pepper, "worth more than gold," and make his own fortune. This transformation and that of the peasants are foreshadowed in this film by a two-part scene in which the mother cares for a child with dengue fever, followed by a meeting with a large group of peasants during which the Malay domestic ("le caporal") translates the mother's exhortation that they all work together to create new and stronger levees in order to make the land profitable and permit all of them to pay their taxes and keep their land from the greedy land agents, "bloody bureaucrats" in the words of the mother, who had taken her money for the arid property on the floodplain in the first place (figure 4.1).

At the same time, there is an awareness on the part of the mother and her family that they are interlopers in this geographic space. Shortly after a visit by the land agents who threaten to repossess her land if she does not pay her mortgage, the mother laments, "I'm ashamed of being French!" Near the end of the film Suzanne relates to Joseph the short exchange she had had off-screen with M. Jo, who accuses them of being immoral. Joseph says that M. Jo was right. And when the elegant woman comes to take Joseph away with her, the mother tells him to go ("Just go, Joseph"). After he has left, she admits to Suzanne that they have no reason to be on the plain anymore. Symbolically, then, the mother dies, in essence taking her leave from the colony.

FIGURE 4.1. The mother talking to the local peasants with the caporal acting as translator

FIGURE 4.2. The peasants reacting to M. Khing's informing them of their expropriation

The mother's scene of exhortation nevertheless suggests a solidarity between the French family and the neighboring peasants, engaged in growing rice for their common good. In this reconfiguration, the Malay caporal/domestic, deaf and essentially mute in the novel, is given a voice and plays a crucial role as link and translator. Near the film's midpoint, he warns, "M. Jo no good—snake in the grass."[38] When the French land agents arrive to tell the peasants that their land has been sold to a M. Khing, the front for M. Jo, they get angry and begin throwing rocks at those who would take their land (figure 4.2). The following scenes show various aspects of a violent peasant revolt, with shots fired and buildings

FIGURE 4.3. Suzanne dressed in Khmer clothing

torched. Running through the forest, the domestic comes upon the head of one of the land agents on a pike. After several intervening scenes, we next see the peasants being forcibly marched, tied together as prisoners. In a symbolic gesture, the Malay who has escaped this fate, gives water to the prisoners. Eventually, the peasants will take refuge on the mother's land, at the levee.

While the promise of a people's resistance closes the novel as Joseph gives his guns to the peasants, their revolt is fully realized in Panh's screen version. And though the family's anti–French colonial mentality is apparent in Duras's text, Panh carries it to its logical conclusion, expressing this attitude in part through an assumption of Khmer indigeneity. The mother struggles to survive alongside the Khmer rice farmers with a passionate intensity that aligns her with the besieged Khmer heroines of Panh's earliest feature film, *Rice People* (1994). Their connection with the land, their dependency on it, and their determination to live from it are one and the same in both narratives; their struggle is shared.[39] As Panh's *The Sea Wall* moves toward its conclusion, the mother dies and is honored with Khmer funeral rites. Finally, in the closing scenes, Suzanne gradually dons pieces of Khmer clothing until she is dressed entirely in the blouse, long wrapped skirt, and headscarf (worn at the neck in this scene) of the peasant women around her (figure 4.3). We also become aware of her ability to speak Khmer. And it is Suzanne who inherits the land, albeit in her quasi-Khmer guise, resonating to some extent with the fate of the eldest daughter, Sokha, in the closing scenes of *Rice People*. In these ways, Panh effectively appropriates Duras's novel, reinventing her text as his own creation and setting it in dialogue with other work in his oeuvre. At the same time, he may well be suggesting the potential of a postcolonial solidarity among those born on this same land.

In an interview for *Cinémoi*, Rithy Panh declares that what appealed to him in the Duras novel was not the love story but rather the portrayal of colonialism in Indochina. That it was a story tied to known history, to a lived reality, made it all the more engaging for him. Thus, as we see in the film, the love story becomes ancillary to the larger political landscape and the family story abstracted to some degree. The alignment of the mother with the Khmer women deflects from the exploitation paralleling colonialism of the mother and her children, apparent in the novel but downplayed in the film. Panh is therefore faithful to certain aspects of the novel and had to make choices about the story as all filmmakers must in the transfer of a rich written text to the screen, choices that would include, for example, a focus on the colonization of the Khmer people with the message that the violence of colonization itself will end also with a violent break. One might also say that if Panh transforms and reinvents Duras, Duras herself authorizes these reimaginings as they resonate with her own practice, the rewriting of the story of the mother and her children in successive texts and, one might add, the displacement of the love story to Japan in *Hiroshima, mon amour* (1959). At the same time, he also implicitly comments on the genre of film adaptation and challenges the colonial family melodrama as presented in such films as Régis Wargnier's big-budget *Indochine* (1992).

In fact, Panh seems to set up his critique carefully, juxtaposing Isabelle Huppert, famous for her challenging films,[40] and Catherine Deneuve, France's best-known star, the model for Marianne statues in front of city halls across France and its overseas departments; a family on the skids and the rich landowners of a rubber plantation; a mother and her children and an heiress and her adopted Vietnamese daughter; a suggestive, nuanced narrative and one that is heavy-handedly epic; a revolution emerging from the people without the help of a Jean-Baptiste. We see Rithy Panh's film as possibly parodic on some level, in its use of, say, swelling romantic strains at dramatic junctures that echo *Indochine*'s portentous if not pretentious moments. Panh's adaptation of *The Sea Wall* serves also, then, as a compelling corrective to *Indochine*'s seductive nostalgia for a bygone colonial era.

NOTES

1. Marguerite Duras, *Un barrage contre le Pacifique* (Paris: Gallimard, 1950); references here are to the Folio edition. Panivong Norindr, *Phantasmatic Indochina: French Colonial Ideology in Architecture, Film, and Literature* (Durham, NC: Duke University Press, 1996), 11.
2. The words "d'après le roman de Marguerite Duras" (adapted from the novel by Marguerite Duras) appear just before the title of the film.
3. Eric Jennings also notes these aspects of the film in his review. Eric T. Jennings, "*The Sea Wall*," *Fiction and Film for Scholars of France: A Cultural Bulletin* 4 (2009), http://h-france.net/ffth/classics/indochine-and-the-sea-wall/. It is worth noting, however, that Jennings reads

these revisions as a reticence on the part of Panh to confront the full horrors of French colonialism in the way that Duras achieves in her portrayal of Saigon. As Jennings remarks: "Several students told me that they found Panh's film to be, overall, oddly more suffused with colonial nostalgia than Régis Wargnier's *Indochine*." He concludes: "If my class was any indication, most found that the film fell headlong into the 'Indochic' tropes and trap." Our reading of the film in the current essay takes an opposing view, arguing for the nuance of Panh's engagement with the colonial.

4. Both Jane Bradley Winston and Leslie Barnes point this out in their landmark studies of Duras and Malraux, and Duras and Lê, respectively. Jane Bradley Winston, *Postcolonial Duras: Cultural Memory in Postwar France* (New York: Palgrave, 2001); Leslie Barnes, *Vietnam and the Colonial Condition of French Literature* (Lincoln: University of Nebraska Press, 2014).

5. Duras, *Un barrage*, 167–169; Marguerite Duras, *The Sea Wall*, trans. Herma Briffault (New York: Harper and Row, 1952), 135–137.

6. Duras, *The Sea Wall*, 135.

7. Elsewhere in this chapter, references to the English translation will be indicated by page number; page numbers followed by F refer to the original text.

8. Duras, *The Sea Wall*, 135 (167F).

9. Duras, 136 (168F).

10. Duras, 136 (168F).

11. Duras, 135 (167–168F).

12. Duras, 136 (168–169F).

13. Duras, 136 (168–169F); Aimé Césaire, *Discourse on Colonialism*, trans. Joan Pinkham (New York: Monthly Review Press, 1972), 21; Aimé Césaire, *Discours sur le colonialisme* (Paris: Présence Africaine, 1955), 19.

14. Duras, *The Sea Wall*, 15–16 (21F), 220–221 (280F), 238–239 (302F).

15. Duras, 16 (21F).

16. Duras, 180 (225F); 85 (108F); 136 (168–169F).

17. Duras, 155 passim (195F passim), 204 (258F).

18. Duras, 178 (223–224F).

19. Duras, (226–227F). See also Winston's brilliant analysis of these pages in *Postcolonial Duras*, 177–178.

20. The name Ream is used in the film, with the words "CAMBODGE-INDOCHINE FRANÇAISE 1931, Plaine de Ream" appearing as the story begins.

21. Duras, *The Sea Wall*, 32 (41–42F).

22. Duras, 32–33 (42F).

23. Duras, 33. The ellipsis in this quote stands for an earlier scene in the novel when Joseph notices the car outside the canteen (30–31 [39–40F]) and describes M. Jo: "'Cripes, what a cattle-truck [set on wheels],' said Joseph. Then he added: 'But that's about all he's got. He looks like an ape'" (33 [42F]).

24. Duras, 34 (44F).

25. Duras, 49 (62–63F).

26. Duras, 50 (64F).

27. Duras, 51 (64F).

28. Duras, 60 (77F).

29. Duras, 60 (76F).

30. Duras, 193–202 (243–255F).

31. Duras, 202 (255F).

32. Duras, 17 (23F); 47 (59F).

33. Duras, 123 (154F).

34. The entire quotation reads as follows: "Certains lecteurs de Duras pensent que Monsieur Jo est un Blanc. Dans le texte, elle ne dit rien sur sa nationalité. Mais dans ses interviews elle parle d'un Chinois. Je l'ai imaginé comme un Sino-Cambodgien issu d'une riche famille de commerçants, et que son père aurait envoyé faire des études en France. Il parle français sans accent. Il se sent à la fois enraciné et déraciné. Il n'est pas occidental, mais occidentalisé. C'est ce genre de types qui exploitent le mieux leurs compatriotes, c'est sur cette classe de nantis locaux que s'appuient toujours les administrations coloniales. Lui, toute sa logique n'est qu'une logique d'exploitation: des terres, des paysans et de Suzanne. M. Jo respire l'ambiguïté comme l'aventure du colonialisme" (76F); [Certain readers of Duras think that M. Jo is white. In the text she says nothing about his nationality. But in her interviews she speaks of a Chinese man. I imagined him as a Sino-Cambodian from a rich family of businessmen sent by his father to study in France. He speaks French without an accent. He feels rooted and uprooted. He's not Western but Westernized. It's those kind of guys who exploit their compatriots the best, and colonial administrations always depend on this class of well-off locals. For him, his whole logic is one of exploitation, of land, peasants, and Suzanne. M. Jo breathes the same ambiguity as the adventure of colonialism. Our translation.] "Un barrage contre le Pacifique," accessed December 9, 2020, http://www.allocine.fr/film/fichefilm-125109/secrets-tournage/. We thank Leslie Barnes for passing along this reference.

35. Our translation. The original line from the film, "On n'est pas des singes ici, hein?," is translated in the subtitles as "Chinks [*sic*] get all the attention here," an intriguing departure from the French that seems to pull in the critique Rithy Panh wants to emphasize of multiple colonizations in Cambodia.

36. Duras, *The Sea Wall*, 56–57 (72–73F).

37. "Vous êtes une ordure" is Suzanne's line verbatim in both the film and the novel. "You're trash" in the film's subtitles is more accurate than "You're a beast" from the translation of the novel. As Suzanne implies, this opinion of M. Jo was first suggested by Joseph, known for his crude language. Duras, 57 (73F).

38. Our translation of "M. Jo pas bon—serpent dans la forêt." "M. Jo is no good—like a snake in the grass" from the English subtitles does not accurately reflect the caporal's French.

39. See Boreth Ly's chapter in this volume for an analysis of the mother's struggle in *Rice People* and, more generally, for an exploration of the incapacitated mother figure as metaphor for the nation.

40. Isabelle Huppert also stars in Claire Denis's film *White Material* (2009), which focuses on a daughter-in-law's struggle to save the family's threatened coffee plantation in an unnamed Francophone African country. In this respect the resemblances to both *Un barrage* and *Indochine* are striking.

5 • RITHY PANH AS *CHASSEUR D'IMAGES*

JENNIFER CAZENAVE

> Cinema was and remains one of the spearheads of empire.
>
> —Scott MacDonald, *A Critical Cinema*

In 1933, the year the original *King Kong* arrived on the big screen, the French cameraman Félix Mesguich published a memoir titled *Tours de manivelle: Souvenirs d'un chasseur d'images* (Turns of the crank: Memories of an image hunter). First hired by the Lumière brothers in 1896 to promote their newly invented cinematograph in America and Russia, Mesguich spent nearly two decades working as a *chasseur d'images* and "storing up the world on film."[1] His memoir reads as one long traveling shot across the globe, encompassing the battlefields of the Russo-Japanese War; a wondrous encounter with Jerusalem; the rubber trees of British Ceylon; the first-ever moving images of the temples of Angkor; the Taj Mahal; and the geishas of Kyoto. In his introduction, the Algerian-born Mesguich, who had served as a Zouave before becoming a *chasseur d'images*, compares himself to the wandering Jew. In 1933, he could have borrowed the title of his memoir from another wandering Jew of early French film history: Albert Kahn and his Archives de la Planète, a vast collection of mostly unedited films captured around the world between 1908 and 1931.

In *Tours de manivelle*, Mesguich never reflects on his status as Other within a post–Dreyfus Affair and imperialist Europe. In a narrative traversed by animal-hunt spectacles, which intimate the violent domination of nature and land underlying the colonial project, he also never comments on the real-life scenes (*actualités*) he witnesses and films in countless French and British colonies. Only once does he briefly remark, "But the life of an image hunter is not always made up of charming scenes and pleasant sensations."[2] Yet, much like a sequence near the beginning of *King Kong* that offers a shot reverse shot of a white director recording indigenous islanders, Mesguich's memoir evinces the intersection—oft relegated to the margins of French film history—of moving images and imperial expansion. The proliferation of travelogues and ethnographic films in the first decades of the twentieth century evidences the entwined narratives of early cinema and empire; the symbolic year of 1895 alone marked the birth of the cinematograph and the consecration of the *mission civilisatrice* (civilizing mission) as France's official ideology in the colonies.[3] Thus, as Paula Amad notes, Kahn's contemporaneous film collection might have been more aptly titled "the Archives of the *French Colonial* Planet."[4]

Almost a century after the premiere of *King Kong* and the publication of *Tours de manivelle*, Rithy Panh released *La France est notre patrie* ("France is our homeland," 2015). Setting aside his own camera, he turns in this documentary to the task of a second-generation *chasseur d'images*: he retrieves archived films, like those made by Mesguich, left behind by decades of imperialism while questioning the legacy of this cinematic past.[5] A contemporary Franco-Cambodian director born after decolonization, Panh reassembles moving images principally of Indochina—only occasionally interspersing footage of other colonies—recorded by amateur and professional cameras from the silent era to the wars of independence. In *La France est notre patrie*, he draws from a vast colonial image bank encompassing canonical and noncanonical nonfiction cinema: on the one hand, the early actualities captured by *chasseurs d'images* sent to Indochina, among them Lumière operator Gabriel Veyre and Albert Kahn cameraman Léon Busy; on the other, the films of soldiers, sailors, traders, administrators, missionaries, and ethnographers. In compiling a broad array of visual memories of empire that primarily denounce sexual and ecological exploitation in the colonies, *La France est notre patrie* bears witness to the centrality of Southeast Asia in the French imaginary of the early twentieth century: what Panivong Norindr terms the "colonial phantasmatic," or production of "mythologized images of erotic and exotic Indochina" disseminated by diverse media, from literature to cinema to the Paris colonial exhibition in 1931 that included a replica of Angkor Wat.[6]

The film's title, a phrase written by teachers and children on the blackboards of schools visible in documentaries such as *France Is an Empire* (1939), illuminates the role Indochina once played as "the capstone of both the French colonial educational system and educational cinema."[7] It also alludes to the work of the filmmaker's father, a teacher and admirer of Jules Ferry who served as a civil servant for the French Ministry of Education under colonialism. The phrase thus casts a personal note on this documentary made directly after Panh's autobiographical account of the Cambodian genocide, *The Missing Picture* (2013), which recovers childhood memories of his father and his subsequent death in a Khmer Rouge labor camp. At the same time, the title posits France as the homeland, or inventor, of both the cinematograph and an aggressive civilizing mission—a twofold history perfectly encapsulated in the *mission cinématographique* (cinematographic mission) undertaken between 1920 and 1922 by the governor-general of

Indochina, Albert Sarraut.[8] Finally, the possessive pronoun in Panh's title gestures toward the complex filmic legacy of imperialism, largely reduced to archival footage and dismissed—or safely distanced—as propaganda. In *La France est notre patrie*, the colonies return as the earliest laboratories and studios of cinema beyond the metropole. While cameramen like Mesguich experimented with and perfected camera movements such as the close-up and the traveling shot, indigenous populations, as well as exotic animals and landscapes, served as actors and spectacles *malgré eux*.

In the wake of the sixtieth anniversary of the fall of Điện Biên Phủ, Panh undertakes a rare incursion into the colonial past that frames imperialism as a project of cultural, sexual, and ecological domination and exploitation. To date, his filmography has chiefly centered on the Cambodian genocide and its aftermath, with the exception of a 2008 adaptation of Marguerite Duras's *The Sea Wall*. If *La France est notre patrie* belongs to a periodic exploration of Cambodia's other violent history before the Khmer Rouge, why did Panh choose—beyond an apparent commemorative purpose—to make this documentary immediately after *The Missing Picture*? Can we not read in the recuperation of "missing pictures" of colonialism an elaboration of Panh's previous engagement with and reconfiguration of French discourses on aesthetic limits to representing historical horror, particularly Jacques Rivette's famous 1961 condemnation of "le travelling de *Kapo*"? As a contemporary *chasseur d'images*, Panh unearths archived footage not just to reconstruct a violent history *through* cinema. His imagined silent film also recuperates a seldom shown history *of* cinema to ultimately posit the visual legacy of imperialism as a missing (motion) picture.

"SOMETIMES HISTORY IS VOICELESS"

Panh is not the first filmmaker to recover the history of the moving image as an artifact of imperialism. In 1986, Italian collaborators Yervant Gianikian (a second-generation Armenian immigrant) and Angela Ricci Lucchi recycled and reedited *From the Pole to the Equator*, an early Italian documentary composed of footage captured in European colonies. Gianikian and Ricci Lucchi constructed their eponymous film around "the metaphor of amnesia," that is, "the general 'amnesia' about primitive cinema, and the desire of early audiences for exotic spectacles, which reflected their dreams of conquest and cultural pillage."[9] A similar legacy of amnesia underlies Panh's undertaking, particularly in the context of contemporary France, where a museum of colonial history has yet to be established.[10] In fact, the complicity of the camera in the construction of the racialized and sexualized exotic Other dictates the necessary fiction at play in the seventy-four-minute-long *La France est notre patrie*. Rather than merely compile archival footage into a documentary, Panh rearranges the colonial image bank as a silent film to call attention to the missing motion pictures of colonialism in the canon of

French cinema. His editing strategy further accentuates the conjunction of cinema and imperialism through the inclusion of an original score by Marc Marder and narrative intertitles utilizing the rhetoric of France's civilizing mission.

In *The Missing Picture*, Panh cut against the grain of an ethics of *exclusion* (of realism, of fictional reconstruction, of archival images) underlying French discourses on the limits of representation inaugurated by Rivette's critique of Gillo Pontecorvo's Holocaust fiction *Kapo*.[11] Framing the Cambodian catastrophe as an event unseen by the West and a memory displaced by other genocides, Panh introduced instead an ethics of *inclusion*. Accordingly, his autobiographical film reconstructed unwitnessed traumatic scenes—such as the forced displacements of populations to the countryside—by means of silent clay figurines set in dioramas. *La France est notre patrie* stages a comparable visual confrontation with the traumatic colonial past anticipated by the opening credits of *The Missing Picture*, which show a room filled with discarded movie cans and reels.

Although indissociable, in cinephilic circles, from Rivette's vilification of "le travelling de *Kapo*," the traveling shot officially entered the French language in 1921.[12] Tinged with foreignness, this borrowed English word invokes an era of tourism and colonialism, as well as a desire, on the part of early cinema, "to carry the viewer into the image" and "to recreate the actual penetration of space traveling involves."[13] Yet, whether in the virtual voyages enabled by nonfiction genres such as the travelogue or the colonial appropriation of lands, populations, and cultures, traveling always entails much more than journeying through time and space. It also functions, as Amad observes in relation to Les Archives de la Planète, "as a conduit for training, knowing, thinking, belonging, and viewing as a modern French citizen."[14]

Panh's silent movie reframes the question of viewing and belonging in the twenty-first century by recovering the missing pictures of imperialism. On the one hand, *La France est notre patrie* uncovers the visual mythologies of empire, above all the constructed, appropriated Other, perpetually opposed to the celebrated "civilized" Westerner. On the other hand, it interrogates the legacy of this visual colonial past, questioning in particular which moving images constitute cinema and belong to its official history. Panh composes his documentary from a broad array of black-and-white, as well as tinted and color, archived footage devoid of either a date, a title, a location, or a cameraman. Moreover, while the film's narrative progresses from colonization to decolonization, these moving images from both the silent era and the "talkies" do not appear in any particular chronological order. *La France est notre patrie* effectively abolishes distinctions and hierarchies between nonfiction genres: all moving images—whether actualities, amateur footage, propaganda films, or scientific documentaries—form the broad institutional matrix of French cinema.

In choosing to present these moving images as a silent film (and some, therefore, anachronistically so), Panh willingly orients the spectator's gaze to early cinema, at once the beginnings of a filmic encounter with the Other and an era "of naïveté in which elements [of imperialism] that later become camouflaged are frankly displayed."[15] For much of the twentieth century, as Tom Gunning observes, the official history of documentary cinema repressed this inaugural voyeurism. Early nonfiction filmmaking remained "undiscussed, as if shrouded by a collective amnesia," subsisting for decades as a missing picture in between the inaugural views of the Lumière brothers and the silent classics of Robert Flaherty.[16] The opening sequence of *La France est notre patrie* suggests as much. The film begins not with the past but with the present: color images of a forgotten and abandoned edifice, overgrown by immense tree roots in a Cambodian forest, reveal empty window and door frames that evoke an off-screen history before cutting to amateur footage of French couples happily dancing in the colonies.

The banality of home movies, rather than the commissioned footage of French colonial documentaries, constitutes our first glimpse into Indochina in *La France est notre patrie*. Composed of several scenes of domestic bliss, such personal and seemingly inconsequential moments depicting laughing couples and playing children momentarily eclipse the local populations and the brutal reality of imperialism. The amateur footage introduces instead the main characters of the French empire: the colonizer as maker of images and locus of civility against which all other bodies and cultures are to be encountered, measured, and framed. These images also make manifest what Françoise Vergès describes as the "colonial family romance" underlying the civilizing mission and premised on "two fixed categories, the giving colonizers and the receiving colonized."[17] This necessary fiction, whereby the French nation posits itself as the sole "parent" of its imperial subjects, to whom it imparts the ideals of the republic, effectively conceals all that the empire takes and extracts in return, including moving images and natural resources. Through compilations of vignettes separated by title cards that reiterate the civilizing vocation, *La France est notre patrie* progressively overturns this "colonial family romance," specifically in bringing into focus the dominated imperial bodies: on the one hand, the exploitation of and control over colonized women, whose visual evidence exposes the voyeurism of early cinema; on the other, the exploitation of and control over nature and labor, which attests to a conception of colonialism as a "social-ecological project."[18]

The film's opening sequence moves from images of colonizers to footage of an indigenous woman, the Tonkinoise of the imperial imaginary, being pushed toward the camera by three laughing Frenchmen. Immediately preceding the title, the final close-up of her face intimates the illusion of morality and domesticity in the colonies, while placing at the center of the frame—and of *La France est notre patrie*—the unacknowledged protagonists of early cinema. "Sometimes history is voiceless," the last title card of the film reads, suggesting a cinematographic undertaking premised on the missing testimonies (beneath the rhetoric of the civilizing mission) and the missing gazes of the colonized (behind the camera). This phrase also illuminates Panh's decision to present this history of cinema as a silent film devoid of a voice-over narration, a formal device that effectively mediates a confrontation, in the twenty-first century, between the spectator and this visual heritage.

Akin to the close-up of the Tonkinoise in the opening sequence, this confrontation is further facilitated by the prevalence of direct address in early nonfiction cinema. Returned gazes abound in *La France est notre patrie*: they invoke, on the one hand, the photograph of Bophana that recurs in Panh's filmography and, on the other, a familiar interpretive move in postcolonial studies to retrospectively read into the look at the camera ambivalence, resistance, and agency.[19] In an essay devoted to the returned gaze, Amad interprets the prevalence of this critical gesture in film studies as "the fetishized trace of our contemporary desire for—based on the historical lack of—the irrecoverable reverse shot of the Other's view of the world."[20] *La France est notre patrie* attempts to retrieve this other side of history, as suggested by the film's final title card in which Panh also explains having assembled these images "in my native way" (à ma façon d'indigène). Much like the device of the silent film, he deploys the returned gaze as part of a necessary fiction that imagines the missing reverse shots of the colonized reacting to the customs of the colonizer. In one sequence accompanied by a jazzy tune, for instance, French women donning dresses, gloves, and jewels parade like movie stars in Hollywood through the Indochinese countryside, evidencing the ways in which white women in the empire "accentuat[ed] the refinements of privilege and new etiquettes of racial difference."[21] Wishing to momentarily reverse the ethnographic spectacle of early cinema and its objectification of indigenous peoples, Panh interrupts this footage and the soundtrack in order to interpose several silent looks of native women staring bewilderedly at the camera. This montage enables him to retrospectively introduce the missing returned gaze of indigenous women, here made to fictitiously look back at the camera as though perplexed by the frivolity of the colonial wives.

In the imperial imaginary of the early twentieth century, white women embodied icons of domesticity and morality, tasked with promoting the ideals of the civilizing mission and providing a safeguard against debauchery. A single well-known *actualité* shot by Gabriel Veyre in 1900 for the Lumière brothers perfectly captures this imperial imaginary: two Western women wearing white dresses toss coins at Vietnamese children. By contrast, indigenous women constituted a reverse image as objects of male fantasy, endlessly viewed, represented, and appropriated through a voyeuristic eye. In turn, centuries of colonial conquest and cohabitation engendered a colossal and violent visual archive of sexual domination and exploitation composed of paintings, advertisements, photographs, postcards, and moving images. An imposing French volume titled *Sexe, race & colonies* (2018) documents this seldom shown history of violence. Approximating Panh's work as a contemporary *chasseur d'images,* the nearly 600-page book resembling an imaginary museum of colonial history moves from the fifteenth century to the present. Cinema enters the scene only in the mid-1920s in *Sexe, race & colonies,* which reproduces, among others, the 1933 poster for *King Kong.*[22]

La France est notre patrie recuperates the lesser-known genre of amateur cinema in the colonies facilitated in the early period by the creation of affordable cameras such as the Pathé Baby launched in 1923. In particular, the amateur footage assembled by Panh bears witness to the practice of concubinage, an ambiguous term encompassing varied domestic arrangements, from sexual access to labor.[23] "Each chooses his *petite épouse,*" an intertitle reads, referring to the name given to concubines across the French empire (in Indochina, the French also coined the pejorative verb *s'encongayer,* from the Vietnamese word *con gái* for young girl, to describe this cohabitation outside marriage).[24] At this moment in the film, Panh once more deploys the trope of the returned gaze to stage a shot reverse shot that frames concubinage as the missing picture of home movies. After the intertitle introducing the *petite épouse,* he seamlessly juxtaposes black-and-white amateur footage of smiling French soldiers looking at the camera with several scenes of local women undressing and posing. The film then cuts back to the returned male gaze, this time showing two men drinking in the foreground while another one forcibly kisses a non-European woman in the background; echoing the previous scene, footage of dancing concubines ensues. Panh concludes this vignette with four nearly identical takes of French sailors walking arm in arm with their *petites épouses* toward the camera—a repetition, like the amateur footage, that accentuates the banality of this colonial scene.

"It was a paradise": thus reads the title card that immediately follows the scenes of French women glamorously parading like the Marilyn Monroes and Audrey Hepburns of Indochina. With this short phrase, Panh introduces a four-minute montage composed of both ethnographic and amateur films depicting the idyllic land-based lifestyles of natives across the empire. After numerous shots of half-naked women engaging in daily activities, he cuts to "Scène de déshabillage, Tonkin" (Undressing scene, Tonkin), a film made by Léon Busy in 1921 for the Albert Kahn archives. Shot entirely out of focus, the black-and-white footage shows a Vietnamese woman undressing completely, briefly looking at the camera, and putting her traditional clothing back on. Panh then inserts amateur footage of a French woman in a bathing suit running toward the camera before placing her hand over the lens. This gesture evincing varying ethics of representation of the female body heightens the voyeurism of "Scène de déshabillage, Tonkin" and the scenes that preceded it, effectively undoing—as Amad remarks in her analysis of the Busy film—the anthropological alibi of early cinema.[25]

"IT IS A STORY OF PICTURES AND A STORY IN PICTURES"

"All the great events, all the great revolutions have been the work of the white race, the only creator among all the races." This quote attributed to a certain "Dr. Legendre" constitutes the film's first intertitle. Embodying the scientific racism integral to and promoted by colonialism, the French doctor affirms a few instants later: "The yellow race is an interbreeding of the white and black race that has perpetuated for a millennium." Aimé-François Legendre (1867–1951) was a physician-major stationed in Tonkin and Sichuan Province, as well as an explorer of China. A prolific writer, Legendre produced travelogues and articles that elaborated racial classifications based on the study of cranial measurements.[26] In *La France est notre patrie*, his scientific voice immediately confronts the spectator with, on the one hand, the primitive/civilized binary used to justify colonization and, on the other, an early film history that blurred the distinction between science and spectacle, ethnography and entertainment, anthropology and voyeurism. The modern concept of race, as Fatimah Tobing Rony reminds us, "was an invention of the nineteenth century and became the defining problem for early anthropology," a discipline deeply imbricated not only with imperial expansion but also with the emergence of the moving image.[27] Anthropology, like cinema, created experiences of travel for spectators. It also staged visual encounters with indigenous peoples by means of dioramas and the French practice of displaying ethnographic bodies in "native villages," first at the Jardin d'Acclimation in 1870 and then, in subsequent decades, at the Exposition Universelle.[28] (Recast through the lens of *La France est notre patrie*, the dioramas of *The Missing Picture* representing scenes of everyday life in Cambodia before the Khmer Rouge appear as a reappropriation of such ethnographic exhibits.)

Derived from Greek roots meaning "writing with motion," the cinematograph constituted a medium of "true scientific inscription" for Félix-Louis Regnault, a French physician and contemporary of Legendre who believed movement evidenced racial difference.[29] Regnault belonged to the Société d'anthropologie de Paris, an institution that legitimated the normative imperial gaze through measurements and classifications of colonized populations. The Société's *Bulletins et Mémoires* published, between 1910 and 1913, five articles by Legendre based on his anthropometric studies. In *La France est notre patrie*, the careful editing around his theories bears witness to the appropriation of both the body and the moving image as sites of supposed racial inscriptions. Immediately following the intertitle displaying Legendre's account of "the yellow race," the film cuts to a medium close-up of a woman in Southeast Asia who, under the scrutiny of an off-frame scientific gaze, is prompted to first face the camera and then turn around. Similarly, in between the title of the film and the first excerpt from Legendre's writings, Panh inserts a minute-long montage of scenes showing women and men

FIGURE 5.1. Children joyfully "exiting the factory"

across the French colonial empire performing ceremonial dances and trance rituals seemingly incomprehensible to the Western eye. This early sequence emphasizes the role of the cinematograph as a tool for inscribing motion (and, for anthropologists like Regnault, race) and the association, through colonization, of disparate peoples around the globe. It also recovers the trope of performance in early nonfiction films: what Alison Griffiths identifies as "the centrality of the ethnographic subject as a body-to-be-performed for nonnative audiences," whereby "savage" populations are made into spectacles and "civilized" spectators into remote ethnographers.[30]

In *La France est notre patrie*, the textual accompaniment moves from the scientific voice of "Dr. Legendre" to intertitles written in the language of the civilizing mission. "Where poverty and ignorance reigned, our homeland offers freedom and knowledge," one title card reads before cutting to a brief sequence displaying the French narrative of progress. After showing colonized women and men working in embroidery factories in Indochina, the footage cuts to a take of children who appear, following Panh's continuity editing, to be joyfully "exiting the factory," to borrow the title of the canonical film shot by the Lumière brothers in Lyon in 1895, which this scene calls to mind (figure 5.1). If the somber notes of Marder's soundtrack during this montage cast a shadow over the civilizing mission, the extradiegetic writing, sounds, and music deployed throughout

La France est notre patrie recuperate and reappropriate the varied techniques—from lecturers, or *bonimenteurs,* reminiscent of "Dr. Legendre" to explanatory intertitles to original scores—used in early nonfiction films "to explain, convince, keep order."[31]

In the closing moments of *La France est notre patrie,* when the story reaches the wars of decolonization and moving images of natives dancing now appear as performances of victory, Panh introduces a textual split. Signaled by the changed font of the title cards, the interrupted narration marks the passage from the voice of the colonizer to the voice of the colonized rebelling against the empire and, finally, to the voice of the Cambodian-born filmmaker. "It is a story of pictures and a story in pictures, beautiful and toxic," Panh affirms in the penultimate intertitle. While the elegant opening theme for piano and violin of Marder's original score returns, the director of *La France est notre patrie* cuts to a final sequence of archived film: strikingly out-of-focus footage of soldiers lowering a French flag, of a burning colonial building, and of a woman running away from the camera, followed by a canted shot of brush in a field. These images gesture toward a certain history of cinema that ended with decolonization, and toward nonfiction films made outside the metropole that faded into the background, never fully integrated or accounted for in a narrative that begins with the legendary invention of the Lumière brothers.

In *La France est notre patrie,* this other history of the moving image offers a reverse shot or colonial counterpart to collective memories of early cinema. Beyond "Exiting the Factory," numerous shots of moving trains and crowded platforms in Indochina conjure the Lumières' "Arrival of a Train at La Ciotat" (1895), while recasting railroads as a tool of imperial expansion used not only to connect cities and region, but also to "promote the exchange of peoples, currencies, commodities, and ideas."[32] Moreover, repeated depictions of travel in *La France est notre patrie*—by boat, train, or rickshaw, on horseback, and riding an elephant—connote a history of exploration and exploitation, further accentuated by innovative traveling shots. For instance, while a jazzy melody evocative of the 1920s is heard, scenes of men and women in Indochina digging the earth and pushing carts on metal tracks in an open-air mine (including an excerpt from Veyre's 1899 *actualité* "The Coal Mines of Hongay") culminate in a pioneering traveling shot captured, to the astonishment of the workers, from a mine cart going up a canyon (figure 5.2). The traveling shot unearthed by Panh approximates in its originality "Le village de Namo," the better-known fifty-second *actualité* recorded on a moving rickshaw by Veyre in Indochina in 1900. If Bertrand Tavernier considers this take showing laughing children running after the off-screen *chasseur d'images* of the Lumière brothers "absolutely perfect" in its composition, "Le village de Namo" bears witness, much like the archived films of *La France est notre patrie,* to the function of the empire as a laboratory for the experimentation of cinematic techniques at the turn of the twentieth century.[33]

FIGURE 5.2. A traveling shot from a mine cart

At once "beautiful and toxic," the traveling shot from the mine cart encapsulates the incessant extraction of moving images and natural resources underlying the "colonial family romance." In fact, this scene is one of many in a fifteen-minute sequence near the beginning of *La France est notre patrie* that documents all that the empire took in return for its civilizing mission: rubber, coal, silk, rice, tea, coffee, animals, and labor. "France seeks neither possessions nor glory. Its vision of mankind is fraternal and generous," reads the intertitle introducing the entwined ecological and economic facets of imperialism, which move from interventionist agricultural practices evidencing European mastery over nature to the creation of rubber and silk factories to the exportation of goods to the metropole. Beyond crates labeled "caoutchouc" and bags of rice, the colonial logic of inexhaustible extraction culminates in a striking early film of the Lumière brothers in Vietnam showing a cow being lifted from a raft unto a ship.[34] By means of its editing, *La France est notre patrie* also retraces the transformation of millions of hectares of rain forest in Southeast Asia into rubber plantations facilitated by an abundance of land and labor. As evidenced in the footage Panh utilizes, the introduction of the Brazilian *havea* seed in Indochina engendered habitat destruction and even a "forest without birds" (following the disappearance of fruit trees) intimated in these scenes by the artificial addition of chirping birds to the soundtrack.[35]

Ultimately, the "social-ecological project" of imperialism to which *La France est notre patrie* bears witness returns as a "story of pictures" marked by the aestheticization of laboring bodies. Panh's montage emphasizes in particular the repetition of the gestures of chopping wood and digging the earth performed in front of the camera by workers across the colonies. These moving images invoke the imperial bodies observed by French poet and diplomat Paul Claudel in 1920s Indochina, bodies seemingly "assimilated into the landscape and presented as part of an aesthetically ravishing exotic system, the disposable bits and parts of a well-oiled machine designed to efficiently work the rice paddies, the rubber plantations, and the open-air mines."[36] The repetition staged from one archived film to the next in *La France est notre patrie* inevitably calls to mind the gesture of digging the earth, reenacted time and again in *The Missing Picture*, that exemplifies, on the one hand, Pol Pot's agricultural revolution and, on the other, the ensuing endless burial of the dead. In Panh's filmography, this gesture also returns in a postcolonial context of globalization and exploitation depicted in *The Land of the Wandering Souls* (2000), which follows migrant workers digging trenches to install the country's first fiber-optic cable.[37] If this gesture recuperates a succession of traumatic histories, from colonization to genocide to civil war, it also conjures the work of Rithy Panh as a contemporary *chasseur d'images* who, perpetually in search of archives, excavates the buried reels of French film history.

NOTES

Epigraph: Scott MacDonald, *A Critical Cinema 3: Interviews with Independent Filmmakers* (Berkeley: University of California Press, 1998), 276.

1. Félix Mesguich, *Tours de manivelle: Souvenirs d'un chasseur d'images* (Paris: Editions Bernard Grasset, 1933), xii. All translations are mine.
2. Mesguich, 216.
3. Alice Conklin, *A Mission to Civilize: The Republican Idea of Empire in France and West Africa, 1895–1930* (Stanford, CA: Stanford University Press, 1997), 11.
4. Paula Amad, *Counter-archive: Film, the Everyday, and Albert Kahn's Archives de la Planète* (New York: Columbia University Press, 2010), 268.
5. For a description of Mesguich's films in Indochina, see Mesguich, *Tours de manivelle*, 222–229.
6. Panivong Norindr, *Phantasmatic Indochina: French Colonial Ideology in Architecture, Film, and Literature* (Durham, NC: Duke University Press, 1996), 13.
7. Peter J. Bloom, *French Colonial Documentary: Mythologies of Humanitarianism* (Minneapolis: University of Minnesota Press, 2008), 137. For a still from *France Is an Empire* displaying the phrase "France Is Our Homeland," see p. 141.
8. David Henry Slavin, *Colonial Cinema and Imperial France, 1919–1939: White Blind Spots, Male Fantasies, Settler Myths* (Baltimore: Johns Hopkins University Press, 2001), 59.
9. Yervant Gianikian quoted in MacDonald, *A Critical Cinema 3*, 280–281.
10. On the absence of such a museum, see the op-ed of French historian Pascal Blanchard marking the 125th anniversary of the 1894 creation of the Ministry of the Colonies, "Un musée sur l'histoire coloniale: Il est temps," *Libération*, May 29, 2019, https://www.liberation.fr/debats/2019/05/29/un-musee-sur-l-histoire-coloniale-il-est-temps_1730468.

11. Jacques Rivette, "On Abjection," trans. David Phelps and Jeremi Szaniakwi, http://www.dvdbeaver.com/rivette/ok/abjection.html. The original French essay appeared in *Cahiers du Cinéma* no. 120 (June 1961): 54–55.
12. "Travelling," in *Le Robert: Dictionnaire historique de la langue française*, ed. Alain Rey, vol. 3 (Paris: Dictionnaires Le Robert, 2000), 3901.
13. Tom Gunning, "'The Whole World within Reach': Travel Images without Borders," in *Virtual Voyages: Cinema and Travel*, ed. Jeffrey Ruoff (Durham, NC: Duke University Press, 2006), 36.
14. Paula Amad, "Between the 'Familiar Text' and the 'Book of the World,'" in *Virtual Voyages: Cinema and Travel*, ed. Jeffrey Ruoff (Durham, NC: Duke University Press, 2006), 101.
15. Gunning, "'The Whole World within Reach,'" 30.
16. Tom Gunning, "Before Documentary: Early Nonfiction Films and the 'View' Aesthetic," in *Uncharted Territory: Essays on Early Nonfiction Film*, ed. Daan Hertogs and Nico de Klerk (Amsterdam: Stichting Nederlands Filmmuseum, 1997), 24, 12. The scholarship of Fatimah Tobing Rony, Alison Griffiths, Jennifer Lynn Peterson, and Paula Amad aims to recuperate the overlook history of early nonfiction films and question, much like Panh's film, assumptions about which moving images constitute cinema.
17. Françoise Vergès, *Monsters and Revolutionaries: Colonial Family Romance and Metissage* (Durham, NC: Duke University Press, 1999), 7.
18. Corey Ross, *Ecology and Power in the Age of Empire: Europe and the Transformation of the Tropical World* (Oxford: Oxford University Press, 2017), 4.
19. See Vicente Sánchez-Biosca's chapter in this volume for an analysis of Bophana's presence throughout Panh's oeuvre.
20. Paula Amad, "Visual Riposte: Looking Back at the Return of the Gaze as Postcolonial Theory's Gift to Film Studies," *Cinema Journal* 52, no. 3 (Spring 2013): 53, 56. For an analysis of the returned gaze in early cinema as a site of resistance, see Alison Griffiths, *Wondrous Difference: Cinema, Anthropology, and Turn-of-the-Century Visual Culture* (New York: Columbia University Press, 2002), 196–203.
21. Ann Stoler, *Carnal Knowledge and Imperial Power: Race and the Intimate in Colonial Rule* (Berkeley: University of California Press, 2002), 55.
22. Pascal Blanchard et al., eds., *Sexe, race & colonies: La domination des corps du XVe siècle à nos jours* (Paris: Editions La Découverte, 2018), 305.
23. Stoler, *Carnal Knowledge and Imperial Power*, 49.
24. Blanchard et al., *Sexe, race & colonies*, 250.
25. Amad, *Counter-archive*, 285.
26. See, for instance, Aimé-François Legendre, *Le far-west chinois: Deux années au Setchouen* (Paris: Plon, 1905), 476.
27. Fatimah Tobing Rony, *The Third Eye: Race, Cinema, and Ethnographic Spectacle* (Durham, NC: Duke University Press, 1996), 10, 24.
28. Rony, 37.
29. Rony, 45.
30. Griffiths, *Wondrous Difference*, 184, 172.
31. Rony, *Third Eye*, 61.
32. Conklin, *Mission to Civilize*, 6.
33. See Bertrand Tavernier's narration on the DVD *The Lumière Brothers: First Films* (Kino Video, 2003), 55:44–56:31. For an analysis of this film, see Barbara Creed and Jeanette Hoorn, "Memory and History: Early Film, Colonialism, and the French Civilizing Mission in Indochina," *French History and Civilization* 4 (2011): 228–230.

34. This particular film also made a deep impression on Tavernier. See *The Lumière Brothers: First Films*, 43:54–44:23.
35. Ross, *Ecology and Power in the Age of Empire*, 100, 113.
36. Thus Norindr summarizes Claudel's impressions; see Norindr, *Phantasmatic Indochina*, 7.
37. For an analysis of gender, labor, and migration in a globalizing Cambodia, see Leslie Barnes's chapter on *The Land of the Wandering Souls* in this volume.

6 • AERIAL AFTERMATHS AND RECKONINGS FROM BELOW

Reseeing Rithy Panh's *Shiiku, the Catch*

CATHY J. SCHLUND-VIALS

> I work on extreme violence. I work on gestures, on bodies, on words, on how extreme violence affects the bodies of victims as well as the bodies of perpetrators.
>
> —"Rithy Panh: Living the Experience of Genocide in Body and Soul," interview with Thierry Cruvellier

> The war, a long bloody battle on a huge scale, must still have been going on. The war that like a flood washing away flocks of sheep and trimmed lawns in some distant country was never supposed to have reached our village. But it had come. . . . Suddenly, our village was enveloped in the war, and in the tumult I could not breathe.
>
> —Kenzaburō Ōe, *Teach Us How to Outgrow Our Madness*

> I can't escape the chain reaction of war.
>
> —*Shiiku, the Catch* (2011)

> *reckoning (n).*
>
> 1. [uncountable, countable] the act of calculating something, especially in a way that is not very exact.
> 2. [countable, usually singular, uncountable] a time when somebody's actions will be judged to be right or wrong and they may be punished.
>
> —*The Oxford English Dictionary*

Produced by Catherine Dussart, written by Michel Fessler, directed by Rithy Panh, and filmed on location (in and around Siem Reap, Cambodia) over a three-month period (December 2010–February 2011), *Shiiku, the Catch* had its Phnom Penh–based world premiere in March 2011, at the second annual Cambodia International Film Festival (CIFF).[1] Partially funded by the Cambodia Film Commission—which, in conjunction with the Bophana Center and the Cambodian Ministry of Culture and Fine Arts, occupied a prominent CIFF position as a key fiscal cosponsor and program organizer—Panh's fourteenth film enjoyed an enviable screening slot as a festival central showcase.[2] Consonant with the CIFF's stated mission to "promote innovative international filmmaking in various forms" and consistent with its aspirational aim to "present quality productions made in and about Cambodia by national and international filmmakers," *The Catch*'s relatively short production journey from script to screen exemplified the festival's locally driven and nationally concentrated agendas by way of the aforementioned setting, the employment of an entirely Khmer film crew, and the utilization of a predominantly nonprofessional, young Cambodian cast (the sole exception in terms of Khmer-dominant casting involved Paris-born actor Cyril Gueï, who assumed the titular role of a downed American fighter pilot held captive in a small Cambodian village).[3]

Shifting from film production to movie narrative, *The Catch*'s Cambodia-centric purview was made even more salient at the level of film plot and camera shot. Regarding the former, *The Catch*'s narratival emplotments directly engage Cambodian history or the middle to late twentieth century, specifically the Cambodian Civil War (1967–1975), wherein U.S.-supported Lon Nol soldiers battled communist Khmer Rouge forces. In addition, the film offers detailed depictions of rural Cambodian daily life and features realistic cinematography (particularly as it entailed the use of natural lighting and seemingly unedited continuous shots). As the country's most well-known director and diasporic cofounder of Phnom Penh's Bophana Center, Panh's prominent position in the CIFF program was consonant with a by-then-established international reputation as Cambodia's most acclaimed filmmaker and nationally recognized archivist.[4] As significant, the CIFF's aesthetic emphasis on "international filmmaking in various forms" is immediately evident in *The Catch*'s French production team (as epitomized by the respective roles of the press officer turned producer Dussart and screenwriter Fessler), reflected in Panh's unique transnational position as a Cambodian refugee who "came of age" as a filmmaker in Paris at the Institut des Hautes Etudes Cinématographiques (IDHEC, now La Fémis), and refracted in the film's explicit revision of a Japanese source text, Kenzaburō Ōe's short story "The Catch" (1957).

Notwithstanding these local, national, and global registers, which correspondingly render discernible through artistic reputation, geographic location, and material production the multivalent "glocal" connections between director, film, and festival, it is ultimately the CIFF's overriding focus on cinematic "innovation" and implied concomitant attention to narrative experimentation that presage this chapter's general analysis of *The Catch*, a movie that, on the one hand, exemplifies via plot an identifiable continuation of Panh's long-standing cinematic contemplation of Cambodian history. Even so, when situated within the celebrated afterlight of widely praised documentaries such as *S21: The Khmer Rouge Killing Machine* (2003) and the intimately autobiographical, Academy Award–nominated *The Missing Picture* (2013), *The Catch* occupies a markedly less visible position vis-à-vis industry-connected recognitions, critical reviews, and scholarly considerations of Panh's multidecade body of work.[5] A mostly unknown, generally underacknowledged, and largely underreviewed work, *The Catch* did not benefit from extensive regional/international distribution, nor did it have access to a far-reaching promotional campaign. Accordingly, the film's narrow circulation, apparent in its limited screening history at the CIFF and the twenty-fourth annual Tokyo International Film Festival, its noninclusion at other internationally prestigious festivals such as the invitation-only Cannes Film Festival (namely, as chief cinematic conduits for awards, recognitions, and honors), and its relatively low budget offer three possible reasons for *The Catch*'s comparatively marginalized position as one of Panh's "lesser" films.

On the other hand, what significantly differentiates *The Catch* from the majority of works that constitute Panh's filmic oeuvre is its idiosyncratically double-sited negotiation of in-country dynamics (as fixed *to* and generated *from* the Cambodian Civil War) alongside extant U.S. foreign policy (principally vis-à-vis Cold War–guided militarized intervention and Vietnam War–driven illicit bombing campaigns). Hence, notwithstanding the film's relatively minor status in relation to the international film market and despite its proportionally marginal location within Panh's larger artistic portfolio, this chapter maintains that it is precisely *The Catch*'s distinctive engagement with these two complex yet interconnected war narratives by way of cinematic historiography and the blended "docufiction" genre that necessitates a critical return to this sometimes dismissed and forgotten production. If, according to an expression famously coined by the Victorian historian Edward Augustus Freeman (1823–1892), "history is past politics and politics present history," then *The Catch*'s synchronized depictions of in-country polemics, Cold War logics, and U.S. militarization—via setting, shot, plot, and characterization—recollect manifold "casualties of war."[6] Composed of combatants and civilians, symptomatic of losses involving bodies corporeal *and* politic, such casualties militate against euphemistic portrayals of nonspecific "collateral damage" by reifying the all-too-real outcomes of what Panh (in the first epigraph to this chapter) terms "extreme violence." These strategic conflations between bodily harm and political catastrophe—revealed through individual act, factional dictate, and foreign-born military campaign—figuratively cohere with *The Catch*'s hybrid format in ways that bring the corporeal back to history.[7]

Alternatively, as a contextualized analysis and close reading of *The Catch* accentuate, these casualties of war are the direct consequence of Cambodian-U.S.

"past politics." As this chapter contends, it is the film's simultaneous engagement with Cambodia's pre–Democratic Kampuchean history and ruinous U.S. foreign policy that affords audiences an evocative panorama of Panh's previously mentioned notion of "extreme violence." Connotative of an "unbroken view of a whole region," suggestive of a "picture containing a wide view," and indicative of "a complete survey or presentation of a subject," the characterization of *The Catch* through a panoramic schema encompasses the film's diverse depictions of "extreme violence."[8] Such capaciousness with regard to history, cinematography, and narrative occurs despite the film's seemingly simplistic plot, which involves a downed U.S. pilot and his captivity as a prisoner of war in a Cambodian village. It is this panoramic treatment of Cambodian civil war and U.S. foreign conflict, wherein the early 1970s Cambodian state and its countryside denizens are inextricably caught in the catastrophic crosshairs of Cold War realpolitik, that significantly contradistinguishes *The Catch* from Panh's other works, which, notwithstanding narrative diversity, are more often than not solely focused on Cambodian experiences under the Khmer Rouge regime or concentrated on Cambodian daily life in the post–Democratic Kampuchean era. As this chapter subsequently explores, this untenable position—artistically revealed in the panoramic treatment of Cambodian history at the level of plot, reflected in the deliberate incorporation of U.S. archival footage, and refracted in the purposeful use of vertical shots to highlight concurrent violence and violations in the air and on the ground—serves as the basis for an expansive antiwar critique that takes centrally the nuanced polemics of in-country war and the binaried machinations of international Cold War conflict.

To establish the cultural and historical stakes of Panh's antiwar critique, this chapter begins with the bellicose histories at the forefront of *The Catch*, particularly as they intersect with contemporaneous U.S. bombing campaigns, the Cambodian Civil War, and rise of the Khmer Rouge regime. The chapter then shifts to the intertextual dimensions of *Shiiku, the Catch* via Kenzaburō Ōe's original short story and Nagisa Oshima's 1961 same-named film adaptation, which concretize the antiwar dimensions of Panh's version. This historical context and these politically inflected cultural resonances support this chapter's overall contention that *The Catch*—despite its material status as an adapted work and revised film project—is dialogically fixed to the pacifism of Ōe's provocative short story. To further accentuate *The Catch*'s antiwar politics via plot and shot, this chapter draws upon Caren Kaplan's influential work on aerial warfare to lay bare *and* deconstruct the peculiar "world-making propensity" in Panh's cinematic use of multiple "views from above" (e.g., via aerial, high-angle, and low-angle camera shots).[9] According to Kaplan, such propensity is marked by "the sudden realization of both the vast scope and vulnerability of the earth as seen from above"; such a realization, predicated on an overwhelming sense of space and place, on the one hand captivates observers. On the other hand, as Kaplan reminds us, the expansiveness contained in these vertical ways of seeing "begs for rigorous deconstruction" because "what can be seen is never just one thing but always an activity undertaken with the constituting purpose of representation—to discern between things . . . [and] make distinctions."[10] On the whole, this chapter contends that integral to *The Catch*'s antiwar politics is a "rigorous deconstruction" of recent Cambodian history; this deconstructionist project critically juxtaposes the vertical dimensions of distanced war making with its horizontal impacts "on the ground." In so doing, *The Catch* concomitantly recollects the "extreme violence" of Cold War realpolitik and evocatively eschews one-dimensional assignations of wartime via its archival restaging of U.S. militarization, filmic treatment of the U.S.-backed Lon Nol regime, and cinematic depiction of an increasingly authoritarian Khmer Rouge.

COLLATERAL DAMAGES: RESEEING U.S. BOMBING CAMPAIGNS AND THE CAMBODIAN CIVIL WAR

According to Taylor Owen and Ben Kiernan, between October 4, 1965, and August 15, 1973, the United States dropped 2,756,941 tons of munitions on 113,716 Cambodian sites. An estimated 230,516 sorties were flown over Cambodia, which had—through its then head of state, Prince Norodom Sihanouk—hitherto declared a neutral position vis-à-vis the Vietnam War.[11] Of these missions, 3,580 involved "unknown targets," and 8,238 failed to list any target whatsoever. While the Johnson administration's use of air-based munitions and the Nixon administration's bombing of the Cambodian countryside (under the auspices of the B-52 "Menu" campaign, 1969–1973) are widely recognized (particularly in the aftermath of the Pentagon Papers publication and the Kent State shooting), less acknowledged is the extent to which the American War in Viet Nam—from the outset and to restate—time and again involved adjacent Cambodia (along with bordering Thailand, Laos, and Burma).[12] As Owen and Kiernan further synopsize, when President Nixon "telephoned his national security advisor, Henry Kissinger, to discuss the ongoing bombing of Cambodia" on December 9, 1970, the "sideshow to the war in Vietnam, begun in 1965 under the Johnson administration, had already seen 475,515 tons of ordnance on Cambodia."[13]

Suggestive of "a small show or stall at an exhibition, fair, or circus" and "a minor or diverting incident or issue, especially one which distracts attention from something more important," the use of "sideshow" in conjunction with Cambodia purposely belies—by way of historical juxtaposition and military magnitude—the degree to which U.S. bombings had an impact that far exceeded immediate foreign policy objectives (e.g., the disruption of the so-termed Ho Chi Minh Trail, which extended along the Cambodia-Vietnam border).[14] As Owen and Kiernan assert, the civilian casualties that resulted from these bombings (which number between 50,000 and 150,000) "drove an enraged populace into the arms of an insurgency that had enjoyed relatively little support until the bombing began, setting in motion the expansion of the Vietnam War deeper into Cambodia, a *coup d'état* in 1970, the rapid rise of the Khmer Rouge, and ultimately the Cambodian genocide."[15] Such disastrous legacies, which occur notwithstanding Cambodia's geopolitical status as a "sideshow" vis-à-vis the Indochina conflict, bring to light the capaciousness of not only U.S. war making but also the Cold War noncontainment of the American War in Vietnam. Measured by hundreds of thousands of U.S. Air Force sorties and millions of tons of munitions, such warfare fulfills by way of mathematical greatness the far-reaching parameters of the so-termed military sublime. Related to Kaplan's aforementioned arguments concerning the "vastness" of aerial warfare, the "military sublime," as Samina Najmi summarizes, encapsulates "dramatic, large-scale spectacles of war and their accompanying inflated rhetoric."[16] Encompassing an enormity that is inconsistently calculable (via numerical measurement) *and* incalculable (with respect to collateral human cost), to read the American bombing of Cambodia via the military sublime is to acknowledge the pugnacious capaciousness and distanced vistas of U.S. empire, a project marked not by moderate program but by excessive force.

Comparably, such imperial excesses are affectively evident and sublimely apparent in first-person accounts such as the following given by an anonymous Cambodian survivor: "We heard a terrifying noise which shook the ground; it was as if the earth trembled, rose up and opened beneath our feet. Enormous explosions lit up the sky like huge bolts of lightning; it was the American B-52s."[17] Reminiscent of Najmi's "dramatic, large-scale spectacles of war," the survivor's concluding revelation of American B-52s follows ominous, sensory-driven recollections (for instance, "a terrifying noise" and the "trembl[ing]" of earth) and descriptions of cataclysmic conflagrations that resemble "huge bolts of lightning." These intensely personal remembrances of American military power, on the one hand, collapse the geopolitical space between the United States and Cambodia by way of munitions transport (in the case of the former) and natural landscape (with regard to the latter). On the other hand, such non-state-authorized accounts accentuate through sublime characterization and vertiginous categorization the collateral costs of U.S. foreign policy via enormity, confusion, and scale. Accordingly, what is originally "seen" or experienced as natural is subsequently exposed as not only man-made but American. As significant, what is visible from the ground (e.g., conflagration and bomber) is by and large invisible from above.

In comparison and by contrast, the "seen" and "unseen" dimensions of distanced warfare, which in *The Catch* initially converge on large-scale U.S. bombings of the Cambodian countryside, are provocatively subverted in its opening frames. Expressly, *The Catch* begins with previously shot footage of U.S. planes flying over a lush landscape; this footage—originally shot by U.S. military personnel as a means of documenting Vietnam War era campaigns and air-based strikes—is aurally accompanied by defamiliarized military jargon (in English), along with more recognizable plane engine sounds, which function as an opening soundtrack. As the military footage progresses, the speaker's voice becomes more animated, presaging a camera angle shift from a horizontal plane view to vertical perspective. This "view from above" is dominated by the downward release of hundreds of cluster bomb munitions that, upon making impact, produce spectacular, bright yellow conflagrations that punctuate a deeply green landscape. Without direct narration and sans explanatory captioning, the intended bomb target featured in the archival footage is at first unclear; however, as the perspective moves from a vertical air view to horizontal ground perspective, a location and date appear onscreen ("Cambodia, 1972"). The first "real-time" shot involves children playing around a large crater; this seemingly innocuous scene of daily life is quickly undermined by a conversation between two unnamed characters wherein the U.S. bombings are directly mentioned.

This juxtaposition of aerial archival footage and on-the-ground camerawork, replayed and reiterated over the course of *The Catch*, on the one hand concretizes by way of visual representation the film's overt engagement with contemporaneous U.S. foreign policy; this engagement is by no means limited to its opening sequences, nor is its use strictly fixed to U.S. war making. This footage is reused prior to the introduction of Lon Nol troops, who forcefully interrogate the village's denizens and destroy selected domiciles; it is also utilized in a scene that precedes the discovery of the African American pilot by the film's child protagonist (Pang). This recycled footage is employed in scenes that foreground the arrival of Khmer Rouge soldiers and cinematically foreshadows scenes involving increased Khmer Rouge control over the village. Last, but certainly not least, *The Catch* concludes with this footage, which literally brings "full circle" the film's overall engagement with U.S. foreign policy "from above" and its multifaceted impacts "on the ground." Taken together, Panh's strategic use of military film footage assumes the cinematic significance of a politically inflected "establishing shot." Intended to set up subsequent scenes, provide setting details (specifically with regard to temporality and geography), and indicate key relationships between and among characters, establishing shots—or extreme long shots—are deliberately slow-paced. This characterization coheres with Panh's utilization of military footage, which is deployed to convey film-relevant information (e.g., details fixed to the imagined world of the film) while "establishing" a more complex understanding of Cambodia's recent war-driven past.

Such narrative complexity with regard to history, politics, and war, revealed through the critical juxtaposition of archival footage and real-time action, corresponds to foundational Soviet director Sergei Eisenstein's theory of editing and notion of "intellectual cinema" via montage. Focused on intentionality, concerned with sequencing, and concentrated on enhancing a work's analytical impact, Eisenstein's overall characterization of montage pivots on a dialectical deployment of connected images that engender revised ways of comprehending history and politics.[18] Such altered understandings correspondingly function as a key facet of "intellectual cinema," which relies on skilled image curation (by the director) and subsequent viewer interpretation (of sequenced, composite images) to articulate an abstract idea. Situated within the context of *The Catch*'s multivalent contemplation of war-driven collateral damage through military montages and set adjacent to the film's indefatigable negotiation of Cambodia's conflict-ridden past via intermingled formats, what emerges as a key theme and polemic is an abstract yet nevertheless compelling antiwar politics that refuses narrow assignation or causation.

TOWARD AN INTERTEXTUAL CINEMA: *SHIIKU, THE CATCH* AS ADAPTIVE ADAPTATION

Notwithstanding its uniqueness with regard to blended form and despite its potential as a multisited antiwar critique, *The Catch* (to reiterate and expand) was by no means a critical or commercial success despite Panh's established reputation as Cambodia's foremost filmmaker and notwithstanding his well-earned status as an internationally recognized auteur. Nor did Panh's wartime "docufiction" enjoy the same transnational circulation as his 2003 documentary, *S21: The Khmer Rouge Killing Machine*, which in the past decade has received renewed interest due to its indubitable relevance to the United Nations/Khmer Rouge Tribunal (2003–2018). This hybrid tribunal (officially known as the Extraordinary Chambers in the Courts of Cambodia [ECCC]) focused its first deliberation (Case 001) on S-21 and its head warden, Kaing Guek Eav (aka Comrade Duch); two former S-21 prisoners—Vann Nath and Chum Mey—occupied central roles in Panh's documentary and would subsequently serve as key tribunal witnesses.[19] Such timely coherences between cinematic production and juridical dynamic were likewise apparent in Panh's sequel to *S21*, *Duch, Master of the Forges of Hell* (2011), which featured one-on-one interviews between Panh and the former Khmer Rouge prison warden. Situated within a contested juridical context wherein Duch/Eav was the first Khmer Rouge official to be tried and—on July 26, 2010—convicted by the ECCC, both *S21: The Khmer Rouge Killing Machine* and *Duch, Master of the Forges of Hell* emphasize Duch as the main subject and principal narrator, thus increasing the documentary film's archival value as provocative court supplement. By contrast, *The Catch*'s early 1970s setting, its narrative connection to the Second Indochina War (Vietnam War), and strategic preoccupation with the pre–Killing Fields past (as a work concerned with the multivalent ambiguities that brought Democratic Kampuchea into "being" on

April 17, 1975) marked a thematic departure for a director most known for works detailing life "under" and "after" the Khmer Rouge regime.

Set roughly three years *prior* to the start of the Democratic Kampuchea period (1975–1979), *The Catch* is nevertheless haunted by what those outside Cambodia term the "Killing Fields" and those within label "Pol Pot Time." Panh's previous films and his distinct position as a displaced subject and refugee survivor of Khmer Rouge authoritarianism render possible a multifaceted cinematic reimagining of Khmer Rouge totalitarianism alongside extant U.S. militarization. Such explorations into Cambodia's turbulent past—wherein the rise of the Khmer Rouge is connected to U.S. intervention—on one level replicate the narrative promulgated in Roland Joffé's Academy Award–nominated *The Killing Fields* (1984), based on the Pulitzer Prize–winning journalist Sydney Schanberg's *New York Times Magazine* piece "The Death and Life of Dith Pran: A Story of Cambodia" (1980). Like *The Killing Fields, The Catch* (as previously discussed) directly accesses by way of aerial bombing montages and cratered landscapes the "on-the-ground" realities of war. Moreover, the film's tactical iterative narration, vexed war-driven polemics, and vertically determined cinematographic perspectives cross multiple aesthetic and political borders.

What further contradistinguishes *The Catch* with regard to its antiwar politics is its particular connection to its source text: Kenzaburō Ōe's aforementioned short story, "The Catch." Like Panh's previous adaptations of cinematic works—*Rice People* (1994) and *The Sea Wall* (2008)—*The Catch* adheres closely to the source plot and, in this case, its salient antiwar themes; however, as was the case in Panh's earlier *Rice People*, the 2011 adaptation of Ōe's pacifist tale involves a significant revision of the historical setting (in 1972), geopolitical backdrop (specifically with regard to illegal U.S. bombing campaigns and Cambodia's civil war), and physical location (e.g., the Cambodian countryside). To that end, the narrative of *The Catch* commences with the discovery of a downed African American pilot by village children. This seemingly serendipitous encounter, which carries with it the potential of rescue and refuge, is soon transformed into a more ominous exchange involving detention and imprisonment. In the original, as villagers wait for word from Japanese officials as to the pilot's ultimate fate, the children responsible for locating him continue to interact with the soldier, whose presumed political leanings are antithetical to those held by the majority of his captors. When the villagers are instructed to relocate the prisoner to a nearby prefecture, the unnamed child protagonist attempts to warn his carceral charge. However, the protagonist's efforts are subverted when the prisoner takes him hostage; this crisis precipitates a violent exchange with the protagonist's father, who—in the process of attacking the prisoner—injures his son. The prisoner's corpse is subsequently discarded in the surrounding woods. Ōe's short story ends with the protagonist's epigraphic observation that, despite its far-off location from metropolitan hubs and strategic military bases, his village was nevertheless "enveloped in the war."

While Panh's *The Catch* is, in terms of its narratival focus and dramatic structure, indebted to Ōe's literary work, the film is likewise dialogically resonant with Nagisa Oshima's adaptation, *Shiiku* (1961). While the famed Japanese director's version adheres closely to its originating text, it is its "aftermath" release that is most relevant to Panh's more recent filmic version. Produced in the afterlight of Japan's World War II defeat and made soon after the U.S. occupation concluded (in 1952), Oshima's *Shiiku* takes place in May 1945 in Japan. On the one hand, *Shiiku* is a complex retrospective work that—like its short story counterpart—is very much presentist in its antisentimental depiction of systemic racism and concomitant xenophobia. Indeed, it is the pilot's race that functions as both a potent signifier of difference to the Japanese villagers and a problematic justification of his denigration by the child captors. The overt use of racial slurs, coupled with the animalistic qualities that dominate the protagonist's recollections about the prisoner, strikes a contemporaneous chord when situated against a backdrop of militarized integration and U.S. imperial expansion.

On the other hand, Oshima's *Shiiku* provocatively extends Ōe's short story to encompass past grievances alongside present-day concerns. Accordingly, Oshima's adaptation takes centrally the injustices embedded in an economically exploitative, scarcity-driven system of feudalism that circumscribes the futurity of the village and impedes the prosperity of its inhabitants. These inequalities are, as the film progresses, exacerbated by a failing war effort and decreased in country resources. As rations are depleted and the village's economic viability rendered more uncertain, its inhabitants increasingly place their blame on the prisoner; as the film ends and the prisoner's elimination appears imminent, his role in relation to the village has been transformed from mere enemy combatant to wholesale scapegoat for all the village's past struggles and ongoing tribulations.

By contrast, Panh's much later adaptation is set during the previously mentioned Cambodian Civil War at a moment wherein U.S. foreign policy vis-à-vis the Vietnam War was—as the introductory epigraph by President Nixon accentuates—an increasingly collateral damage enterprise (specifically in terms of civilian losses) and a noncontained, illicit endeavor. The African American pilot appears—on first glance—to be a major character, whose presence catalyzes character action and plot developments with regard to xenophobia and discrimination. However, whereas racialization and isolationism serve as intelligible themes in the previously discussed Japanese counterparts, Panh's direction, along with Fessler's adaptation, shifts the emphasis from problematic community dynamics to a troubling authoritative collective (specifically regarding Khmer Rouge ideology). As Panh admits, "I always wanted to depict a situation . . . where a child would be entangled in the revolution and army."[20] Notwithstanding these distinctions, Panh's *The Catch* and its screenplay—at the levels of plot, character development, and bellicose thematic—pay cinematic homage to Ōe's Japanese source text and, to a lesser degree, Oshima's adaptation.

Shifting from a comparative framework and returning to the more recent film's plot, as the narrative progresses, the conflicts between child jailors and their prisoner increase. Regarding the former, the children (especially Pang) struggle to not empathize with the so-termed enemy.[21] The latter does attempt escape following news that he will be located elsewhere, but the escape ends with the suggestion that he will perish at the hands of those charged with caring for him (i.e., Pang and the other village children); instead of an execution scene, the audience is left with a parting image of the pilot, and the film ends with a rescreening of the previously discussed military film footage.

CONCLUSION

Despite the film's reiterative conclusion, as the initial excerpt from Ōe's literary source text reminds and Pang's above-placed provocative missive suggests, a true "war story," as delineated via a discernible first premise and an expanded final deliberation, is one wherein the capacious impacts of mid-twentieth-century distanced warfare are rendered historically visible, complexly discernible, and affectively palpable. To surmise and summarize, the enormity of past and present U.S. militarization abroad and the collateral damage that is part and parcel of large-scale war making necessitate a multivalent analysis consistent with what Pulitzer Prize–winning author Viet Thanh Nguyen maintains should be a key facet of "war stories" as a distinct narrative mode. As Nguyen avers, a "true" war story is one wherein soldier subjectivity is eschewed in favor of civilian loss; instead, a "true" war story is one "not about soldiers"; it is also an account that illustrates how normal war is, how war touches and transforms everything and everybody, including, most of all, civilians.[22] Nguyen's characterization of "true war stories," predicated on a more expansive "re-seeing" of war, conflict, and "collateral damage," productively corresponds to and encapsulates the antiwar politics at the forefront of Panh's *The Catch,* which in its multivalent engagements with in-country conflict and international war cinematically reckons with quotidian dimensions of "extreme violence" and its still-relevant aftermaths.

NOTES

First epigraph: "Rithy Panh: Living the Experience of Genocide in Body and Soul," interview by Thierry Cruvellier, *JusticeInfo.net,* November 27, 2018, https://www.justiceinfo.net/en/justiceinfo-comment-and-debate/in-depth-interviews/39596-rithy-panh-living-the-experience-of-genocide-in-body-and-soul.html; second epigraph: Kenzaburō Ōe, *Teach Us How to Outgrow Our Madness,* trans. John Nathan (New York: Publisher's Group West, 1977), 200. The story in the collection is titled "Prize Stock," though in other translations the title is translated as "The Catch." Originally published in 1957, "The Catch" was awarded the prestigious Akutagawa Prize in 1958, when Ōe was twenty-three years old. Established in 1935, the Akutagawa Prize recognizes the best serious literary story published by a new or emerging

Japanese author. Ōe was awarded the Nobel Prize in Literature in 1994; third epigraph: *Shiiku, the Catch* (2011). This line is spoken by Pang, the main protagonist, a child villager turned soldier; fourth epigraph: *Oxford English Dictionary*, s.v. "reckoning," https://www.oxfordlearnersdictionaries.com/us/definition/english/reckoning.

1. See "Cambodian Film Commission," accessed April 13, 2020, https://cambodia-cfc.org/2011/02/04/the-catch-by-rithy-panh/#:~:text=SHIIKU%2C%20THE%20CATCH%20is%20the%20new%20feature%20by,with%20the%20support%20of%20the%20Cambodia%20Film%20Commission.
2. See "Cambodian International Film Festival," accessed April 29, 2020, filmfreeway.com/CambodiaInternationalFilmFestival.
3. "Cambodian International Film Festival."
4. As Cambodia's largest cultural archive, the Bophana Center occupies a prominent national and international position.
5. Both *S21: The Khmer Rouge Killing Machine* and *The Missing Picture* received awards at the Cannes Film Festival. In addition to other festival honors, *The Missing Picture* would receive an Academy Award nomination for Best Foreign Language Film, representing the first-ever nomination of a Cambodian-directed work.
6. Quoted in James W. Thompson, *A History of Historical Writing*, vol. 2 (New York: Macmillan, 1942), 35. Despite the usefulness of Freeman's characterization of history vis-à-vis this chapter's larger argument concerning Panh's work, his reputation is rightly critiqued due to his overt anti-Semitic proclivities, anti-Black racism, and vehement xenophobia.
7. I am grateful for Joseph Mai's comments with regard to Panh's use of aesthetic hybridity in *The Catch*.
8. *Oxford English Dictionary*, s.v. "panoramic," https://www.oxfordlearnersdictionaries.com/us/definition/english/panoramic.
9. Caren Kaplan, *Aerial Aftermaths: War from Above* (Durham, NC: Duke University Press, 2018), 11.
10. Kaplan, 11.
11. Taylor Owen and Ben Kiernan, "Bombs over Cambodia," *The Walrus*, October 2006, 67.
12. See Cathy J. Schlund-Vials, *War, Genocide, and Justice: Cambodian American Memory Work* (Minneapolis: University of Minnesota Press, 2012).
13. Owen and Kiernan, "Bombs over Cambodia," 66.
14. *Oxford English Dictionary*, s.v. "sideshow," https://www.oxfordlearnersdictionaries.com/us/definition/english/sideshow.
15. Owen and Kiernan, "Bombs over Cambodia," 63. The Khmer Rouge regime began on April 17, 1975, when troops overtook Cambodia's capital, Phnom Penh. Soon after, the Khmer Rouge emptied the nation's cities and relocated its denizens to the countryside, ushering in the so-termed Killing Fields era. Guided by the superseding desire to eliminate all Western influence and create a classless society, the Khmer Rouge prohibited religion, outlawed currency, proscribed education, and strategically targeted those who were most closely allied with the previous regime or deemed "enemies of the people" due to alleged Western affiliations. On January 7, 1979, the Vietnamese ostensibly liberated Cambodia, signaling the end to both regional hostilities and the dissolution of the Khmer Rouge regime. Setting aside the relatively short period of Khmer Rouge rule, its impact was catastrophic: an estimated 1.7 million Cambodians perished due to disease, starvation, forced labor, and execution; 90 percent of Khmer court musicians and dancers were dead; nine judges were left in the country; the majority of the nation's teachers (three-quarters) died or fled the country; and out of an estimated 550 doctors, only 48 survived. To date, only three Khmer Rouge leaders have been successfully tried and convicted of crimes against humanity (in 2010 and 2014, respectively).

16. Samina Najmi, "Naomi Shihab Nye's Aesthetic Smallness and the Military Sublime," *MELUS* 35, no. 2 (2010): 152.
17. Quoted in Owen and Kiernan, "Bombs over Cambodia," 66.
18. According to Eisenstein, the five methods of montage include "metric montage" (which involves shot length and is focused on eliciting an emotional response); "rhythmic montage" (characterized by its attention to time and tempo within a contained scene); "tonal montage" (as signaled through lighting, shadow, and shape); "overtonal montage" (the combination of metric, rhythmic, and tonal montage); and "intellectual/ideological montage" (wherein images are combined to relay an abstract concept). See Sergei Eisenstein, *The Eisenstein Reader*, ed. Richard Taylor, trans. Richard Taylor and William Powell (London: British Film Institute, 1998), 17–20.
19. The United Nations/Khmer Rouge Tribunal was originally formed in 2006; in addition to Kaing Guek Eav, four other Khmer Rouge officials were tried over the course of the next twelve years: Khieu Samphan (former Democratic Kampuchean prime minister); Nuon Chea (chief ideologue whose status in the regime was confirmed via the nickname "Brother 2" [Saloth Sar, aka Pol Pot, occupied the position of "Brother 1"]); Ieng Sary (former Democratic Kampuchea foreign minister); and Ieng Thirith (former Khmer Rouge social minister). The tribunal was composed of three cases: Case 001 (involving Eav's alleged war crimes), Case 001/01 (which extended the war crime allegation to encompass the remaining four defendants), and Case 002 (wherein Sary and Samphan were charged with crimes of genocide). After almost a year of deliberation, Eav was found guilty of war crimes and sentenced to nineteen years in July 2010. Eav appealed his verdict and was subsequently given a much longer sentence (life). Ieng Sary passed away on March 14, 2013; his wife, Ieng Thirith, was deemed mentally incompetent due to advance Alzheimer's disease in 2015. On November 15, 2018, the Extraordinary Chambers in the Courts of Cambodia issued a final verdict for Khieu Samphan and Nuon Chea; both were found guilty of genocide and sentenced to life imprisonment, but Chea passed away the following year (in 2019). Set against a backdrop of overdue prosecution and situated within a context of juridical belatedness, the ruling was quite historic; after all, one of the major points of tribunal contention was whether or not what happened in Cambodia was indeed "genocide" given that the Khmer Rouge—with a few exceptions—targeted not an ethnic or religious affiliation but a class-oriented status (i.e., the middle class and urban denizens).
20. "Master of the Documentary Challenges Kenzaburo Ōe's Masterpiece" (*Shiiku* Q&A), Tiff Tokyo, accessed June 10, 2020, http://2011.tiff-jp.net/news/en/?p=842.
21. Pang's increased allegiance to the Khmer Rouge is not equally replicated by the other children in the village, nor is it a stance that is universally adopted by the village adults. Rather, the film's characters are configured along a spectrum with regard to Khmer Rouge affiliation and Lon Nol regime allegiance. Again, I am grateful to Joseph Mai for the editorial suggestion.
22. Viet Thanh Nguyen, "On True War Stories," in "(Re)Collecting the Vietnam War," ed. Cathy J. Schlund-Vials and Sylvia Shin Huey Chong, special issue, *Asian American Literary Review* 6, no. 2 (Fall 2015): 140–145.

7 • CAMBODIA'S "WANDERING SOULS"

Migrant Labor and the Promise of Connection

LESLIE BARNES

I built the road,
The rice of misery, an iron sun
Clearing, filling, graveling, blasting
Chains at my ankles, the crack of whips
I built the road

We built the road
Stones and blood
Clearing, filling, graveling, blasting
Hunger and malaria
We built the road

Thousands built the road
When the bus comes, we thought
All the riches brought in, ah ah
We'll prosper then.

But after so long on the road,
With no doctor,
We burst our eardrums,
Became deaf
Didn't hear the bus when it came.
No riches.

—Marguerite Duras, "Chant du caporal"

> The first lesson to be gained from these struggles is that the "commoning" of the material means of reproduction is the primary mechanism by which a collective interest and mutual bonds are created. It is also the first line of resistance to a life of enslavement, whether in armies, brothels, or sweatshops.
>
> —Silvia Federici, "Feminism and the Politics of the Common in an Era of Primitive Accumulation"

In the opening sequence of Rithy Panh's *The Land of the Wandering Souls* (2000), a few lines of text superimposed onto scenes of a work site announce the film's overlapping subjects: the technological modernization of Cambodia and the labor opportunities such a project provides. In these scenes, skilled Cambodian workers manipulate cranes, welding equipment, and heavy-duty drilling machines under the direction of Alcatel, the French telecommunications company responsible for laying the fiber-optic cables that would connect Cambodia with the rest of the world. The title shot, however, which appears a few seconds later, reveals a deeper tension at the heart of the film (figure 7.1). Here, a large concrete pipe frames a lone man working the ground with a hoe at the center of the image. Indeed, despite the suggestion of technologically advanced labor in the first few shots, the film follows the migrant workers who traverse the country digging trenches for the cables. Inside the pipe, which offers a visual echo of these cables, we see a crude mattress and a plastic bag, a pile of belongings the worker will carry with him as the trenches advance. Herein lies the tension. The pipe—and the opportunity it represents—is at once that which shelters and that which exposes, that which creates the possibility of work and that which confines the working poor within the conditions of their ongoing exploitation.

Evocative of the Khmer Rouge's forced displacement and murderous abuse of working bodies, *The Land of the Wandering Souls* does not just link the project of modernizing Cambodia through digital communication networks to the thread of labor exploitation running throughout Cambodian history; it also heralds the contemporary migratory labor patterns that see low-skilled and unskilled workers relocating within and across borders for opportunities in the manufacturing, hospitality, construction, and security industries. And in its insistence on the relationship between the free flow of global capital and the limited mobility of the working poor, often expressed in close-ups of the toiling body—disabled, exposed, pregnant, and diseased—the film offers a strident and poetic critique of what is meant by progress in the Global South. This essay draws on Marxist and feminist critiques of labor and develops the metaphors of connectivity and

FIGURE 7.1. Title shot, from inside a concrete pipe

collectivity suggested by the film's subject matter to examine how migratory labor alienates while also creating the conditions for the workers' discovery and expression of a seemingly impossible solidarity. For while the workers and their families are fundamentally disconnected from their labor power, the product and benefit of their labor, and the rapidly evolving society through which they move, they sustain each other and their own human dignity with simple displays of intimacy, care, and camaraderie. In the latter half of my reading, I pay special attention to the ways in which *The Land of the Wandering Souls* interrogates the relation of women to capital. I am particularly interested in the film's focus on reproductive labor—cooking and caring for children, for example—that has traditionally been coded feminine, that remains unremunerated under capitalism, and that Panh repeatedly juxtaposes with waged activity, insisting on its status *as work*. And I suggest that the film gestures toward a commons—however beleaguered, however unattainable—placing women at the center of the struggle against capitalist exploitation.

CONNECTION

In 1999, six years into a structural reform program designed to integrate the nation's struggling economy with the rest of Asia and the world, and four years before admission to the World Trade Organization, Cambodia joined the Association for Southeast Asian Nations (ASEAN) Free Trade Area. This trade bloc formalized economic cooperation in the region by promoting the free circulation of goods and services across member nations. Special Economic Zones in Cambodia, areas of the country that boast preferential laws and regulations pertaining to industry and trade, would follow in 2006. The arrival of Alcatel, a leading provider of submarine fiber-optic cables in the late 1990s and early years of the twenty-first century, should thus be understood in the context of this regional effort to attract foreign direct investment and further consolidate ASEAN's status as a world production center through the elimination of tariffs and other trade barriers. Though we might not consider this an example of the new international division of labor, an economic phenomenon that has seen the relocation of entire industrial outfits, it is no less a manifestation of the shift of labor and capital from the Global North to the Global South.

Economic analysts often defend this trend with recourse to the promise of "capitalism as the great equalizer and promoter of interconnectedness" on a planetary scale.[1] Likewise, in *The Land of the Wandering Souls* the local enterprises employed by Alcatel attempt to convey to the workers the inconceivable power of the cables by likening them to a magic force capable of folding time and space to conjure loved ones scattered around the world. In one early scene, one of these middlemen draws on imagery from the great Cambodian epic, the *Reamker*, to promise instant connections: "Magic eyes, magic ears—that's the cable. Magic eyes—in other words, you're here but you see the United States. You see the whole world. . . . And magic ears? You're here but you hear someone in the United States or in Canada, thanks to this network they call telecommunications. Before, they spoke of magic eyes and ears. Now we've found them." Later, the workers return to a Buddhist cosmology in their attempts to make sense of it all, linking the inner components of the cables to the four great elements and to the human body. They understand the technology "in their way," Panh observes, and trust that they will one day profit from "the riches [that] will flow beneath their country . . . when the broadband becomes earth, water, fire, wind."[2] But, as Hing Tsang suggests, the conversation also reveals a burgeoning social consciousness.[3] The men are not only "beginning to make connections" between traditional and global worldviews; they are reflecting on their relation to the means of production. One explains: "They invest here. But they take from us too. Give and take, nothing is free. Without that, no commerce." But the other, in response, develops an analogy that hints at the imbalance of power undermining free exchange: "[You] loan me 5 units of rice," he says, "but I sell them behind your back and don't pay you." On one level, he is trying to understand how to guarantee returns on an investment such as the one he witnesses around him. But his analogy also offers a poignant description of the worker's alienation, to which I will return later: "They'll do all that . . . to make money?" Moreover, he immediately associates this sense of being robbed with the Khmer Rouge, highlighting the lingering effects of the regime, which not only decimated an entire generation but also deprived it of the right to knowledge and learning: "a mass of ignorant people, beasts . . . we can be nothing other than workers."

In its sustained focus on the labor of the working poor, who travel on foot from camp to camp and who spend their days and often nights bent over the trenches, the film makes explicit connections between the spread of neoliberal capitalism and the exploitative regimes that have marred Cambodia's recent past. The title, as others have noted, plays on this dual possibility: the "wandering souls" traversing the country are at once the workers (displaced by the advancing trenches) and the victims of civil war and the Khmer Rouge (the dead who were never properly buried and thus whose souls were never able to transcend this realm).[4] The film draws such strong visual parallels between these "souls" that the migrant workers appear as the living ghosts of these victims, forced to relive in perpetuity the chasms separating the powerful from the powerless, the years of hunger and forced labor, and the constant threat of death. Interspersed with long shots that underscore the scale of the project and echo archival footage of the Khmer Rouge collectivized agricultural initiatives are repeated medium and close-up shots in which men and women, sparsely clad and often wearing only rubber sandals on their feet, stand covered with dirt in their shallow ditches, as if burying themselves. At moments it appears as though the earth is swallowing them; it is almost difficult to discern where the laboring bodies end and the trenches begin. Early in the film, the camera follows the demining personnel who work just steps ahead of the diggers. The workers uncover unexploded ordinances—bombs and 40 mm grenades, for example—that evoke not only the Cambodian Civil War, the American War in Vietnam, and the rearmament of the Khmer Rouge after 1979, but also the military-run extreme shooting ranges that today accommodate tourists keen to handle an M79 grenade launcher. The fear of literally digging one's own grave returns throughout the film as the workers compare these discoveries, ruminating on contradictory questions of filial responsibility and their own disposability within the labor force.

Nixon and Pol Pot are not the only specters haunting the workers, however. As Panh reminds us, "There was misery in Cambodia before the genocide, and it remains today . . . the poor pay dearly . . . , no matter the regime."[5] The intersecting aims of colonialist expansion—civilization and material gain—also flow through the trenches. A "phase in the spatialization of the world by a capitalism that has yet to live out its history,"[6] the French colonial project proceeded according to a logic of speculation and accumulation, integrating remote colonial markets much in the same way that, here, Cambodia is linked to the rest of the world via telecommunications. These digital pathways echo colonial infrastructure projects like national highways and rail lines, built to facilitate the free circulation of goods and capital. Panh's 2008 adaptation of Marguerite Duras's autobiographical novel, *The Sea Wall* (1950), which is set in southern coastal Cambodia in the 1920s, suggests an acute awareness of the French appropriation of Cambodian land and its exploitation of native labor. The epigraph with which this chapter begins shows Duras already grappling with the false promises of colonial infrastructure projects, a theme she develops in the novel around the figure of the mother's servant, "le caporal." Indeed, the novel itself, as Jane Winston has shown, is the most explicit example of Duras's anticolonial politics and a trenchant critique of "the class-based restriction of rights underpinning bourgeois capitalism."[7] In his treatment of the novel, Panh draws the theme out even further, adding scenes of colonial appropriation, violent native revolt, and colonial suppression in response. Further, Panh casts the Franco-Cambodian actor Randal Douc as M. Jo, the lover who will become Chinese in Duras's later writings but whose ethnicity remains unspecified in this novel, imagining him as a wealthy Sino-Cambodian speculator.[8] In so doing, his version also makes explicit the legacy of Asian intermediaries—the native militiamen of which Duras's corporal speaks or the Cambodian enterprises managing the labor in *The Land of the Wandering Souls*—who profit from the subjugation of local workers.[9]

DISCONNECTION

Like Duras's corporal, like the scores of colonized who labored to generate riches they would never access, the workers in Panh's film are alienated from the product of their labor, from which they are unlikely to profit. Throughout the film, Panh creates visual and aural constellations, that is, series of images and sounds that, in parallel or in juxtaposition, within or across shots and scenes, gesture toward this fundamental disconnect. One such early establishing shot shows a line of workers digging the trench to one side of a major road, a national highway perhaps (figure 7.2). In this shot, parallel lines—colonial and neocolonial, the road and the trenches—converge on the horizon, a future moment of development and benefit. More instructive than the suggested parallel, however, is the contrast established between those who travel the road on motorbikes and in cars and trucks and those who toil alongside it. Here we find the necessary balance of progress and immobility under capitalism. The first group, those with access to means (of production, of circulation), advance toward this promised future; the second group goes nowhere.

Another example can be found in the scene discussed earlier. One of the workers responds to the local intermediary's description of the cable's magic with "I don't have electricity, just a petrol lamp. And . . . I often don't have any petrol." He laughs, as if to share the irony of the situation, or at least to suggest that it has not been lost on him, before continuing: "I don't know when I'll be able to live and to breathe like everyone else . . . never." Cambodia may have found the magic eyes and ears to connect them to the rest of the world, but the

FIGURE 7.2. The road and the trenches: progress and immobility under capitalism

workers responsible for laying the cables in the ground cannot even count on the minimal conditions—shelter, sustenance, power—needed to take advantage of such potential. Another scene, later in the film, further underscores the idea of missed connections, revealing the gulf that separates the working poor from the technological advances surrounding them. In this scene, a woman tries to connect three different people via a satellite phone. The first has received a call but is not there to take it, the second does not understand how to use the phone and is then unable to get the person on the other end of the line to recognize him, and the third cannot reach the person he wishes to call. In each instance, telecommunications appear not as that which connects but as a site of the failure to connect.

Panh's film is not a Marxist denunciation of Alcatel, of technological advancement, or of multinationals, but rather a study of "the effects of liberalization in the process of completely transforming the country." "If the film is about human exploitation," he notes, "I think it's indispensable that it make the human visible."[10] But by focusing his camera on the workers—their bodies in motion and at rest, their interactions, daily struggles, and worries—Panh makes visible not only the *idea* of estranged labor but also the human experience of "sink[ing] to the level of . . . the most wretched of commodities."[11] For Marx, the objectification of labor is the result of its realization: in working, the worker transforms both himself and his activity into alien objects exchanged for wages. But the worker only becomes a commodity as such within specific social relations, just as his hoe only becomes capital within specific social relations. This same worker, this same hoe, "when torn from these relationships . . . is no more [commodity or] capital than gold in itself is *money* or sugar is the price of sugar."[12] In other words, when toiling one's land to feed one's family, the work, the tool, and the product belong to the worker. The migrant worker, however, is by definition separated from land and often family, and in some cases has neither. Entire villages have been abandoned so that the trenches might advance; parents have disappeared into neighboring countries in search of work. One man laments having returned "empty-handed" from twenty years of armed conflict; landless, he and his wife, whose hand is infected from the constant digging—an external manifestation of the deep internal wound of exploitation, perhaps—can only hope to work the land of others.

The Land of the Wandering Souls meditates on the relationship between the physical experience of work and the increasing tenuousness of the worker's survival. Bound to a labor arrangement that at once sustains and annihilates them, the workers in the film are only able to survive as "physical subjects" through their labor power, but it is also only as physical subjects that they have access to work.[13] It is not just the Khmer Rouge that has condemned an entire generation to work as beasts, depriving them of land, family, and education; the transformation of the Cambodian economy—away from communist principles and toward capitalist accumulation—demands such a sacrifice. For, as Marx observes, "The existence of a class which possesses nothing but its capacity to labor is a necessary prerequisite of capital."[14] The workers sell their labor power by the meter dug for a means of subsistence, more or less immediately consumed, while that accumulated labor produces for those paying the wages "a greater value than it previously possessed."[15] Labor power is thus unproductive for the worker, exponentially reproductive for the capitalist. And insofar as the workers' activity belongs to someone else, the workers themselves belong to someone else. As such, for Marx the wage worker is not "freely active in any but his animal functions—eating, drinking, procreating," activities that are universally human but here reduced to animal because "separate[d] from the sphere of all other human activity and turn[ed] into sole and ultimate ends."[16] The workers in *The Land of the Wandering Souls* produce nothing for themselves, managing only to sustain and to reproduce themselves as labor. Many of the scenes not focused on the digging, for example, follow the men, women, and children as they forage for, prepare, consume, and worry about the scarcity and expense of food. Though the film does not examine the capitalist appropriation of land or the commercialization of agriculture through structural adjustment programs, it nevertheless presents food as a metonym for the neoliberal project of separating agricultural producers from their land. It also demonstrates the extent to which "the worker becomes all the poorer the more wealth he produces."[17] As the film progresses, and with every meter dug, the workers are paid less and less. First, wages are temporarily withheld; then, the promised increase in price per meter in the urban centers is not forthcoming. And at the end of the film, when the project is complete and all the meters accumulated, the boss abandons the workers without paying a cent. Many return home poorer, hungrier, and more desperate than they were the day they left, their bodies broken and scarred like the land they leave behind them.

One woman returns nine months pregnant and, in the film's final scene, has given birth to a son—Samnang, meaning "lucky." Feminist critics have long insisted on Marx's failure to account for the gendered experience of capital's dehumanization of the worker. Rithy Panh's films, and this film in particular, often invite gendered readings. Boreth Ly has given one such reading, arguing that the "deepening penetration of neoliberal capitalism" has undermined traditional Cambodian notions of masculinity, which has historically been associated with military power and sexual dominance, with tilling the land and providing for the family.[18] Emasculated by their poverty in a world of "monetary masculinity," the men in Panh's film are acutely aware of their increasing inability to feed their families. The women are too, which may explain why they denigrate their own contributions to the family's survival. "The mother can die," one woman claims; "the father cannot." Indeed, like Marx, who failed to value any work other than commodity production, the women in *The Land of the Wandering Souls* repeatedly downplay the myriad forms of labor they perform, including the time they spend in the trenches. Unremunerated even for their digging, for which compensation goes to the husbands, the women appear to accept, in Silvia Federici's words, "the wage as the dividing line between work and non-work, production and parasitism, potential power and powerlessness."[19] Excluded from the social contract according to which one exchanges labor for a means of subsistence, the women are disciplined to see themselves as burdens, just as their husbands are disciplined by their responsibility as sole breadwinners to return to the trenches each day and night, digging themselves further into poverty with each heave of the hoe.

For Federici, capital conceals reproductive labor by naturalizing it, by transforming it into a feminine act of love or duty.[20] When they are not assisting the men in the trenches, the women perform primarily reproductive tasks. They cook. They wash the clothes. They clean their children and care for their men. In one scene, a woman washes her husband's hair in the river as he teases her about chasing other women. In another, the pregnant woman goes to the market to buy new shoes for her husband, who is missing one foot. In yet another, the camera is fixed on a third woman, who cuts and cleans her six-month-old daughter's nails with a pair of scissors as she recounts the births of her children, each born in camps or on the road, and details their daily existence. Because these activities are unwaged, they are not considered work, but instead, to return to a Marxist

FIGURE 7.3. The mother's labor continues as she rests

frame, forms of "personal service outside capital," in other words, physical, emotional, and sexual servicing within the domestic unit. Rithy Panh's film, which repeatedly juxtaposes reproductive with waged activity, uncovers this work as work. The gendered dimensions of waged and unwaged labor are visible throughout the film but perhaps are made most explicit in a scene where a woman has stopped digging to breastfeed (figure 7.3). The medium shot shows her feet perched on the edge of the trench, a hoe lying beside her; her son has paused as well and looks on. Another man continues to dig. In this moment, Panh's filming insists on the tension between the body at rest and the body at work. Nourishing what Federici deems to be "the most precious product to appear on the capitalist market," in other words, the future workforce, the woman has taken a break from one form of labor only to perform another. The scene thus encourages the viewer not only to identify with the struggles of the wageless worker worldwide but also to reflect on the signal importance of reproduction as "the foundation of every economic and political system."[21]

TOWARD A COLLECTIVE STRUGGLE?

The Land of the Wandering Souls does not leave us with much cause for optimism. Nevertheless, and as is often the case in Panh's oeuvre, it steadfastly affirms the persistence of human dignity in the face of exploitation.[22] Throughout the film, the camera lingers as the workers discover and express a seemingly impossible solidarity, each sustaining the other and themselves with simple displays of human kindness—a lullaby, a consoling gesture, a word of advice. Such gestures reinforce the social fabric of the family and the immediate community, both threatened by structural adjustment programs, which have seen the unraveling of families throughout the developing world as one or more members migrate in search of work. The migrant families also find practical and spiritual support from the communities through which they move. The injured woman receives treatment for her hand, though she will have to dig another section of the trenches before she can pay for it. She and her husband also seek assistance in a local pagoda, where a Buddhist monk counsels them and performs a water blessing. Himself shielded by the sacred script of Cambodian Sak Yant tattoos, the ancient practice of protecting the individual through markings on the body, the monk counters the lingering effects of violence in their lives, "a profound wound that marks a man forever," with sacred water first sprinkled, then poured on the family. "No one thinks of you, a man who has returned from war, who needs help.... That is the injustice: no one thinks of you." Through his gestures, physical and empathic, the monk situates the family's struggle within the larger social problem of poverty and indifference in postwar Cambodia—effectively making the alleviation of individual misery a communal responsibility—and receives the family as part of the spiritual community.[23]

Both men and women perform these acts of solidarity; both strive to hold up the suffering. And yet, it would not be an exaggeration to say that women are at the heart of this film and this effort. For despite their self-assessments, in which they minimize their role, the five or six female protagonists do not merely eclipse their male counterparts in screen time; they lead the way in expressions of resistance, pointing out when they have been underpaid and conspiring briefly to unearth the cables in revolt when they realize they have been cheated at the end of the project. And in their quiet but deliberate commitment to sustain the whole despite the pressing needs of their individual units, the women also embody the spirit of the commons. At its core, the commons is a politics of survival, one that privileges the collective through shared physical and material resources and that reclaims control through "moments of collective reproduction and cooperation."[24] Through simple acts of mutual aid and in the name of a mode of existence outside the exploitative logic of capital, the women forge bonds of solidarity, fostering a sense of shared responsibility within and beyond the migrant community. Families sleep together under the open sky, safer in numbers. One woman teaches another's little girl the correct forms of address while grooming her fingernails, briefly sharing with her mother the responsibility of the child's physical care and social education. Another talks a desperate woman out of leaving the project, despite the ever-deepening hole her family has dug for itself, by reminding her of the small-scale loan arrangements they have among themselves: "If you dig, the others will help you. If not, you won't have anything left." The women work to build a collective, a local, temporary commons within which they do more than economize the cost of reproductive labor and protect each other from exposure; through the commons, they carve out a means of recovering their self-worth within an economic order "that has abandoned them to their difficulties."[25]

Indeed, the most meaningful, though perhaps most paradoxical, connection provided by the Alcatel cables is this bond of mutual aid established among strangers. Early in the film, the pregnant woman visits a nearby village to beg for rice. In so doing, she is also a witness to the scale of the nation's poverty: "In some houses, there is nothing." An older woman, who has barely enough to feed herself, offers a few cups. The gesture is reminiscent of almsgiving, the tradition in Theravada Buddhism of giving food to the monks who wander past each morning, which creates a spiritual connection and a relation of mutual support between the monastic community and the laypeople. Over the course of their conversation, it becomes clear that the woman is motivated less by her own karma than by the material need to pull the country out of poverty and by the realization that this need can only be met by the people. "What little rice we have," she says, "we have to share, so that we can live together. She has nothing. I have nothing." This woman gives so that the future might be different. For her, it is a collective struggle, a battle that must be waged. Turning to the past, she speaks of the three wars she has endured. The first two—Lon Nol's and Pol Pot's—found her deep in the earth, taking cover in wells as opposing forces raged around her and digging canals as part of the Khmer Rouge push to industrialize. She does not name the third war, but I would suggest that it is this collective struggle she identifies before her, embodied in the woman emerged from the trenches to beg for sustenance so that she might return to the trenches. Listening to the young woman talk of her abandoned home, her mutilated husband, her hungry children, and her unborn child, the older woman tells her that they must fight.

Twenty years later, the struggle continues. Cambodia's push to modernize has only intensified, supported by international aid and foreign direct investment. Most of the money financing the most visible area of development today—construction—comes from China, however, which signals an important shift in (neo)colonial dynamics in contemporary Asia.[26] According to the International Labor Organization, construction represented 11 percent of the informal labor market as of 2009 and was the site of four deadly occupational accidents per day.[27] Construction work has also emerged as a theme in contemporary Cambodian art and film. Davy Chou's first feature, *Diamond Island* (2016), follows the young rural workers who migrate to Phnom Penh to find construction work on the eponymous luxury development on the Bassac River.[28] Neak Sophal's photography raises questions about labor and identity, and specifically, the ways in which one's identity is defined by, if not reduced to, the work that one performs. In her "Green Net" series, Sophal weaves threads of the green netting surrounding high-rise construction projects in Phnom Penh into photographs of female construction workers superimposed onto work sites. These images not only push us to reflect on the ways in which Cambodia's building boom, and the Chinese investment returns it ensures, ensnares migrant workers in physically and economically perilous labor conditions; in their deliberately disproportionate scale—the women's bodies tower over the sites of their labor—they also insist on the gendered dimensions of labor and progress in contemporary Cambodia.

Telecommunications and other new technologies play an increasingly central role in movements within the contemporary low-skilled and unskilled labor market. Though a recent study on migrant labor populations suggests that nearly a quarter of migrant workers leave home with no employment leads, it also points to the prevalence of Facebook and the internet in employment recruiting.[29] Of the fourteen human resources managers interviewed in this study, all had Facebook accounts, and only one was without a smartphone. The workers interviewed also indicated an interest in Facebook and smartphones as a means of job seeking. The first line of dialogue in Chou's film, which opens with the young protagonist's rural-to-urban migration, attests to the importance of such technology for the migrant laborer seeking to maintain connections at home while establishing them elsewhere. His mother asks, "Do you have your phone?" A generation on, low-skilled and unskilled migrant workers may have benefited from the cables laid by the men and women in Panh's film, but the magic eyes and ears that now assist them in finding work have done little to change the ongoing socioeconomic precarity in which they live. And it is unclear whether this increased digital connectivity has had any salutary effects on the expression of solidarity among the working poor. *The Land of the Wandering Souls* offers a forceful and enduring challenge to the idea of progress in the Global South, showing its promises to be false while creating a space for those who "pay dearly . . . no matter the regime" to share their struggles and reclaim their dignity. The creation of such a collective—however temporary, however fragile—may be the only resistance against a life of exploitation.

NOTES

First epigraph: Marguerite Duras, "Chant du caporal," Fonds Duras, Institut Mémoires de l'Edition Contemporaine, DRS 30.10, "*Un barrage contre le Pacifique*, textes préparatoires" (translations are mine unless otherwise noted); second epigraph: Silvia Federici, "Feminism and the Politics of the Common in an Era of Primitive Accumulation," in *Revolution at Point Zero: Housework, Reproduction, and the Feminist Struggle* (New York: PM Press, 2012), 144.

1. Silvia Federici, "Reproduction and Feminist Struggle in the New International Division of Labor," in *Revolution at Point Zero*, 67.

2. Rithy Panh, "Au Cambodge, le cinéma est une médicine," interview by Antoine Baecque, *Libération*, October 5, 2005, https://www.liberation.fr/cahier-special/2005/10/05/au-cambodge-le-cinema-est-une-medecine_534510.

3. Hing Tsang, *Semiotics and Documentary Film: The Living Sign in the Cinema* (Berlin: De Gruyter, 2013), 156.

4. See Tsang, 142; Jennifer Cazenave, "Earth as Archive: Reframing Memory and Mourning in *The Missing Picture*," *Cinema Journal* 57, no. 2 (2018): 53.

5. Panh, "Au Cambodge, le cinéma est une médicine."

6. Arif Dirlik, "Rethinking Colonialism: Globalization, Postcolonialism, and the Nation," *Interventions* 4, no. 3 (2002): 430.

7. Jane Bradley Winston, *Postcolonial Duras: Cultural Memory in Postwar France* (New York: Palgrave, 2001), 19.

8. For a further discussion of this figure, and of labor exploitation in *The Sea Wall*, see Rachel Harrison and Jack Yeager's chapter in this volume.

9. Panh notes: "These are the kind of men who best exploit their compatriots, and the colonial administrators always rely on this class of wealthy locals. The entire logic is one only of exploitation: the land, the farmers." "Un barrage contre le Pacifique," *Allociné*, accessed December 9, 2020, http://www.allocine.fr/film/fichefilm-125109/secrets-tournage/.

10. Rithy Panh, "La parole filmée: Pour vaincre la terreur," *Communications* 71 (2001): 378. In a keynote conversation with Vicente Sánchez-Biosca at the Fourteenth Biannual Meeting of the International Association of Genocide Scholars, held in Phnom Penh on July 14–19, 2019, Panh mentioned that he did not know Marx or Mao when Duch referenced them in the interviews conducted for the film *Duch: Master of the Forges of Hell* (2011), eleven years after the release of *The Land of the Wandering Souls*.

11. Karl Marx, "Estranged Labour," in *The Economic and Philosophical Manuscripts*, in *The Marx-Engels Reader*, ed. Robert C. Tucker, 2nd ed. (New York: W. W. Norton, 1978), 70.

12. Karl Marx, "Wage Labour and Capital," in *The Marx-Engels Reader*, 207.

13. Marx, "Estranged Labour," 73.

14. Marx, "Wage Labour and Capital," 208.

15. Marx, 209.

16. Marx, "Estranged Labour," 74.

17. Marx, 71.

18. Boreth Ly, "Screening the Crisis of Monetary Masculinity in Rithy Panh's *One Night after the War* and *Burnt Theatre*," in *Film and Contemporary Southeast Asian Cinema: Cultural Interpretation and Social Intervention*, ed. David C. L. Lim and Hiroyuki Yamamoto (London: Routledge, 2012), 53, 64.

19. Silvia Federici, "Counterplanning from the Kitchen," in *Révolution at Point Zero*, 29.

20. Silvia Federici, "Wages against Housework," in *Revolution at Point Zero*, 17.

21. Federici, 2.

22. Though I do not want to deny the possibility of "chance, love, and hope" suggested with this final scene (Tsang, *Semiotics and Documentary Film*, 158), it is also important to note that despite the collective consciousness developing among the workers throughout the film and the moments of shared responsibility, its final moments find them having returned to the private, domestic space, such that there is still "cooperation at the point of production," but "separation and atomization at the point of reproduction" (Federici, "Feminism and the Politics of the Common," 146).

23. Tsang, *Semiotics and Documentary Film*, 154.

24. Silvia Federici, "The Reproduction of Labor Power in the Global Economy," in *Revolution at Point Zero*, 111.

25. See the description of the "One Dollar Project," a participatory web documentary project focused on the lives of the working poor and aiming to "create a global dialogue about economic injustice." http://onedollar.bophana.org/en/about.

26. See "Construction," *Open Development Cambodia*, May 12, 2016, https://opendevelopment cambodia.net/topics/construction/; Philip Heijmans, "Chinese Money Is Driving One of Asia's Fastest Property Booms," *Bloomberg*, September 11, 2018, https://www.bloomberg.com /news/features/2018-09-10/chinese-money-is-driving-a-property-boom-in-cambodia.

27. International Labour Organization, "Enhancing Occupational Safety and Health Standards in Construction Sector in Cambodia," accessed December 9, 2020, https://www.ilo.org /asia/projects/WCMS_577102/lang--en/index.htm. Of the fifty workers interviewed in a more recent study, only half had signed contracts in their current jobs; not one of these twenty-five were working in construction. See the USAID Counter Trafficking-in-Persons Program's *Internal Migration for Low-Skilled or Unskilled Work in Cambodia: Preliminary Qualitative Results*, Open Institute, June 2016, https://www.open.org.kh/research/Internal_Migra tion-Qualitative_Results-June2016.pdf (22). In June 2019, a nearly completed building in Sihanoukville collapsed on the fifty-five to sixty workers using it as their accommodation, killing just over a dozen workers. See "Building Construction Site in Cambodia Collapses, Killing at Least 13 and Trapping Dozens," ABC News, June 23, 2019, https://www.abc.net.au/news/2019 -06-22/cambodia-building-collapse-kills-and-injures-workers/11238284.

28. The Cambodian production company Anti-Archive, of which Chou is a founding member, has a number of projects that explore labor in relation to family and tradition (Douglas Seok's *Turn Left Turn Right*, 2016); desire and consumption (Keang Navich's *New Land Broken Road*, 2018); and modernization, heritage, and the growing Cambodian middle class (Steve Chen's *Dream Land*, 2015). This is not to suggest that the interest in labor is new, however; Panh's films have examined agricultural labor (*Rice People*, 1994), creative work (*The Burnt Theatre*, 2005), and sex work (*Paper Cannot Wrap Ember*, 2007). He has also raised questions of forced and ideological labor under the Khmer Rouge (*S21: The Khmer Rouge Killing Machine*, 2003; *Duch: The Master of the Forges of Hell*, 2011; *The Missing Picture*, 2013).

29. USAID Counter Trafficking-in-Persons Program, *Internal Migration for Low-Skilled or Unskilled Work*, 26–27.

PART 3 THE QUESTION OF JUSTICE

8 • ARCHIVING THE PERPETRATOR

STÉPHANIE BENZAQUEN-GAUTIER
AND JOHN KLEINEN

Early 1972, in the midst of the civil war opposing the Khmer Rouge guerrillas and the Republican troops of Marshal Lon Nol, French historian Serge Thion, a supporter of "anti-imperialist" struggles, was invited for a study tour in the Khmer Rouge–controlled areas.[1] He was the first Westerner to be allowed in the "liberated zones," and his report was published in the newspaper *Le Monde* in April 1972. In the province of Kampong Chhnang, Thion came across a cadre school where villagers were taught Marxist-Leninist concepts. He marveled at this vision of political education, whereby the everyday Khmer spoken by farmers was replaced with a new language adjusted to the "specific rationality of a modern liberation struggle."[2] For Thion, this substitution made it possible for the villagers "to rethink their condition and articulate it to broader questions of national politics." He concluded: "Before, through daily words, people could only think at the village level; now . . . they can think at the nation level."[3]

It was not only the language the Khmer Rouge aimed to transform.[4] They also wanted to reshape Cambodian bodies and society. This radical undertaking did not escape Sarin Ith, a school education inspector who spent nine months in 1972 in the bush as a candidate party member.[5] In his account about life in the "liberated zones," he describes the new gestures people living in these areas had to learn and perform, such as the salute to the party's flag.[6] Manual work was compulsory for party members with an intellectual background and was regarded "as of the prime necessity in 'building' yourself to become a proletariat, a worker," and developing "a revolutionary consciousness."[7]

After the Khmer Rouge takeover in April 1975, this policy of remolding the political, social, and physical Cambodian body was applied nationwide. Khmer Rouge gestures included those by which the extermination of nearly 20 percent of the population was carried out. However, unlike the "redeeming" gestures of manual labor featuring centrally in Democratic Kampuchea's propaganda, the gestures of killing remain invisible. In 1976–1978, several pictures of execution circulated in the international mainstream newspapers, but it turned out they had been staged and taken in Thailand by intelligence services.[8] Archival research is ongoing in Cambodia, and to date, some of the few photographic records of extermination available are photographs of prisoners at the detention and interrogation center S-21 in Phnom Penh, in particular the pictures showing specific inmates killed after being tortured.[9] Yet, these gruesome images show the outcome, not the process itself.

One must return to gestures of killing, film director Rithy Panh says, "because, if genocide is ideology-driven it is carried through gestures."[10] Body language becomes thus a means to understand the mechanics of violence in Democratic Kampuchea in depth. But in the absence of visual documentation, how is it possible to recapture these gestures? According to philosopher Giorgio Agamben, cinema plays a crucial role in this undertaking.[11] Retrieving, documenting, and archiving the body language of perpetrators is at the core of Panh's films *S21: The Khmer Rouge Killing Machine* (2003) and *Duch, Master of the Forges of Hell* (2011). The director's work spans almost three decades, a period during which the representation and perception of the perpetrator, itself a figure in transition, underwent dramatic changes. Building on visual anthropology, film and media studies, and perpetrator studies, this chapter seeks to situate Panh's work within these dynamics and shed light on its contribution to this process.

The first section zooms out and looks at different attempts to film perpetrators in Cambodia and other parts of Southeast Asia, and the role gestures play in these attempts. While the modalities and functions of this recording vary from one film to another, the comparison points to a shared space revolving around the gesture's potential to complete, challenge, or transform word and image. The second section zooms in and discusses Panh's specificity in terms of methodology and objectives. Agamben's analysis of gesture and cinema provides the conceptual framework for the discussion. More specifically, the question of polarity, as discussed by the philosopher, shows how Panh is concerned not only with the documentary dimension of filming gestures of killing but also, and more important, with the ethical one. Agamben stresses the tension, conveyed by the image, between on the one hand gestures that manifest as reified layers, the emergence of which pertains to voluntary memory, and on the other hand gestures that breach these layers and irrupt as involuntary memory.[12] The challenge is to overcome this tension and ascribe the recorded gesture the function of a medium between past and present, repression and recollection, extermination and responsibility. The chapter explores the extent to which this understanding of cinema's operation leads to a specific act of archiving and how the latter becomes the condition for transforming communicative memory into cultural memory and producing new forms for the mediation and transmission of the past.[13]

ZOOM OUT: FILMING PERPETRATORS AND THEIR BODIES

"Why did you kill? How many people did you kill?" journalist John Pilger asks two Khmer Rouge prisoners in the documentary movie *Year Zero: The Silent Death of Cambodia* (1979). The camera does a close-up on their faces, which betray nothing. The men appear to be brainwashed executioners who just obeyed orders. Over the years, the image of Khmer Rouge perpetrators has become more complex, especially from the beginning of the twenty-first century onward, with the trials at the Extraordinary Chambers in the Courts of Cambodia (ECCC). Testimonies at the tribunal together with paradigm shifts in academic research, especially anthropology, about Democratic Kampuchea have helped turn attention away from Khmer Rouge leaders and toward the personal stories of midranking and low-ranking ones.[14] Moreover, facilitated by new economic and publishing conditions as well as journalistic interest, the recent growth of perpetrator testimonial literature has filled the void of the previous years,[15] when the only Khmer Rouge accounts available were those related to the prosecution (in absentia) of Pol Pot and Ieng Sary at the People's Revolutionary Tribunal (1979). These new approaches have dramatically altered the initial depiction of Khmer Rouge perpetrators as indoctrinated robots. They have also contributed to the emergence of narrative "gray zones" articulated around the study of agency and motivations, and the potential "victim status" of some Khmer Rouge, notably child soldiers.[16] As will be seen now, the documentary cinema production (in Cambodia and beyond) in that period reflects these changes of perspective.

JAN KROGSGAARD AND THOMAS WEBER CARLSEN, *VOICES OF KHMER ROUGE*

Between December 2002 and May 2003, Danish filmmakers Jan Krogsgaard and Thomas Weber Carlsen interviewed thirty ex–Khmer Rouge soldiers and low-ranking cadres (eighteen men and twelve women) aged between thirty-eight and seventy and coming from peasant and lower-middle-class backgrounds.[17] All were defectors from the northwestern part of Cambodia, who had surrendered to the government in the late 1990s.[18] The interviews were edited, translated, and subtitled in 2004–2008 and finalized in 2011. The result was a forty-three-hour-long video installation with films lasting from twenty-five minutes up to two hours. By giving "ordinary Khmer Rouge members" a chance "to relate their own personal accounts," Krogsgaard and Carlsen wanted to bring nuances to the monolithic depiction of the Khmer Rouge as a "unified mass of killers."[19] The interviews were articulated chronologically from childhood to the present day. To preserve the flow of the stories, the directors edited the material as little as possible and tried to stay "true to the original document, where playing time equals recorded time."[20] This emphasis on their minimal intervention in the process is connected to their objective of producing "a study document" for future research.[21] For Krogsgaard and Carlsen, the value of their project was to preserve on the record the first time personal stories from within the Khmer Rouge were told (at least to outsiders). Yet, the spontaneity of this first-time telling is debatable. The interviews were conducted while negotiations on the establishment of the ECCC were still underway, and the identity of those to be put on the prosecution list remained unclear. Knowing that their words were video recorded, and could thus become incriminating in case of a trial, certainly made the interviewees cautious.

In these conditions, how credible are their accounts? The question is particularly bothersome since Krogsgaard and Carlsen's interview methodology may be found wanting. For example, the directors did not ask the questions themselves but worked with a translator, Leang Kham, himself a former Khmer Rouge cadre. Moreover, the encounter remained a onetime event. Krogsgaard and Carlsen did not come back for a second or third interview, or engage in a follow-up process. Reliability is thus a major issue when it comes to *Voices of Khmer Rouge*. Viewers have no point of reference for assessing what they hear. In this context, body language might provide additional clues. Krogsgaard and Carlsen certainly were aware of this potential of gestures, and they did their best to capture the attitude of the interviewees. They worked with two cameras: one fixed on a tripod filmed the individual in his or her daily environment; the other, handheld, focused on the face and expression.[22]

The videos offer a wide range of body language. There is, for example, the woman from a transportation unit who moved across the Thai border several times over the years. Her attitude during the interview indicates her uneasiness at recounting her story. Her knees twitch; she continually crosses and uncrosses her hands and fiddles with her wedding ring. In contrast, there is the man who joined the Khmer Rouge forces in 1970 and worked as a journalist for the movement's newspaper. In 1980 he became part of the close circle of Pol Pot until the latter's death in 1998. The man is undeniably a seasoned storyteller, emphasizing important moments of his life story with hand movements. When he tells anecdotes about the later years, he does impersonations of Pol Pot. This quasi-theatrical performance calls the account's spontaneity into question. The story, if not rehearsed, has probably been told several times, unlike that of the woman whose nervous, uncontrolled gestures suggest that she is not used to telling what happened to her (especially to strangers) and make her more credible. Of course, it is difficult to draw any conclusions on such a basis, particularly without accounting for possible gender differences. Still, gestures might indicate the interviewee's status (or lack thereof) within the movement and consequently point to what is at stake for her or him in this interview, thereby giving access to something beyond words.

THET SAMBATH AND ROB LEMKIN, *ENEMIES OF THE PEOPLE* AND *ANATOMY OF A MASSACRE: ONE DAY AT PO CHREY*

Cambodian journalist Thet Sambath lost both parents and his older brother during the Democratic Kampuchea period. The first movie he made in collaboration with British film director Rob Lemkin, *Enemies of the People* (2009), was an attempt to understand why so many people had been killed.[23] For Thet, it was essential to understand the chain of command. Therefore, he interviewed both ends of it, Khmer Rouge leader Nuon Chea and rank-and-file executioners Suon and Khoun. Unlike Krogsgaard and Carlsen's interviews, Thet and Lemkin's working process spans a long period. For six years, Thet visited Nuon Chea weekly in his house in Pailin, accumulating more than a thousand hours of recordings in the process. The archival dimension of *Enemies of the People* is clear. Nuon Chea's account is "for history, not for evidence."[24] This is why Thet and Lemkin refused to deposit the film as evidence at the ECCC in the case against Nuon Chea, even when the judges threatened them with subpoenas. It was crucial for Thet that former Khmer Rouge keep speaking candidly to him because "they believe that my project is neutral and genuinely interested in creating an archive for future generations."[25] This archive is conceived of as a layered structure enabling the comparison between successive stages of storytelling. In their second collaboration, *Anatomy of a Massacre: One Day at Po Chrey* (2012), which investigates the killing of Republican civil servants and military at Po Chrey (Pursat Province) in late April 1975, Thet and Lemkin rely on the same structure. The movie includes statements made at different periods by Nuon Chea with regard to the massacre, revealing the old Khmer Rouge's remarkable capacity to adjust his discourse to the changing political and juridical environment.

In both movies, Thet and Lemkin explore how narratives can be reactivated through bodily memory, for instance, by returning to killing sites with the perpetrators. In *Anatomy of a Massacre*, with In Thoeun, Thet visits the pond at Tuol Po Chrey where thousands of Lon Nol officials, soldiers, and civilians were slaughtered. The former Khmer Rouge shows him how he walked the place, making some detours to avoid the areas where corpses were piled. However, very few gestures of killing are recorded. In *Anatomy of a Massacre*, Thet interviews Po Chean, a villager who witnessed the transportation of the victims by truck to the site of execution. Thet wants to understand how people were tied together and put in line. He and a neighbor volunteer as guinea pigs for Po to show how the knots were made. In *Enemies of the People*, Thet asks Suon, a former militia commander who admitted to slaughtering 200 people, to show him how he killed people. Embarrassed, Suon refuses to perform the act on Thet himself. Instead, he grabs a young man and mimes the slicing of his throat: "You hold them like this so that they cannot scream." In both cases, Thet's will to have the "act of killing" performed via his own body goes beyond the investigative function. It points to his quest for an experiential or even sensory contact with the past.

This quest takes a special form when it comes to Nuon Chea. The latter did not kill people with his own hands. Moreover, he is a man in full control of what he says and does, not prone to emotional outbursts. Therefore, it is less his body language than an "atmosphere" around him—and what it may reveal about the Khmer Rouge psyche—that Thet and Lemkin capture. Journalist Seth Mydans rightly stresses the extent to which secrecy pervades *Enemies of the People*. Nuon Chea urges Thet to keep their meetings secret, even from his family—Thet says that "even in his prayers, he has not yet told the souls of his parents, on whose behalf he has been searching."[26] Conversely, Thet hides his family story from Nuon Chea until the very end in 2007. What *Enemies of the People* manages to record, in part at least, is the Khmer Rouge culture of secrecy, formed over decades of underground activities. Thet comes dangerously close to experiencing what Nuon Chea lived during his years of struggle before and after the Democratic Kampuchea period—defiance, caution, dissimulation, and also, more problematically, a sense of comradeship and closeness—thereby opening up a gray zone of personal connection between victim and perpetrator.[27]

JOSHUA OPPENHEIMER, *THE ACT OF KILLING*

The representation and perception of perpetrators through body language are not unique to Cambodia. In the period discussed here, there is another emblematic work: Joshua Oppenheimer's *The Act of Killing* (2012). The linkage with Panh's cinema is often underlined. Indeed, Oppenheimer has acknowledged his debt to the Cambodian film director on several occasions and also interviewed Panh for the book *Killer Images* (2012). In his movie, Oppenheimer exclusively used the staged memory of criminal and paramilitary vigilantes who did the dirty business for the Indonesian army and politicians who toppled President Sukarno in 1965. The Kudeta of September 30, 1965, brought Suharto's military junta to power. In a wave of killings lasting five months, members of the Special Forces, ad hoc criminal gangs, and religious Muslim fanatics destroyed the lives of at least half a million people. Unlike the Khmer Rouge leaders, these people were never brought to justice. Instead, they continue to be feared and in a certain way respected, still enjoying the admiration of many in Indonesia. The two protagonists of *The Act of Killing*, Anwar Kongo (seventy-two) and Adi Zulkadry (sixty-nine), reenact their own roles during the events. Anwar was then a petty thug, trafficking in movie tickets. Adi was a leading founder of the paramilitary Pancasila Youth and a member of its elite death unit, the Frog Squad. Oppenheimer shows the extent of impunity enjoyed by the perpetrators. Current-day politician Jusuf Kalla is seen congratulating members of Indonesia's youth movement, Pemuda Pancasila, for their share in exterminating Indonesian communism. The audience of a television talk show visibly enjoys and applauds to Anwar's stories of his killing sprees. Adi reminds the viewer of the victor's justice: "War crimes are defined by the victors. We won."

The hubris of those interviewed, and of the stories made public by the military supporters of the New Order, is shown through overacted reenactments. One wonders, though, what the perpetrators' gestures mean in a different cultural context, fifty years after the events, and whether they take the form of sheer mimicry as an attempt to become part of a particular picture rather than one imitating a preexisting image.[28] Mimicry is thus not a reproduction of the original but, as Homi Bhabha describes it, a mix of attraction and repulsion or, as Jean Rouch shows in his film *Les maîtres fous* (1955), a blurred copy of the original as an ambivalent representation of the relationship between colonizer and colonized, in this case between perpetrator and victim.[29] The phantasmatic shots of a bizarre opera buffa near Toba Lake is particularly disturbing because it seems to suggest that civilian psychopaths or lunatics were mainly responsible for the act of killing. In his book *The Killing Compartments* (2015), the Dutch sociologist Abram de Swaan makes a more convincing argument. Organized mass killings in the last century have been possible only in societies where a deliberate cutting of social contacts between the majority and a condemned minority has taken place through physical or symbolic compartmentalization. But this does not mean that everybody becomes a killer when circumstances are "right," de Swaan warns. What process or system is needed? This question haunts Panh's work, and gestures provide a key to answer them, as will be seen in the next section.

ZOOM IN: NOTES ON THE PERPETRATOR'S GESTURE

In the opening scene of *S21: The Khmer Rouge Killing Machine*, former S-21 deputy head Him Houy sits with his parents. The leaders were evil, he says, but "I remained a good man, today still." He claims that he did what he was ordered because he was afraid for his life. This scene explains in part why gestures are critical to Panh's cinematic project. They help breach the wall carefully constructed by those who took part in the extermination of their fellow countrymen and "open up a piece of their memory, often locked in the universal defense of the man who just obeyed orders for fear of being killed."[30] Performing anew the gestures of the past forces the perpetrators to reach out to a layer of memory that cannot be verbalized or rationalized. As discussed in the previous section, gestures operate in a number of ways in films dealing with perpetrators. As embodied evidence, contradiction, supplement, or clue, they create a complex web of relations with both speech and the act of recording/archiving. These aspects are all present in Panh's work, but his cinema is unique in that it makes body language a method of inquiry at the interplay of two processes. One is the reflection about the human dimension of genocide, in its individual form. The other is the reflection about the system that transforms people into killers. Panh does not place gestures in the "false alternative between ends and means" but deploys them for what they are—as "the exhibition of a mediality," in this case, the mediality of extermination as it was carried out at the Khmer Rouge prison code-named S-21 in Phnom Penh.[31] Gestures become the medium that renders the psychological and structural mechanics of violence visible, and thereby provide access to a complex form of historical understanding. Archiving them via films is thus the reinscription of an undocumented process into the realm of knowledge and witnessing.

S21: THE KHMER ROUGE KILLING MACHINE

More than 18,000 men, women, and children lost their lives in S-21 between mid-1975 and January 1979. How did this happen? What indoctrination enabled such violence? How did S-21 guards and interrogators become used to seeing and inflicting so much suffering? Filmed at the Tuol Sleng Genocide Museum (established in 1979 in some of the buildings that formed the S-21 complex), Panh's *S21* documents the disciplinary gestures performed at the different stages of the extermination process: arrest, interrogation, humiliation, and destruction. To understand the chronology of destruction, the film director brought back to Tuol Sleng a group of former guards (Khieu "Poeuv" Ches, Tcheam Seûr, Nhieb Ho, Som Meth) alongside higher echelons of the prison staff, including Him, interrogator Prâk Khân, and head of registers Sours Thi. Panh's idea was to "put the daily gestures of crimes back in their original territory" and "plunge [the perpetrators] again into the reality of that period."[32] *S21* was shot in different rooms of the site as well as at Choeung Ek, the orchard outside Phnom Penh where S-21 prisoners were killed and buried in mass graves. Through the use of objects (table, typewriter) and archival material (identification photographs and "confessions" of the prisoners, execution lists, interrogator's manual), Panh combines description and reconstruction to delve into the detailed mechanics of extermination, up to the slaughtering of inmates at Choeung Ek. He asks the guards to "do the gestures" in front of the camera. "I make it clear: I don't ask them to 'act' but to 'do the gestures'—as a means to expand words. If necessary, they do it again ten times. Twenty times. Reflexes come back: I see what really happened. . . . The extermination appears in its methodology and its truth."[33]

As mentioned earlier, the polarity inherent in the act of recording gestures is a central issue. What happens in the image? What do we see? Are these gestures of the past so "automatic" that they can be recalled at any time? Are they so deeply repressed that they resurface only as flashes of memory? If gestures are to be "the key for understanding the perpetrator's behavior," they have to be freed from this polarity.[34] The five-minute sequence in which former guard Poeuv performs anew the routine of his night watch of three collective cells is a good illustration of how Panh achieves this result. It shows Poeuv pacing the corridor, opening and locking the cell doors, bringing back a prisoner who has just been tortured, or the ammunition boxes the inmates were forced to use as toilets. Inmates struggle over water; a prisoner tries to steal gruel from another. As Poeuv relives these situations, he seems to lose contact with reality, immersing himself in the past. He enters the cells to discipline the men, yells orders like "Shut up or I take the club!" and "I said no mess. You will see what you get if you continue." However, the Khmer Rouge songs that play in the background preclude this scene from becoming a reenactment (a term Panh does not like because of its theatrical connotations, hence its potential to threaten the very act of documenting). They create a discordance against which gestures can be deployed as traces to be recorded, neither as flashes nor as remnants of ideology but dialectically with the filming process, as a means of investigation.

"The memory of gestures, having them performed, the craftsmanship of death—that's what I am interested in. One cannot say that this death machine is inhuman. It is profoundly human. When you think that Khân wrote in his palm the number of the prisoner and the cell not to forget them—that's where Man lies, in this reflection on how to organize work in this concentrationary universe," Panh writes.[35] In his view, gestures must give access to something more: "This work will maybe help us catch sight of what is the human part of this crime, what happened in their mind when they performed these gestures." It is not a historian's work; Panh admits that he does not have enough distance for that and does not even try to be objective. Rather, he sees his contribution as a "reflection on the psychological dimension of this mass crime."[36] Therefore, he also creates situations that force the Khmer Rouge to think about their acts.[37] Artist Vann Nath, one of the few prisoners who survived S-21, plays a crucial role in this process. His intervention continually unhinges the former guards and disrupts the narratives by which they seem to have come to terms with their responsibility. Vann confronts them with evidence. He reads aloud archival documents, shows them photographs, and takes them to see his paintings (which describe the ordeal of the S-21 inmates). With persistence, he asks Prâk, Him, and the others how they see themselves, how they see the victims, and how they could even believe in the "confessions" they extracted from the prisoners. This confrontation between victim and perpetrators, which could be seen as a form of liberating energy, helps reconnect the gestures of killing to a repressed layer of emotions. Vann reads the "confession" of Nay Nân, a nineteen-year-old girl tortured by Prâk. Shocked by the absurdity of the girl's self-accusations of sabotage, Vann turns to Prâk and states: "Your reflection as a man, you had lost it" (after Prâk told him again that, at the time, he was indoctrinated, just obeying the party's orders, and that the party knew what they were doing). "Where did your feelings, your education go?" Vann asks him. He then brings up the notion of a "robot." In this case, though, it is not the ideological robot depicted by Pilger forty years earlier but something deeper, in which Good and Bad, and the faculty of distinguishing between the two, are central. Becoming a robot means losing one's morality and ethics.[38] How can these be regained, if ever? Vann's questions seem to touch upon something deep in the psyche of the perpetrators. Indeed, the whole issue of female prisoners remains, apparently, a highly sensitive topic for the former staff. As Khân recounts the story of the torture of Nay Nân, he progressively unravels the complexity of his feelings for the girl, how pity, love, sexual desire, and frustration fueled his violence against her. In this lies the human remnant of the gesture of killing, a remnant that can be rediscovered—and perhaps recovered—beyond words. This points to an additional function of the archive created by Panh, as the latter documents and preserves the fleeting moments when perpetrators, however reluctantly, acknowledge their deeds.

DUCH, MASTER OF THE FORGES OF HELL

The Khmer Rouge included a substantive number of teachers in its ranks. This explains, in part, why dehumanization through education (or indoctrination) is so critical an issue for Panh. Former S-21 commander Duch (Kaing Guek Eav) was a math teacher. How does a man who received an enlightened education (Duch quotes Vigny and Balzac in French) turn into the organizer of the extermination of at least 18,000 people (not including the victims at the security center M-13 he commanded during the 1970–1975 civil war)? For this reason, *Duch, Master of the Forges of Hell* is essential to Panh's investigation of the Khmer Rouge killing machine. It also supplies a missing piece in his inquest, since he was not able to interview the ex-prison commander when he was making *S21*.[39] The film opens and ends with Duch's gestures. The first sequence shows the man's early morning ritual in his cell, making his coffee and drinking it while he looks out the window. The closing scene shows him doing physical exercise, eating, and praying (he converted to evangelical Christianity in the 1990s). Between the two sequences, Panh takes the viewer on a long journey through the system of administration, interrogation, and killing at S-21, as seen from the upper level of authority at the prison.

Throughout the film, Duch is in full control of his body language. Still, there are moments when he lets something escape. These are the gestures of embarrassment and denial that Panh's camera captures—when Duch is in a difficult position, for example, he rubs his face or breathes loudly.[40] As well, the confrontation with evidence (S-21 documents, photographs and "confessions" of prisoners, Khmer Rouge propaganda footage, excerpts of the movie *S21*) helps breach the protective shell Duch has built. Looking at the photo of the investiture of the national army leads him to enact the salute of the party's flag, with his fist raised to his temple. Panh cuts to an archival image of a group of Khmer Rouge saluting the flag and then back to Duch, who seems lost in the past and repeats the words: "I pledge to serve the party, the country, the people." Still, Duch's gestures remain sparse. This possibly reflects his attempt to maintain a clear division between theory/ideology (his realm as "technician of the revolution") and the physical field whereby ideology was implemented through physical violence. For instance, he dismisses, with a laugh, the accusation made by some of the S-21 staff members (in Panh's footage shown to him) that he interrogated prisoners himself. He did not, he tells Panh, because interrogating creates ties with the victim and the S-21 personnel. Then, you would end up being judged by them: "How to beat a prisoner in a way that can serve as model?"

Over the course of the film, however, a more complex oscillation in his relation to gestures appears, and Duch contradicts himself a number of times. For example, he admits that he oversaw the interrogation of Koy Thourn (Central Committee member, minister of commerce, secretary of the Northern Zone, arrested and killed in 1977). He succeeded in reaching out to Koy Thourn through kindness and words. Duch spoke to him nicely, waited, and smiled and in this way coaxed him into writing his "confession." "My spear, these are my words," Duch claims, making the gesture of pushing a spear into the air. Annotating lists and handing them over to the staff (Duch performs the gesture) mean that he was a criminal, because this gesture transformed free human beings into prisoners, living into dead. Gesture is the "communication of communicability," Agamben writes, "because being-in-language is not something that could be said in sentences, the gesture is essentially always a gesture of not being able to figure something out in language."[41] Pushed by Panh, Duch reveals the performative dimension of words in Democratic Kampuchea—they can kill. There is thus an unbreakable link between words and gestures, which Duch fully embodies. His work (or his *métier*, as he calls it in French) is to "transfer the language of killing on paper by irrigating the thoughts of his subordinates."

Like the salute to the party flag, another scene shows the hold Khmer Rouge ideology still has on Duch. Panh presents him with a photograph of himself sitting in front of a microphone during a political training session for S-21 staff members. Scrutinizing the picture, Duch describes his face on the image as "avid to explain the essence of this language. This language of killing . . . of proletarian dictatorship, I disseminated it at S-21. . . . Don't hesitate! These are the words of the Party. The Party guides you. You hesitate? Why?" He relives the moment: "The Party, it's me!" he shouts, sticking out his chest and pointing a finger at himself. Then, he laughs and apologizes to Panh: "Excuse me, I play the big man!" *Duch* is, thus, the attempt to reconnect the words and gestures that Duch tried so carefully to keep apart. Recording, Agamben warns, can interrupt the gesture and suspend it in a state of being only a means. Therefore, it is crucial to reintroduce its finality and weave it anew into the web of meanings in which it was initially enmeshed. This is exactly what Panh does when he asks Duch to read Khmer Rouge slogans written on sheets of paper, then cuts to archival images of Democratic Kampuchea propaganda movies and sequences of *S21* in which the former staff perform their prison gestures. "Politics is a scream," Panh writes.[42] Yet, as Agamben reminds us, politics is also the "absolute and complete gesturality of human beings."[43] By intertwining discourses and acts, Panh exhibits the gesturality of extermination in its entirety. In so doing, he transforms "a *res* into a *res gesta*."[44] This opens the door to a new language, at the same time psychological, anthropological, historiographical, and judicial.

CONCLUSION

Zooming out, this chapter tried to give Panh's work a broader context and situate his unique perspective in relation to the documentary practices of other directors who filmed perpetrators in Cambodia and Indonesia. Zooming in, the chapter discussed how Panh documents, in both *S21* and *Duch*, a multilevel interaction between word and gesture, the process of transformation of the language of killing into the act itself, and the ways in which the act in turn affects the perpetrators' narratives about their role in the ordeal of the Cambodian population. "Because cinema has its center in the gesture and not in the image, it belongs essentially to the realm of ethics and politics (i.e., not simply to that of aesthetics)," Agamben writes.[45] If the gesture exhibited in its mediality becomes, according to the philosopher, a new pleasure for the audience, in the ethical cinema of Panh it becomes for the viewer a means to access a different level of witnessing and understanding. Moreover, the bodily language of extermination thus archived opens up for Khmer Rouge perpetrators the possibility to recognize what they have done. "As long as one does not acknowledge one's gestures, there is no individual responsibility, hence no possible way of asking for forgiveness," Panh says.[46] It does not mean that forgiveness will be granted, but it means at least that victims will be given a choice when there was none before.

NOTES

Acknowledgments: Part of the research for this paper was made possible through the Cultures of Occupation in Twentieth-Century Asia Project, and therefore received funding from the European Research Council under the European Union's Horizon 2020 research and innovation program (grant no. 682081).

1. The Khmer Rouge was known then as the National United Front of Kampuchea (FUNK), the alliance they had formed for tactical reasons in March 1970 with former head of state Norodom Sihanouk, after the latter was ousted in the bloodless coup engineered by Prince Sirik Matak and Lon Nol on March 18, 1970.
2. Serge Thion, *Un témoignage occidental: Dans les maquis cambodgiens* (Editions F.U.N.C., 1972), 12–13. All translations provided by Stéphanie Benzaquen-Gautier.

3. Thion, 13.
4. See, e.g., Henri Locard, *Le "Petit Livre Rouge" de Pol Pot ou les paroles de l'Angkar entendues dans le Cambodge des Khmers Rouges du 17 avril 1975 au 7 janvier 1979* (Paris: L'Harmattan, 1997); Laurence Picq, *Le piège Khmer Rouge* (Paris: Buchet Castel, 2013); François Ponchaud, *Cambodge année zéro* (Paris: Julliard, 1977).
5. As explained by Kenneth Quinn in his PhD dissertation "The Origins and Development of Radical Cambodian Communism" (University of Maryland, 1982), this experience in the "liberated zones" turned Ith into a dedicated anticommunist. A clear-headed observer of the Khmer Rouge system, he wrote the book *Sranaoh Pralung Khmer* (Regrets for the Khmer soul), in which he warned of the threat they posed to Cambodia. However, the Lon Nol regime banned the book and threw Ith into jail. Elizabeth Becker, *When the War Was Over: Cambodia and the Khmer Rouge Revolution* (New York: Simon and Schuster, 1986), 141.
6. Sarin Ith, "Life in the Bureaus (Offices) of the Khmer Rouge," in *Communist Party Power in Kampuchea (Cambodia): Documents and Discussion*, comp. and ed. Timothy Michael Carney, data paper no. 106, Southeast Asia Program, Department of Asian Studies, Cornell University, January 1977, 53.
7. Ith, 46, 49.
8. Roel Burgler, *The Eyes of the Pineapple: Revolutionary Intellectuals and Terror in Democratic Kampuchea* (Saarbrucken: Verlag Breitenbach, 1990), 1–2.
9. Prisoners were photographed upon arrival and the picture attached to their file. Thousands of negatives survived the fall of Democratic Kampuchea because S-21 commander Duch did not have the time to destroy them before fleeing the Vietnamese advance in January 1979.
10. Philippe Mangeot, Jean-Philippe Renouard, and Isabelle Saint-Saëns, "La parole des tueurs: Une mémoire des corps: Entretien avec Jean Hatzfeld et Rithy Panh," *Vacarme* 2, no. 27 (2004): 35.
11. Giorgio Agamben, "Notes on Gesture," in *Means without End: Notes on Politics*, trans. Vincenzo Binetti and Cesare Casarino (Minneapolis: University of Minnesota Press, 2000), 53.
12. Agamben, 54.
13. Jan Assmann, "Communicative and Cultural Memory," in *Cultural Memory Studies: An International and Interdisciplinary Handbook*, ed. Astrid Erll and Ansgar Nünning (Berlin: De Gruyter, 2008), 109–118.
14. See, e.g., Meng-Try Ea and Sorya Sim, *Victims and Perpetrators? Testimony of Young Khmer Rouge Comrades* (Phnom Penh: Documentation Center of Cambodia, 2001); Alexander Laban Hinton, *Why Did They Kill? Cambodia in the Shadow of Genocide* (Berkeley: University of California Press, 2005).
15. See, e.g., En Nhem and Dara Duong, *Nhem En: The Khmer Rouge's Photographer at S-21: Under the Khmer Rouge Genocide: Personal Memoir* (Cambodia: self-published, 2014); Sikoeun Suong, *Itinéraire d'un intellectuel Khmer Rouge* (Paris: Les Editions du Cerf, 2013).
16. On the subject, see Julie Bernath, "'Complex Political Victims' in the Aftermath of Mass Atrocity: Reflections on the Khmer Rouge Tribunal in Cambodia," *International Journal of Transitional Justice* 10, no. 1 (2016): 46–66.
17. The project was supported by the Center for Kulturog Udvikling (CKU) and the Danish Centre for Culture and Development (DCCD).
18. They asked their names not be used. Roth Meas, "Khmer Rouge Soldiers Voice Views on Film," *Phnom Penh Post*, February 28, 2011, https://www.phnompenhpost.com/lifestyle/kr-soldiers-voice-views-film.
19. Jan Krogsgaard and Thomas Weber Carlsen, "Voices of the Khmer Rouge," Austro Sino Art Program, accessed November 7, 2019, http://www.austrosinoartsprogram.org/blog/jan-krogsgaard-thomas-weber-carlsen-voices-khmer-rouge.

20. Krogsgaard and Carlsen.
21. Krogsgaard and Carlsen.
22. Krogsgaard and Carlsen.
23. For further discussion of the movie, see for example: Deirdre Boyle, "Interviewing the Devil: Interrogating Masters of the Cambodian Genocide," in *A Companion to Contemporary Documentary Film* (UK; Wiley Blackwell, 2015); Gina Chon and Thet Sambath, *Behind the Killing Fields: A Khmer Rouge Leader and One of his Victims* (Philadelphia, Oxford: University of Pennsylvania Press, 2010); Alvin Lim, *Cambodia and the Politics of Aesthetics* (New York and London: Routledge, 2013).
24. Seth Mydans, "In a Cambodian Friendship, a Secret Quest," *New York Times*, August 6, 2010, https://www.nytimes.com/2010/08/07/world/asia/07cambo.html.
25. Thet Sambath, "The Truth about the Khmer Rouge Is Too Big for One Court Case," *The Guardian*, June 27, 2011, https://www.theguardian.com/law/2011/jun/27/truth-khmer-rouge-court-case.
26. Quoted by Mydans, "In a Cambodian Friendship."
27. Thet expressed on several occasions how close he felt to Nuon Chea, visiting him in prison and getting messages from him through the old Khmer Rouge cadre's wife. Gina Chon and Thet Sambath, *Behind the Killing Fields*, 158.
28. Oppenheimer's approach is not completely new, as is shown by other directors such as Abbas Kiarostami and Werner Herzog, who used the same techniques in *Close-Up* (1990) and *Little Dieter Needs to Fly (Escape from Laos)* (1997), respectively. Errol Morris used reenactments in *The Thin Blue Line* (1988) that came close to Akira Kurosawa's *Rashomon* (1950).
29. Homi K. Bhabha, "Of Mimicry and Man: The Ambivalence of Colonial Discourse," in *The Location of Culture* (London: Routledge, 1994). For a critique of Rouch, see James G. Ferguson, "Of Mimicry and Membership: Africans and the 'New World Society,'" *Cultural Anthropology* 17, no. 4 (2002): 551–569.
30. Rithy Panh with Christine Chaumeau, *La machine Khmère Rouge: Monti Santésok S-21* (Paris: Flammarion, 2003), 87.
31. Agamben, "Notes on Gesture," 56, 57.
32. Panh, *La machine Khmère Rouge*, 87.
33. Rithy Panh with Christophe Bataille, *L'élimination* (Paris: Grasset, 2012), 120–121.
34. Panh, *La machine Khmère Rouge*, 43.
35. Panh, 199.
36. Panh, 88.
37. Panh, *L'élimination*, 19.
38. Panh, *La machine Khmère Rouge*, 296–297.
39. Panh, *L'élimination*, 18.
40. Panh, 50.
41. Agamben, "Notes on Gesture," 58.
42. Panh, *L'élimination*, 86.
43. Agamben, "Notes on Gesture," 59.
44. Agamben, 59.
45. Agamben, 55.
46. Mangeot, Renouard, and Saint-Saëns, "La parole des tueurs," 32.

9 • CREATING DUCH

The Projects of Duch, François Bizot, and Rithy Panh

DONALD REID

Duch, the nom de guerre of Kaing Guek Eav, was the first Khmer Rouge official to be tried by the Extraordinary Chambers in the Courts of Cambodia (ECCC).[1] The court saw in Duch an ideologically committed bureaucrat responsible for the deaths of well over 12,000 men, women, and children between 1975 and 1979. However, other dimensions to Duch's character are revealed in the two most important efforts to analyze and present him as he was during the 1970s, those of François Bizot and Rithy Panh: this was the Duch on trial, not the Duch in the courtroom facing charges of crimes against humanity three decades later. Bizot's focus on humanity and Panh's on crimes enable us to see the perpetrator in new ways.

Duch was born in 1942, the son of an indebted businessman. Taken under the wing by radical teachers, he pledged allegiance in 1967 to the Cambodian Communist Party, the Khmer Rouge. In a world of privilege denied to Duch, the Khmer Rouge appreciated him and gave him hope.[2] Arrested and imprisoned for political activity in 1968, Duch was released in 1970 after Lon Nol overthrew Prince Sihanouk. Duch joined the maquis and in 1971 was put in charge of the M-13 camp, where those accused of collaborating with the government or spying for opponents of the Khmer Rouge were interrogated and executed. When the Khmer Rouge came to power in April 1975, it named Duch second-in-command of the S-21 security group. S-21 dealt initially with those who had worked for the Lon Nol regime. At the end of March 1976, the Khmer Rouge named Duch head of S-21 and made its mission to handle traitors within the party. Duch established S-21 in new quarters in a former lycée in Phnom Penh, Tuol Sleng.

After Phnom Penh fell to Vietnam in January 1979, Duch remained active in the Khmer Rouge for a decade and a half, until its demise was apparent and it no longer had a place for him. "If the party had won," he says in Rithy Panh's film *Duch, Master of the Forges of Hell,* he would have remained the "most determined" of its disciples. Duch left the Khmer Rouge for evangelical Christianity. Baptized in January 1996, he worked under a new name for Christian refugee groups until 1999, when he was recognized and the Cambodian government arrested him. In 2010 the ECCC convicted Duch of crimes against humanity for his actions as director at S-21; in 2012 the appeals court sentenced Duch to life imprisonment. His embrace of Christianity resonates with the commitment he had made to the Khmer Rouge. At his trial, he said, "If Cambodian traditions so allow, I would gladly agree to be stoned like St. Stephen and St. James were after the death of Christ." Duch believes that Deng Xiaoping was a Christian as well, but had to keep this secret from the Chinese Communist Party.[3]

DUCH AT S-21

Economic failures and the disastrous war with Vietnam had led some Khmer Rouge militants to question the policies pursued by the leadership of Democratic Kampuchea, Angkar. Unwilling to tolerate opposition from within, Angkar designated party members for arrest. Security agents brought them and their families to S-21 to be interrogated and executed. Angkar interpreted dissent as treason and wanted evidence of this treason from the arrested; the staff tortured prisoners to make them confess to sabotage and to spying for their choice of the CIA, the KGB, or the Vietnamese.[4] The plausibility of these confessions was not a concern. What was important was to get the arrested to name coconspirators. Many of those arrested had almost certainly not criticized Angkar, but they had the misfortune of showing up in the chain of names drawn from the prisoners who had preceded them. When Duch judged an interrogation complete, he had the prisoner and family taken to be executed at the killing field of Choeung Ek that he set up outside of Phnom Penh.

What motivated Duch? He was not a sadist, but he derived great pleasure from creating order out of the cacophony of denunciations. To explain this as the work of a bureaucrat in the unbureaucratic world of patronage at the core of Khmer Rouge rule should not obscure the personal satisfaction Duch took from aligning the disparate revelations in the confessions. His chef d'oeuvre, "The Last Joint Plan," a report prepared for Angkar in which he put together the networks of betrayal uncovered in interrogations at S-21, shows this clearly.[5] Duch frequently visited a couple of prisoners who survived as artists producing portraits of Pol Pot. The task he gave them of painting pictures that matched photos exactly, yet did away with imperfections in the subject's appearance revealed in the photos, was of a piece with his project of rendering an impeccable product using confessions wrenched from tortured individuals.

At Duch's trial, prosecutors responded to his defense in terms of obedience and fear by saying he acted out of belief. However, they did not analyze how Duch understood this belief. The Khmer Rouge was a Marxist-Leninist party and as such it would direct the proletariat to make a socialist revolution. However, in a society without a proletariat, the situation in Cambodia, it is only the party that knows "proletarian truth": "the primacy of proletarian truth," Duch tells us, means that "whatever is the truth, the proletarian class had to be victorious."[6] As Duch made clear in court, there was nothing of importance external to the party. Brother Number 2, Nuon Chea, explained in July 1978, "The leadership apparatus must be defended at any price. If we lose members but retain the leadership, we can continue to win victories."[7] Creation of Communist Cambodia could require the death of a large part of the population, Duch told François Bizot in 1971; this, he explained, was something the party could live with.[8]

In interviews in 1999 and at his trial, Duch said that perhaps 20 percent of what was in prisoners' confessions was true. The words of the arrested were the ore that Duch refined to extract what the party found valuable. If a prisoner named a member of the Khmer Rouge leadership, Duch consulted with his superiors to determine if the prisoner should rewrite the confession without this information.[9] Duch was, in Panh's words, "afflicted with a 'disease of purity.'"[10] The purity of the party required purification of the confessions. Duch's total lack of empathy allowed him to fulfill his allegiance to Angkar, whose inscrutable ways were, he believed, the only path to revolution in Cambodia. For Bizot, "Duch's role was that of a great magician, charged with guaranteeing the survival of his idols (i.e., the 'historic heroes of the revolution') and to exorcise their paranoia."[11] Khmer Rouge ideology was incarnated in the leadership. Duch's faith in this ideology was inseparable from his faith in the leaders, and he abandoned it only when he came to feel, long after defeat by the Vietnamese, that they had betrayed their mission and his role in it. This was evident, he realized, when shortly before Duch's arrest, Brother Number 1, Pol Pot, claimed that he knew nothing of S-21 and later, when fellow Khmer Rouge leader Khieu Samphan said that he was not fully aware of "the atrociously brutal character" of Khmer Rouge rule until he saw Panh's film *S21: The Khmer Rouge Death Machine*.[12]

At his trial, Duch evaded discussing the specifics of what he had done. He expressed remorse but preferred to talk about superiors who ordered him and subordinates whom he had perform acts of inhumanity in response to these orders: as a Khmer Rouge official, he was no longer an individual, but an agent of the party and therefore lacked personal agency. In his closing argument, Duch's attorney, Kar Savuth, asserted that the Khmer Rouge leadership should be tried, but not his client. Duch's final statement to the court was a history of the Communist Party of Cambodia; he concluded by reading the thirty-four footnotes to the court, one by one. Duch's defense became that he had been imprisoned in the Khmer Rouge. While he acknowledged the actions he took then, he asserted that no one could judge him because no one today can penetrate S-21 to see the individual they claim to judge. However, François Bizot and Rithy Panh do seek to take us to the Duch who is being judged—the Duch active in the Khmer Rouge—not as lawyers, but as representatives of the humanity Duch asks to reenter.

FRANÇOIS BIZOT

François Bizot is a prominent French ethnologist, known for his work on Buddhism in Cambodia. Khmer Rouge forces arrested him in October 1971 and took him to M-13, where he was held for two and a half months. Duch questioned Bizot and came to believe that he was not a CIA agent, although Duch's immediate superior thought he must be and should be executed. Based on a report Duch prepared for the party leadership, the Khmer Rouge released Bizot in late December 1971. Duch contacted him on the eve of his arrest in 1999. Bizot went to see Duch in Cambodia and in 2000 published *The Gate*, which includes an account of his experience at M-13. Marcel Lemonde, a judge in Duch's trial, was surprised to find that Bizot had made no mention of Duch in the report he filed with the French embassy after his release.[13] Duch assumed importance for Bizot when he reflected back on the experience in M-13 and what it revealed to him. In *The Gate*, Bizot presents Duch as "one of those fervent idealists who yearned above all for truth."[14] Duch was a faithful party member, but Bizot believes Duch understood this differently when he held Bizot than he would as director of S-21. Duch's assessment of Bizot in 1971 is the only time of which we have a record before 1999 that Duch appears to seek the "truth" as it would be understood outside the Khmer Rouge, and can do so without seeing this as a betrayal of the party.

When he was captured, Bizot saw himself as standing for Khmer culture against external forces, whether these took the form of Lon Nol's American-equipped soldiers, the Americans who bombed Cambodia, the Khmer Rouge who wanted to save Cambodia by destroying it first, French intellectuals who supported the Khmer Rouge without attempting to know what it was, or the North Vietnamese, who sought control of Cambodia. Bizot was a Frenchman immersed in rural Cambodian Buddhism that he knew better than Duch, who lived alongside it but was not of it. Duch could not find in Bizot the crimes that marked other prisoners for him. The fascination was mutual. In his novel *Le saut du Varan* (2006), Bizot creates a Duch who defends not the Khmer Rouge but an embodiment of the culture Bizot studies. In the novel, the French ethnologist Rénot sees himself as a "medium" for native informants rather than a researcher. He is fascinated by accounts of an isolated kingdom in the jungle where Angkor civilization survives in its purity. In 1970, Rénot meets guerrillas led by Duch who guard the kingdom from alien intrusions. They shoot Rénot with poison arrows. The kingdom takes care of him, but Rénot, Duch, and the kingdom itself are destroyed by American bombing.[15]

After Bizot's liberation from M-13 had been decided, he and Duch have a conversation around the fire on Christmas Eve in 1971. In the thousands of pages of memoirs, interviews, and trial transcripts, and the many hours of film, it is the only time that we see Duch speaking with an individual in a roughly equal position of power. At one point, Bizot asks Duch about torture at M-13. Bizot knew that torture took place there, but he is shocked to learn that Duch practices it, brutally beating prisoners he suspects of lying. Bizot believes that in telling him this, Duch is revealing his inner self: "The fervent revolutionary had opened my eyes to that which I was thousands of miles from suspecting, eradicating any sort of optimism from me. By exposing his distress to me—by taking the chance of lifting the veil from the darkest parts of his being—Duch had knowingly wanted to show me the outline of my own, as one warns a traveler of the perils that lie ahead. He was setting off an alarm whose import and scope was exactly the sort of danger sign he had found lacking on his own journey, but that he did not doubt I would need myself."[16] If others try to reconcile the individual they see on trial with his actions as director of S-21, Bizot attempted to do this with the Duch he knew before he ran S-21.

Bizot begins *Facing the Torturer*, published after Duch's trial, with a confession that he had killed with his bare hands a pet fennec he had brought back from his service in the Algerian War because he saw that caring for it would interfere with his desire to travel; his journey to Cambodia began years before with this act of cruelty. It is not monsters, but "normal" people like himself, who can do terrible, inhumane things: "My Cambodian ordeal . . . opened my eyes to a threatening piece of intimate mathematics: what is inside me equals the worst of what there is in others." Duch, wrote Bizot, "remained my fellow man," even when directing S-21.[17] Bizot moved from seeing in Duch his Communist friends in Paris to seeing himself. He wrote of going to see Duch in prison: "Talking freely with him seemed the only way to open new perspectives on myself."[18] Other Western intellectuals without Bizot's experience draw the same conclusion as he did: to understand Duch committing crimes against humanity, one must look at oneself.[19]

RITHY PANH

Rithy Panh has filmed and written extensively on his horrific experiences and those of his nation under Khmer Rouge rule. In his more than 300 hours of filming for *Duch, Master of the Forges of Hell*, Panh gains no new perspectives on himself like those of Bizot. Panh produced *Le temps des aveux*, the film drawn from Bizot's *The Gate*, but it has no place for the self-analysis by Bizot (or Duch) at the heart of Bizot's interpretation of his experience. In Bizot's telling of Duch, Bizot figures prominently; Duch never appears alone. Panh, on the other hand, is totally absent from *Duch*. Panh recognizes violence within himself. However, he considers this not as a human universal but as the product of his experiences and something that confrontation with those experiences enables him to overcome.[20] When Panh interviews Duch in prison, he recognizes that Duch felt himself superior to Panh and his film crew composed of survivors.[21] Panh never has the conversation of relative equals like that of Duch and Bizot that leads to Bizot's epiphany. It means something different for Westerners to look at the perpetrator of Khmer Rouge crimes, and then to themselves, than for a Khmer like Panh, a victim who does not have this distance and does not want it and who feels that identifying with Duch takes us away from the particularity of his crimes. When Him Huy, the former joint chief of security at S-21, whom Panh filmed in *S21*, tried to convince him that "there is evil in each of us, and that we could all have become murderers," Panh replies that he would not know; he was in a forced labor camp.[22] For Panh, that all could do evil is a banal observation or a dangerous escape. His goal is not self-exploration or the revelation of universal human qualities, but to grasp what falls outside both survivors' accounts of loss and the most diligent accounting by lawyers and historians of acts of inhumanity.

The Khmer Rouge were obsessed with secrecy. Their term for executions like those of the S-21, *kamtech*, is usually translated in English as "smash," but Panh makes clear that it means "to reduce to dust," to leave no trace.[23] As Duch explains in *Duch*, the Khmer Rouge did not return the body of the executed to the family. "There was no mourning. This was the Khmer Rouge tradition. *Kamtech* means to destroy the name, the image, the body, everything. We destroyed the old world to build the new." For Duch, the Great Leap Forward of the Khmer Rouge was not about economic development, but the destruction of the old as a precondition for creating the new. Duch was the perfect practitioner of *kamtech* until he was not. When the Vietnamese entered Phnom Penh in 1979, he fled, without destroying either the archive that documented activities at S-21 or the few surviving prisoners. Duch left *kamtech* incomplete, and this provides Panh a point of entry. He does not question Duch in the film; archival documents and filmed interviews with those who escaped *kamtech*, or practiced it as Duch's subordinates, perform this role.

Panh's earlier film *S21* brings together interrogators and guards with survivors of Tuol Sleng in an effort to access their responsibilities and responsibility, their remorse and repentance. Panh did not create "reconstitutions" like those done later at Choeung Ek and S-21 for Duch's trial. His goal was not to reenact historical events. The S-21 staff, who cannot speak of what they did, recall the gestures they made back in the day; after ten or twenty times, "their reflexes return, [Panh] sees what really happened."[24] He deftly calls up their corporeal memory of daily acts in Tuol Sleng to present to viewers what no archives or testimony contains. When Judge Lemonde criticized the court for showing an extract of *S21* as being like having *Schindler's List* screened at the Nuremburg trials, he got it totally wrong.[25] The individuals themselves, not actors, revisited their past selves, rather than performing assigned roles.

Duch presented a different and more challenging case than the S-21 staff, who did not face going on trial for their actions. Panh had eschewed filming Khmer Rouge leaders; their denials of knowledge of what went on and of responsibility disgusted him.[26] However, Duch, the man who created the staff interviewed in *S21*, was the absent presence of that film. The film Panh devotes to Duch is in this sense a prequel to *S21*. Citing the Khmer Rouge dictate that "only the newborn child is pure," Duch tells of indoctrinating youths of modest peasant origins. Rather than teaching them to read and write, he trained them to staff M-13 and S-21; they were loyal because they knew nothing else. Eighty-two of the 111 who staffed Tuol Sleng in early 1977 were aged between seventeen and twenty-one.[27] These are the men we see reinhabit their Tuol Sleng selves in Panh's *S21*. Duch believed that their class background allowed them to carry out without qualms their revolutionary mission of killing those who stood in the way of the dictatorship of the proletariat. However, as one of the educated, Duch explains that he did not find this easy. The Khmer Rouge sustained a hierarchy in which agents drawn from the peasantry destroyed; the party told them who to destroy. Those who cannot do, teach. Duch tells of his eagerness to convey the "rhetoric of killing" to his students. This is what leads Panh to say that educated individuals like Duch made a choice and "consciously performed their functions as criminals, who knew very well what they were doing."[28] Although S-21 staff discuss Duch's participation in the torture and abuse of prisoners in footage Duch watches on a laptop in *Duch*, he denies this. Duch refers in the film to his "double crime" of claiming not to have committed acts, while working hard to forget them. Duch's claim to have arranged not to see what was troubling reveals that he knew what he did not want to see.

In *S21*, the survivor Vann Nath—a painter who had produced portraits of Pol Pot—articulates Panh's vision.[29] In *Duch*, there is no figure like this. Instead, as Panh makes clear, his filming and editing play this role. Duch, Panh explains, "doesn't know that montage is a politics and a morality unto itself"; "Thanks to cinema the truth comes out: montage versus mendacity."[30] Reflecting on how Duch "reinvents his truth in order to survive"—Panh believes that Duch used telling his story to him to prepare for his trial—Panh responds by editing his film "against Duch."[31] Panh spliced into *Duch* Khmer Rouge footage of orderly laborers and smiling leaders. These clips are themselves contrasted with still photographs of the arrested when they entered Tuol Sleng and their lifeless, tortured bodies when they exited, and of Vann Nath's dramatic paintings of the abuse that took place there for which there are no stirring propaganda films. Panh is neither a therapist nor a historian, neither a lawyer nor a judge. He is an artist, and his film is an alternative to the trial, an effort to contest *kamtech* rather than the impossible effort to understand, explain, or render a verdict on Duch.

In the logorrhea Panh induces, Duch reveals the director of S-21 he has never left behind. Referring to Duch's assessment of the truth contained in the confessions prisoners made at S-21, Panh "think[s] about what he said to me: 'In every lie, there's some truth. In every truth, there's some lie. The most important thing is that the prisoner denounces his collaborators.'"[32] Panh seeks to get behind Duch's ready denunciation of his collaborators above him and his questioning of the accounts of those below, to reach the Duch of S-21 himself; this is the kind of exercise that had not concerned Duch when he analyzed prisoners' confessions. Panh created a scale to measure what he assessed as Duch's truthfulness during filming. In the early interviews, he saw Duch as telling the truth 20 percent of the time—the same figure Duch gave for the truth content of the confessions at Tuol Sleng—and he never saw Duch achieving the passing grade he would need to "get back his humanity and dignity."[33] Even when Duch defends himself, he reminds us of who he was and remains. Duch recites to Panh and others Alfred de Vigny's poem, "La mort du loup," in which he claims the role of the wolf who sacrifices himself so his family can escape the hunter. Yet, at S-21, Duch had been the hunter who treated those arrested as animals and assured that they could not save their families.[34]

Getting the prison staff in *S21* to revisit repeatedly their actions at Tuol Sleng uncovers the practice of their inhumanity there. Panh wants the same from Duch, not the legal evidence to make a case for or against him. Panh asks Duch to read a multitude of Khmer Rouge slogans, what Duch calls "the framework for their thought." Asked to pick one, he selects "To keep you, we gain nothing; if we eliminate you, we lose nothing," a guide to acting without making choices that undergirds the political culture in which he operated. Panh gives Duch the file of Bophana, whose arrest and execution had been the subject of one of his earlier films: "You can still perceive [in Duch], after thirty years, the combativeness, the hatred, the perversity, an excitement that resembles desire."[35] Panh allows viewers to see what those at the trial did not.

At the time Panh filmed him, Duch had long before renounced the Khmer Rouge and experienced a loss of faith in its leadership. However, Panh is successful getting him to tap into the words and gestures of Duch the Khmer Rouge official. Both Duch and the S-21 staff can only think of torture and deaths from within the context of Khmer Rouge culture, so that whenever they go beyond an affirmation of remorse, they revert to this language; they believe that their acts exist in this sphere and cannot be understood outside of it. Like the prison personnel in *S21* who communicate through their gestures the past that inhabits them, Duch comes to attention and gives the Khmer Rouge party salute as he tells of pledging allegiance to the revolution, revealing the need to reenter a world he never fully left in order to speak of it. In prison, when he saw Nuon

Chea, a Khmer Rouge leader Duch had disparaged after leaving the party, he went down on his knees, explaining that Nuon Chea remained his superior.[36]

As Panh shows, Duch can easily launch into the persona of the S-21 director speaking to his staff: "Whoever was arrested by the party must be considered an enemy. Don't go weak at the knees! These are the party's words. The party is guiding you. Not me! I'm the party." At this point Duch himself seems taken aback by how easy this performance has been and asks for a break in the filming. While attributing responsibility for the criminal acts performed at S-21 to the party, he cannot avoid telling viewers that he is the party. Elsewhere in Panh's film, Duch thinks as the director of S-21 about his situation after S-21. The one prisoner Duch admits to interrogating (playing on his obedience to the party, but not laying a hand on him) was the Central Committee member Koy Thourn. Because S-21 was the only prison where Central Committee members—"those very people with blood on their hands"—were executed, he suggests that what he had done was what the court that is trying him now seeks to do: "I'm not saying S-21 did the right thing because it killed criminals, but it was thugs wiping out other thugs." You can take Duch out of S-21, but Panh shows you cannot take S-21 out of Duch.

Duch tells viewers that "proletarian truth" means "You may kill anyone for the proletariat to prevail." Morality was a matter of loyalty to the party to which he had sworn allegiance, not one of a shared humanity. This is the ideology he embraced, not the fine points of Marxism, which appear in bizarre forms in the film.[37] In a telling passage, Duch describes the Khmer Rouge as moving toward Communism: "From each according to his ability, to each according to his needs," he says in French, adding that he was not paid according to his work operating the means of destruction, but was supplied with what he needed to do this work—cigarettes.[38] Later in the film Duch draws on "class principles" from Marx and Engels for his theory that attractive women were "sexual instruments" that could distract a revolutionary from his duties.

Duch's defense is that he was afraid that if he challenged the party leaders, he would be executed. But the brilliance of Panh's *Duch* is to reveal how Duch understood this when directing S-21. He would not be distracted. Duch recounts that he had three strikes against him—he was Sino-Khmer, educated, and not a member of a central network in the party. Yet, he explains, "I didn't die like so many others because I am dedicated," suggesting that there was an order at work in the Khmer Rouge based on commitment, and that party members who were executed were at fault: their crime was a lack of dedication.

Arrest was an occupational hazard of work in the Khmer Rouge. This did not lead Duch to question the party; instead, like a skilled worker in a dangerous trade, he dedicated himself to job safety. He had all who were brought to S-21 photographed to assure they could be caught if they escaped. As Duch explains in Panh's film, he worked hard "to avoid being betrayed or killed for no reason"; he did not arrest an interrogator who had broken the rules governing questioning by sexually assaulting Duch's primary school teacher for fear that he would be accused of "individualism." Duch did not conduct interrogations himself because if he did not get the desired results, he would be shamed and others would say he was past his prime. The success of Panh is to capture Duch thinking as he did at S-21.

Panh also reveals Duch's sense that he was not sufficiently appreciated for his work at S-21. Other state offices were identified with three-digit numbers, but M-13 and S-21 had two-digit numbers. Although Duch had no reason to think a higher number had any significance, he asked, "Why did the security services have fewer digits than the others?"[39] The time that Duch gets the most upset in the film is when he tells of a superior ordering him to dig up a corpse and photograph it to prove that S-21 had carried out the execution. "If they don't trust us, why use us?" When the Khmer Rouge leadership appreciated members' work, they referred to them as "pure instruments of the party"; a pained Duch reported that at S-21, they were never given this honor.[40] The film makes us see that for Duch there are more grievances from the time than those of his victims.

Everyone remarks on Duch's laughter. To show his inhumanity, the prosecutor at Duch's trial asked Bizot about the time at M-13 when Duch had told him the party leadership had found him guilty. Bizot had collapsed, and then Duch laughed and revealed that Bizot had been judged innocent. But Bizot responded to what he called the prosecutor's "magic trick" by saying that Duch's "need to laugh . . . this need to joke, with the guards or even with the prisoners, was precisely the most distinct, but also the most tragic, proof of Duch's humanity."[41] Panh does not buy this. He sees Duch's laughter as an effort to avoid certain subjects or to infer an intimacy with a questioner. If laughter is a human trait, when Duch laughs in Panh's film, it is the closest he comes to being a monster.[42]

In pleading for a reduced sentence, Duch's lawyer, François Roux, had asked the court to allow a penitent Duch to reenter humanity. Panh thought this was an admirable goal, but that it was not a question of a blanket apology rewarded with forgiveness.[43] It was up to Duch to act, not the court or other gatekeepers to humanity. As far as Panh was concerned, in neither the filming nor the trial did Duch ever come close to acknowledging "*in detail*" what he had done; he remains within the Khmer Rouge culture that *Duch* reveals.[44] Panh told Roux that during the trial Duch had achieved only 5 percent on the humanity scale based on his truthfulness, a fall from the 20 percent when he began filming.[45] Panh ends his film with Duch contrasting karma—what individuals do decides their future fate—to absolution by God for those who express remorse and ask to be forgiven. When Duch embraced the Khmer Rouge project of establishing the dictatorship of the proletariat, he originally thought of it as directed against usurers, like those who had victimized his father, and thieves. In Panh's film, Duch identifies himself with the thief crucified alongside Christ who repents and asks the

Lord to take him to heaven. For Panh, however, the reentry to humanity follows a different path; it is a matter of acknowledging the choices one makes and accepting one's karma.

A GREAT MAGICIAN

At his trial, Duch sought forgiveness as a Christian, but he did so in terms that were never free of a party logic. In *Duch*, he says he acted at S-21 in line with Khmer Rouge ideology whose fundamental principle was obedience to party leadership. Duch's assertion that ideology can be "criminal," but not "wicked or cruel"—"I don't know the meaning of those words," Duch adds, thinking as director of S-21—makes it impossible for him to express the remorse and responsibility that the court and the civil parties seek for the acts of wickedness and cruelty he committed at S-21.

François Bizot and Rithy Panh transport us to the time when Duch played an important role in the Khmer Rouge. Bizot takes us there and then to the universality of human experience. Like all, he has committed regrettable acts, and he owes a debt of gratitude to Duch for helping him to understand himself. However, Bizot does not demand of Duch that he see the evil and cruel nature of his own acts as other than a consequence of eating the fruit of the tree of ideology. Panh has no sense that Duch can enable him to see who he is. Panh felt, in turn, that Duch refused the opportunity he gave him to see himself. Bizot believed that if Duch had once been totally enmeshed in the Khmer Rouge, "in his cell, the spirit of the prisoner no longer came from anyone."[46] Bizot makes the imprisoned Duch the blank slate on which he can inscribe what he believes Duch has revealed to him. Panh has a different project. He calls up the spirit that animated Duch at S-21 that the archives he left behind cannot fully reveal. Bizot refers to Duch as "a great magician" at Tuol Sleng, but it took another one to reveal Duch when he had been its director.

NOTES

1. There are a number of good studies of Duch and his trial. These include Thierry Cruvellier, *The Master of Confessions: The Making of a Khmer Rouge Torturer*, trans. Alex Gilly (New York: HarperCollins, 2014); Nic Dunlop, *The Lost Executioner: The Story of Comrade Duch and the Khmer Rouge* (London: Bloomsbury, 2005); and Alexander Laban Hinton, *Man or Monster? The Trial of a Khmer Rouge Torturer* (Durham, NC: Duke University Press, 2016).
2. Youk Chhang in *Camarade Duch: Bienvenu en enfer*, directed by Adrian Maben (Paris: Arte Éditions, 2012), DVD.
3. Chy Terith, *When the Criminal Laughs* (Phnom Penh: Documentation Center of Cambodia, 2014), 42, 102.
4. Ben Kiernan, *The Pol Pot Regime: Race, Power, and Genocide in Cambodia under the Khmer Rouge, 1975–79* (New Haven, CT: Yale University Press, 1996), 350.

5. Duch, "The Last Joint Plan," in Karl Jackson, ed., *Cambodia 1975–1978* (Princeton, NJ: Princeton University Press, 1992), 299–314.

6. Rithy Panh with Christophe Bataille, *The Elimination: A Survivor of the Khmer Rouge Confronts His Past and the Commandant of the Killing Fields*, trans. John Cullen (New York: Other Press, 2013), 91; Christophe Peschoux and Haing Kheng Heng, *Itinerary of an Ordinary Torturer: Interview with Duch, Former Khmer Rouge Commander of S-21* (Chiang Mai: Silkworm Books, 2016), 128.

7. David Chandler, *Voices from S-21: Terror and History in Pol Pot's Secret Prison* (Berkeley: University of California Press, 1999), 16.

8. François Bizot, *The Gate*, trans. Ewan Cameron (New York: Random House, 2003), 116.

9. Peschoux and Kheng Heng, *Itinerary of an Ordinary Torturer*, 121, 144–145.

10. Robert Carmichael, *When Clouds Fell from the Sky: A Disappearance, a Daughter's Search and Cambodia's First War Criminal* (London: Mason-McDonald Press, 2015), 319.

11. François Bizot, "Préface," in David Chandler, *S-21 ou Le crime impuni des Khmers rouges* (Paris: Autrement, 2002), 10.

12. Khieu Samphan, *L'histoire récente du Cambodge et mes prises de position* (Paris: L'Harmattan, 2004), 132.

13. Marcel Lemonde, *Un juge face aux Khmers Rouges* (Paris: Le Seuil, 2013), 105.

14. Bizot, *The Gate*, 83.

15. Bizot, *Le saut du Varan* (Paris: Flammarion, 2006). After talking to Bizot about his experiences, John Le Carré created the character Hansen in *The Secret Pilgrim* (1990). Hansen researches Buddhism in areas "liberated" by the Khmer Rouge in northern Cambodia. With this as his cover, he works for British intelligence, supplying information that the Americans use to bomb villages that shelter Vietnamese troops.

16. François Bizot, *Facing the Torturer*, trans. Charlotte Mandell and Antoine Audouard (New York: Knopf, 2012), 86–87.

17. Bizot, 18, 21.

18. Bizot, 94.

19. Hinton, *Man or Monster?*, 33; Peschoux and Kheng Heng, *Itinerary of an Ordinary Torturer*, 28.

20. Panh, *The Elimination*, 6.

21. Amandine Scherrer, "Filmer pour voir: Ombres et lumières sur le génocide Khmer," *Cultures & Conflits* 97 (Spring 2015): 152.

22. Rithy Panh, "Epilogue," in *Bringing the Khmer Rouge to Justice*, ed. Jaya Ramji and Beth Van Schaack (Lewiston, NY: Edwin Mellen Press, 2005), 431.

23. Panh, *The Elimination*, 103–104; Rithy Panh with Christine Chaumeau, *La machine Khmère Rouge: Monti Santésok S-21* (Paris: Flammarion, 2003), 234–237.

24. Panh, *The Elimination*, 91; Panh, *La machine Khmère Rouge*, 87–88. Stéphanie Benzaquen-Gautier and John Kleinen's chapter in this volume examines in detail the signal importance of these "gestures of killing."

25. Lemonde, *Un juge face aux Khmers Rouges*, 230–231. What an S-21 interrogator like Prâk Khân said at the trial of Duch is "dismayingly benign" compared with his revelations in *S21*. Cruvellier, *The Master of Confessions*, 36.

26. Panh, "Epilogue," 430–431.

27. Kiernan, *The Pol Pot Regime*, 316.

28. Rithy Panh, "La parole filmée: Pour vaincre la terreur," *Communications* 71 (2001): 384.

29. Alexander Hinton sees Vann Nath's testimony as the turning point in Duch's trial because he so convincingly presented actions that Duch had denied. Hinton, *Man or Monster?*, 181.

30. Panh, *The Elimination*, 113–114, 255

31. Panh, 17–18, 186.
32. Panh, 186.
33. Carmichael, *When Clouds Fell from the Sky*, 317–318.
34. Panh, *The Elimination*, 208–210.
35. Panh, 16.
36. Lemonde, *Un juge face aux Khmers Rouges*, 153.
37. Duch referred constantly to Marxism, forcing Panh to take a break in filming to read or reread works by Marx, Louis Althusser, and Etienne Balibar. Pascal Merigeau, "Rithy Panh passe 'Duch' à la question," *L'Obs*, October 23, 2014, https://www.nouvelobs.com/cinema/20120104.CIN0404/rithy-panh-passe-duch-a-la-question.html.
38. Every afternoon at S-21, Duch would take a break and pour himself a glass of coconut milk with Cointreau. Panh, *The Elimination*, 260–261.
39. Panh, 129.
40. Panh, 71.
41. Bizot, *Facing the Torturer*, 120–121.
42. Panh, *The Elimination*, 65, 119, 130, 133, 216, 257.
43. Carmichael, *When Clouds Fell from the Sky*, 315–316.
44. Panh, *The Elimination*, 257.
45. Carmichael, *When Clouds Fell from the Sky*, 318.
46. Bizot, *Facing the Torturer*, 100.

10 · RITHY PANH, JEAN AMÉRY, AND THE PARADIGM OF MORAL RESENTMENT

RAYA MORAG

The regeneration of the New (post–Khmer Rouge mainly documentary) Cambodian Cinema during the first decade of the twenty-first century is based, I claim, on an irresolvable tension between two radically different attitudes toward Cambodia's unassimilated genocidal past: reconciliation and resentment. The evolution of the reconciliation paradigm in genocide scholarship, developed mainly during and after the work of the South African Truth and Reconciliation Commission (TRC) and prior to the establishment of the Khmer Rouge tribunal (the Extraordinary Chambers in the Courts of Cambodia [ECCC]), reveals that the conceptualization of reconciliation continues to be a source of great perplexity.[1] Nevertheless, most scholars who advocate reconciliation stress social stability, which according to prevailing views relates to, and should impact, society's postgenocide present and future. Thus, they promote justice, mercy, and forgiveness; the end of the past and the marking of a new beginning; a radical change in the present; and so on.

FROM FORGIVENESS TO RESENTMENT: DERRIDA, SCHELER, AMÉRY

In contrast, in his seminal work "On Forgiveness," Jacques Derrida opposes the arguments underlying the reconciliation paradigm and extends its perspectives, including coming out against the "ceremony of culpability."[2] He illuminates the tensions between ethics and politics (therefore reflecting more extensively on the problematic aspects raised by the major works on reconciliation) and proposes a sharp differentiation between forgiveness and all related themes, such as regret, excuse, reconciliation, and amnesty. Dissatisfied with existing models, he introduces a notion of forgiveness based on a radical purity.

In order to unravel this radical perception, Derrida discusses a 1967 essay by the French philosopher Vladimir Jankélévitch ("Should We Pardon Them?"). Alluding to Germans, Jankélévitch passionately argues that the terrible deeds committed during the Holocaust are irreparable, inexpiable, and unforgivable. While Derrida agrees with Jankélévitch that forgiveness is impossible, in contrast to Jankélévitch (and Hannah Arendt in *The Human Condition*),[3] he defines the paradox of forgiveness: for Derrida, "forgiveness forgives only the unforgivable" and "forgiveness must announce itself as impossibility itself."[4]

Striving to circumvent the useful mystification, abusive rhetoric, inauthenticity, corruption, and trivialization of forgiveness, and the (mostly made by the nation-state) calculated transactions of reconciliation that inevitably entail conditions agreed to in advance, Derrida emphasizes the contrast between responsible ethics and irresponsible politics that stands at the heart of his thought: "Each time forgiveness is at the service of a finality, be it noble and spiritual (atonement or redemption, reconciliation, salvation), each time that it aims to re-establish a normality (social, national, political, psychological) by a work of mourning, by some therapy or ecology of memory, then the 'forgiveness' is not pure—nor is its concept. Forgiveness is not, it *should not be*, normal, normative, normalising. It *should* remain exceptional and extraordinary, in the face of the impossible: as if it interrupted the ordinary course of historical temporality."[5] Emphasizing what he perceives as the Abrahamic language (juxtaposing Judaism, the Christianities, and the Islams) to discuss forgiveness, Derrida stages the aporia between a conditional forgiveness, which he associates with reconciliation, and a pure forgiveness, arising from a Levinasian unconditional ethical injunction. He stresses that pure forgiveness is an effect of relations and differences based on these poles, the unconditional and the conditional, and that these poles are heterogeneous, irreducible, and indissociable. Thus, "Forgiveness is mad . . . a madness of the impossible."[6]

Can Derrida's deconstructive rearticulation of forgiveness and his hyperbolic ethics, which "carries itself beyond laws, norms, or any obligation. Ethics beyond ethics,"[7] pave the way in a world in which "the proliferation of scenes of repentance, or of asking 'forgiveness,' signifies, no doubt, a *universal urgency* of memory"? And, if "*it is necessary* to turn toward the past; and *it is necessary* to take this act of memory, of self-accusation, of 'repentance,' of appearance [*comparution*] at the same time beyond the juridical instance, or that of the Nation-State," how will this act be carried out?[8]

Given that "the concept of the 'crime against humanity' remains on the horizon of the entire geopolitics of forgiveness,"[9] Derrida claims that "forgiveness must engage two singularities: the guilty (the 'perpetrator' as they say in South

Africa) and the victim. As soon as a third party intervenes, one can again speak of amnesty, reconciliation, reparation, etc., but certainly not of pure forgiveness."[10] Elaborating and repeating this creed, Derrida contends, "If anyone has the right to forgive, it is only the victim, and not a tertiary institution. For, in addition, even if this spouse is also a victim, well, the absolute victim, if one can say that, remains her dead husband. Only the dead man could legitimately consider forgiveness. The survivor is not ready to substitute herself, abusively, for the dead."[11]

The imperative against the Third,[12] which usually means an affirmation of sovereignty, closes Derrida's essay on forgiveness: "What I dream of, what I try to think as the 'purity' of a forgiveness worthy of its name, would be a forgiveness without power: *unconditional but without sovereignty*. The most difficult task, at once necessary and apparently impossible, would be to dissociate *unconditionality* and *sovereignty*."[13] Breaking what he regards as a dangerous cathexis, Derrida uses the metaphor of the abyss to indicate the site of responsibility. I suggest that the radical reworking of this basic Levinasian term, finally described as metaphor, is highly pertinent to the Cambodian autogenocide:

> There could be, in effect, all sorts of proximity (where the crime is between people who know each other): language, neighborhood, familiarity, even family, etc. But in order for evil to emerge, "radical evil" and perhaps worse again, the unforgivable evil, the only one which would make the question of forgiveness emerge, it is necessary that at the most intimate of that intimacy an absolute hatred would come to interrupt the peace. This destructive hostility can only aim at what Levinas calls the "face" of the Other, the similar other, the closest neighbor, between the Bosnians and Serbs, for example, within the same quarter, the same house, sometimes in the same family. Must forgiveness saturate the abyss?[14]

Cambodian cinema's acknowledgment of the relationships within Cambodian society regarding perpetration (and collaboration), simultaneous with the impracticality of bringing to trial all Khmer Rouge cadres, generated two historically and ideologically interrelated phenomena, which are conspicuous in Rithy Panh's films that represent encounters with perpetrators: *S21: The Khmer Rouge Death Machine* (2003); *Duch, Master of the Forges of Hell* (2011); and *Graves without a Name* (2018). The first phenomenon is the transformation of the spectators' ethical consciousness by defying the twentieth-century legacy of reconciliation and forgiveness; the second is the presentation in the films of what I propose to call nonvindictive moral resentment,[15] following Holocaust survivor and writer Jean Améry's perspective in his collection of essays from 1966, *At the Mind's Limits: Contemplations by a Survivor on Auschwitz and Its Realities*.[16]

AMÉRY AND PANH

Améry and Panh share the subjective state of the victim in a world that is mostly dominated by those Améry calls "nonvictims," which I regard as the basis for their shared perspectives concerning reconciliation and forgiveness, exemplified particularly in Améry's essay "Resentments" and *Radical Humanism: Selected Essays*,[17] in Panh's films *Duch, Master of the Forges of Hell* and *Graves without a Name*,[18] and his memoir *The Elimination: A Survivor of the Khmer Rouge Confronts His Past and the Commandant of the Killing Fields*.[19] The affinity revealed in Améry's and Panh's creative works attests to Panh's perspective not only on survival but on society's deep obligation to its past.

The biographies of these two genocide survivors will help us understand their affinity: Rithy Panh was born in a suburb of Phnom Penh in 1962, one of nine children. His father, to whom he dedicates *Duch*, was heavily involved in governmental work, first as a schoolteacher and primary school inspector and then as a senator and an undersecretary at the Ministry of Education. In Panh's thirteenth year, on April 17, 1975, the Khmer Rouge entered the capital. His family, now labeled "New People," was deported to the northwest Cambodia countryside.[20] He was witness to the suffering and slow death of his parents, siblings, and other relatives from reeducation, overwork, disease, and famine. His father eventually refused to eat "anything that doesn't resemble food fit for human beings" and gradually stopped eating at all, until he too died.[21] Panh first worked in a number of labor camps and then was assigned to a hospital, where he worked as a cleaner and later a gravedigger in charge of burying the hospital's dead. In 1979, he escaped to the jungle and was able to reach a refugee camp at Mai Rut, Thailand. In Paris, he was reunited with two of his siblings, became interested in filmmaking, and graduated from the Institut des Hautes Etudes Cinématographiques (IDHEC, now La Fémis). His first documentary, *Site 2* (on Cambodian refugees), won several international awards. Since then, Panh's unique oeuvre has expanded to include both nonfiction and fiction films that for the most part deal with the traumatic history of the Khmer Rouge regime. He was central to founding the Bophana Audiovisual Resource Center in Phnom Penh. Known as a cinema activist, he has undertaken a number of postgenocide projects, perhaps the most important of which is the mentoring of the young generation of Cambodian filmmakers.

Hanns Chaim Mayer (later, Jean Améry) was born in Vienna, Austria, in 1912. His mother was Catholic and his father Jewish. After his father's death in action during World War I, his mother raised him as a Roman Catholic. After the March 1938 Anschluss, he fled first to France and then to Belgium with his Jewish wife. The Belgians initially deported him to France as a German foreigner, where he was interned at the Gurs camp in the south of the country. After escaping, he joined the Resistance in Belgium. In July 1943, the Gestapo arrested him for distributing anti-Nazi propaganda among the German occupation forces; he was first tortured and then sent to Auschwitz, but as a Jew and not a political prisoner. He endured a year in Auschwitz III, the Buna-Monowitz labor camp, working at hard labor: digging dirt, laying cables, lugging sacks of cement and iron crossbeams. He was evacuated first to Buchenwald and then to Bergen-Belsen ahead of the advancing Red Army and was liberated from Belsen in April 1945. After the war, to symbolize his dissociation from German culture and alliance with French culture, the former Hanns Mayer changed his name to Jean Améry. He lived in Brussels and worked as a culture journalist for German-language newspapers in Switzerland, refusing to publish in Germany or Austria until 1964, when he delivered a radio address on the intellectual in Auschwitz. This address became the opening essay in his collection, *Beyond Guilt and Atonement*, which was translated into English in 1966 as *At the Mind's Limits: Contemplations by a Survivor on Auschwitz and Its Realities*. He writes in the preface to the first edition of the book, "When the big Auschwitz trial began in Frankfurt in 1964, I wrote the first essay on my experiences in the Third Reich, after twenty years of silence."[22] As Myers claims, being "an autobiographical and philosophical essayist whose texts are notoriously intransigent—hard to categorize," and even harder to embrace, his challenge to a "fashionable victimhood"—Améry's principal contribution to understanding the Holocaust "is his concept of *losing trust in the world*. Starting with *At the Mind's Limits*, all of his books venture into the 'closed world' of suffering, declining to offer 'cheap consolation' or to find a redemptive message in suffering. His approach instead is unsparing, relentlessly bleak, 'disconsoling.'"[23] The novelty of this approach makes him one of the most highly regarded of Holocaust writers.

According to the Amérian experience, after a short postwar period in which he felt that Holocaust victims were listened to and respected in Germany and Europe, the politics of forgetting became so hegemonic that what he calls his "camp-self"/"victim-self" dominated the much-desired "survivor-self." When victimhood was again repressed politically, the camp-self, feeling loneliness and social isolation, came to the fore. In 1976, thirty-one years after the end of World War II (and a decade before the "Historians Debate" [*Historikerstreit*] broke out in Germany), Améry wrote: "Nothing has healed, and what perhaps was already on the point of healing in 1964 is bursting open again as an infected wound."[24]

At the heart of his thought, Améry stages the political conflict between collective progress and survivors' struggle with the past, between the victims' need for recognition and (both German and European) society's political urge to promote social stability through reconciliation—consequently, I maintain, in line with Jacques Derrida's contention that politics sabotages pure forgiveness, society's need to assure expected political transactions and financial gains.

The victims' immense sense of betrayal harbors Améry's resentment. However, this is neither the Nietzschean nor the Max Schelerian resentment/*ressentiment* embodying the mental attitude of the weak and powerless—the *schelechtwegekommene*—against their aristocratic masters.[25] Regardless of the differences between the conceptions of these two preeminent resentment/*ressentiment* writers, Nietzsche's influential view became paradigmatic in Western thought, claiming that because slaves cannot revolt openly against noble men, they try to discredit them and their achievements, leading to a falsification of all genuine sensations and compensating themselves indulgingly with an imaginary revenge. Opposing both Nietzsche's and Scheler's dominant conceptualizations, Améry's innovation lies in his definition of resentment not as an unconscious uncontrollable negative impulse of human nature, but as a highly self-conscious state of personal morality. Enabling an insightful introspection into the humanness of resentment, Améry repudiates Nietzsche for despising victims, whom he regards as weak, inferior, and cowardly, and instead elevates the dignity of the victim, having been forced by circumstances beyond their control. Moreover, Améry, in an exceedingly bold move, rejects the entire psychological-moralist tradition that follows the Nietzschean premise and which sees resentment as a kind of sickness that harms the "patient" while repressing its ethics.

This repression, I suggest, is still discerned in post-Amérian criticism by most scholars (such as Aleida Assmann, Arne Johan Vetlesen, Jeffrey K. Olick, Magdalena Zolkos, and Thomas Brudholm) unable to resist Améry's radicalism to the level of constituting a "reconcilable resentment."[26] However, a politically sanctioned program of forgiveness guided by commonality such as took place in the TRC (most famously, Archbishop Desmond Tutu's book *No Future without Forgiveness*) has not been realized in Cambodia. For the victims of violence and torture, the pressure to overcome, repress, or otherwise deny their identity, suggests Améry, is immoral.

Pointing to the irreconcilable conflict between victims' unreadiness to forget and forgive and a society's privileging of forgiveness, Améry raises a vital conceptualization of time, which, I suggest, is embodied in Panh's structuring of time sense as well:

> Natural consciousness of time actually is rooted in the physiological process of wound-healing and became part of the social conception of reality. But precisely for this reason it is not only extramoral, but also antimoral in character. Man has the right and the privilege to declare himself to be in disagreement with every natural occurrence, including the biological healing that time brings about. What happened, happened. This sentence is just as true as it is hostile to morals and intellect. The moral power to resist contains the protest, the revolt against reality, which is rational only as long as it is moral. The moral person demands annulment of time—in the particular case under question, by nailing the criminal to his deed.[27]

Assmann notes that for Améry, "The political rehabilitation of Germany is accompanied by a new sense of time, which Améry calls 'natural,' 'biological' or 'social' time, oriented towards forgetting. It is the time in which life goes on, wounds are healed and grass eventually covers everything. This shape of time enforces the law of life, not of truth. Its opposite is 'moral' time . . . where there can be . . . only a remorseless return to the crimes and the wish for their public acknowledgement."[28]

Reflecting on the affinity between Améry's polemical writing and Rithy Panh's polemical filmmaking and editing, I suggest that in Panh's films an Amérian-inspired unvindictive epistemology of moral resentment is embodied in a new cinematic rendering of time and temporality. As such, it is unique in world cinema. What Assmann calls "'moral' time . . . where there can be . . . only a remorseless return to the crimes" is, in fact, a reconstruction of the genocidal time and a remodeling of its dynamics. Based on an epistemic faith, it is not an act of turning back or a mere reversal but, I suggest, an act of "Being Then," in the past.[29]

In *Duch, Master of the Forges of Hell*, Panh uses three major strategies during his interview with Duch for a rearticulated understanding of the relationship between past, present, and future. Projecting resentment, these strategies construct the representation of the Cambodian past as a moral time for Duch. The first strategy is to demand that spectators reshape their conception of time by showing very short video clips or still photos from the Khmer Rouge past that are inserted into the interviewing process. Confronting Duch, these materials reveal his responses to be lies but also, and simultaneously, incessantly take the spectator back to the past. The representation of these materials does not last more than a few seconds; thus, for the spectators, they function as flickers of time consciousness, marking their difference from the conventional undemanding easiness of cinematic flashbacks. Flickering sometimes so quickly (for instance, a four-second shot of hands examining a button taken from a pile of dead prisoners' clothes), as if almost ungraspable, they are nevertheless engraved on the spectators' consciousness due to their contrasting content and the repetition of the technique.

His second strategy, meant to modify our perception of time as a major component of expressing moral resentment toward Cambodia's past, is the use of materials placed on a desk at the center of the mise-en-scène. These materials, consisting mostly of written documents and still photographs taken from S-21, the notorious torture and execution center Tuol Sleng, which Duch commanded, are orchestrated on Duch's desk such that at intervals some are more noticeable than others (figure 10.1). Through Duch's reading them, pointing at his signature, looking at them, and reflecting on them, he is returned again and again into the past. Since Duch had read these execution accounts while he was the director of S-21 and regarded them as true confessions, Panh's requirement that he reread them becomes a form of reenactment of Duch's deeds through the speech act. Duch rereads the documents, which attest to torture that he refuses to admit he took part in and are based on (false) self-incrimination he enforced

FIGURE 10.1. Duch returns to the records and to the past

on the prisoners. Thus, in an inverse move, his rereading becomes a substitute for his unperformed confession, for his obstinate refusal to acknowledge responsibility for his crimes. The rereading is also a substitute for—and ironically, also refutes—Duch's lies. In contrast to the bodily reenactments by camp guards in Panh's *S21: The Khmer Rouge Killing Machine*, Duch's rereading of these records is not performed automatically.[30] In further contrast to the guards, he is neither possessed by the past nor reliving it. On the contrary, his rereading is saturated with denial and negation, using Khmer Rouge rhetoric as a major tool of his determined confrontation with Panh. Thus, Panh's constant and relentless use of these materials has major significance in terms of the new epistemology. Whenever Duch refrains from looking, the camera's gaze forces the spectators to gaze at a document, Duch's signature, comments in red ink (like "Exterminate!"), or the expressions of the soon-to-be-dead-prisoners in the mug shots. As Panh writes: "Duch asks me why I'm always showing him photographs. 'What's the point?' he asks, in that tone of his. I answer, 'But the thing is . . . they're listening to you. Koy Thourn is here. Bophana's here. Taing Siv Leang too. I believe they're listening to you.'"[31]

The third strategy, which transforms the perception of time for both Duch and the spectator, is Panh's avoidance of appearing before the camera such that the conjuring act, which makes the dead play the Third, meaningful

Other during the interview, is at the center, while repeatedly reflecting on the "time of the dead."

The use of these strategies to build a polemical narrative through counterediting of course aims at refuting, contradicting, opposing, and disproving the perpetrator's lies. Its primary significance, however, lies in reconstructing the genocidal time into a form of resentment. In other words, *Duch, Master of the Forges of Hell* (and to a lesser degree Panh's earlier film *S21: The Khmer Rouge Death Machine*) constitutes an epistemology of moral resentment that demands an ethical response from both the perpetrator and the spectator. The spectator's embrace of moral resentment (especially if he or she is Cambodian) is, of course, totally different in scope and intensity of responsibility from that of Duch. The immediacy of Panh's cinema is realized in a call for intervention by taking the perpetrator back to the problematic points in the temporality he inhabits, disrupting a world that is unacquainted with the moral dimension of time. It is assumed, however, that the production of time that connects him or her again and again to the dead, the Third, is incessantly performed by both him (reluctantly) and the spectator (willingly).

I claim that Panh's concrete and constant battle with Duch is meant not only to overcome the perpetrator's psychological reactions, inner mind structures, propaganda techniques, explicit and implicit strategies, and dynamics of argumentations and language—all of which have been described by genocide scholars from Leo Kuper to Israel Charny and others—but also to embody resentment.[32] The film thus becomes a sort of absolute recording of this time and temporality, demanding the spectator's acknowledgment of moral resentment each time that it is screened/viewed. Panh's cinema becomes an index of this tie, forcing the spectator to experience the time of resentment, resisting the world of "nonvictims."

Panh, no less than Améry, proposes resentment as a radical conceptualization of survival morality based on a new relation to the past. Améry believes that time must be disordered to become moral: "I hope that my resentment—which is my personal protest against the antimoral natural process of healing that time brings about, and by which I make the genuinely humane and absurd demand that time be turned back—will also perform a historical function."[33] Thus, during the survivor-perpetrator encounter, Panh's resentment, I claim, has a threefold interrelated embodiment: as a constitution of the victim's position vis-à-vis the perpetrator; as an act of conjuring the dead, who are transformed into the meaningful Other; and as a reconstruction of the genocidal time and a remodeling of its dynamics.

It is not only the refusal of future reconciliation and the disordering of temporality in order to bring the perpetrator back to his past deeds that form the main component of Panh's ideology of resentment. Returning to the past as an act of resentment also means rupturing the moment of the everlasting Now that is rooted in denial. The Now in *Duch, Master of the Forges of Hell* is the time of denial realized as a continuous mindset of tactics and manipulations. After all, the "willing executioner" unfolds his denial of the past in the present; the "twilight state of knowing and not-knowing," as Stanley Cohen calls it,[34] happens in the present, while blocking out the past. In this regard, rupturing the attachment between denial and the Now as its dominant temporalization elevates resentment's value and makes it more coherent than Améry suggests: "Resentment is not only unnatural but also a logically inconsistent condition. It nails every one of us onto the cross of his ruined past. Absurdly, it demands that the irreversible be turned around, that the event be undone. Resentment blocks the exit to the genuine human dimension, the future. I know that the time-sense of the person trapped in resentment is twisted around, dis-ordered, if you wish, for it desires two impossible things: regression into the past and nullification of what happened."[35]

Panh's meticulous work of editing (combining insertions like still photographs, "flickering" short clips, and archival clips presented as videos) attests to his commitment to a moral regression to the past, creating a resentment that "blocks the exit to the genuine human dimension, the future . . . for this reason the man of resentment cannot join in the unisonous peace chorus all around him, which cheerfully proposes: not backward let us look but forward, to a better, common future!"[36] The belief in being somewhat fundamentally conditioned by the past, shared by Panh and Améry, stands in contrast to Duch's constant denials declared repetitively. His reaction to the proliferation of materials presented by Panh is revealed to be rooted in a total unacknowledgment that has characterized all the years Panh spent shooting the film. Thus, it is obvious that Panh refrains from anchoring the confrontation in the discourse of reconciliation, forgiveness, and similitude, and that his objection to this discourse is revealed through embracing the discourse of responsibility, accountability, justice, and difference as part of the Amérian philosophy of resentment. According to Panh's perpetrator documentary cinema, the perpetrator's story should be told in different terms than that of the survivor (or of the victim). In other words, the necropolitics of the Cambodian genocide are transformed through the perpetrator's perspective of time in which the perpetrator is called to imagine himself a member of a response-able community.

Unlike *Duch, Graves without a Name* is not based on a direct confrontation with perpetrators. Nevertheless, Panh's ethics of moral resentment, which calls for the spectator's engagement, is evidenced in the film's constant conjuring of the dead, the Third. Buddhist and shaman rituals, local-indigenous beliefs, and mediums' trances are called upon to assist the director in his spiritual journey through Cambodia's killing fields to discover the lost burial sites of his family. The poetic narration (written by Panh with Christophe Bataille) incessantly reflects on the boundaries of mourning, questioning the relationships between a mourning that is part of the killing site and mourning that is siteless, "disembodied." In this way, the repetitiousness of the conjuring rituals transforms the commentary texts from texts speaking about mourning to being "themselves texts *of* or *in* mourning."[37]

This necromantic embodying of the dead reflects as well on a unique form of mourning as described by Derrida in *The Work of Mourning,* in which he invokes "the unbearable paradox of fidelity" to the dead,[38] according to which the source of our responsibility is the impossibility of the interiorization of the dead, who is "living in me."[39] Thus, if the dead is revealed to us through his image, and the "image looks at us," "We are all looked at. . . . He looks at us. *In us.* He looks in us. And from now on more than ever."[40] In Derridean mourning, conceived as a healthy process of attachment to the dead (unlike Freudian-influenced schools), we honor the Otherness of the dead and our continuous engagement with them. This conception, which is dominant in Panh's position as a survivor who seeks his (and the spectators') attachment to the past, is elaborated on in Derrida's earlier work *The Gift of Death,* in which he argues that death is the place of one's irreplaceability and responsibility,[41] which in Levinasian terms is always oriented toward the Other. Keeping the singularity and the presence of the dead "in me," as Derrida conceives it, becomes, thus, the only way to mourn. The presence of Panh's body and voice (delivered by Panh's regular narrator Randal Douc) allows his voice to be that of the many dead whose mourning, which accentuates their presentness, becomes part of the new temporality.

The "meetings" with the spirits of the dead, mediated through various trances and voices, are juxtaposed with the accounts of two low-ranked perpetrators who still live in the village. While Panh's camera (he is a co-photographer with Prum Mesar) captures their bodily posture alongside a huge machete, they give accounts that validate major traumatic events of the genocide, some of which, vestiges of the KR regime, are still considered taboo in Cambodian society, such as the devastating hunger in the communes, the brutality of the Khmer Rouge cadres, forced marriages, rape, and cannibalism. Between the accounts, moral resentment is realized in symbolic imagery of the killing fields: a high-angle shot of dozens of ants eating the small baked sculptures that symbolize the dead, the naked bodies thrown into the killing fields (figure 10.2); similarly, a shot of a dry tree that resembles a human figure is shown left on the bank of a small, dry river, and the photos of Panh's family members are placed at their presumed burial sites. This imagery takes the spectator repetitively to the past, reflecting on both the Derridean "dead in me" and the unrepentant attitude of the perpetrators, at times referring to themselves as victims.

The commentary taken from Panh's *Elimination* as well as from the script of Alain Resnais's *Night and Fog* (1956), written by concentration camp survivor Jean Cayrol, finally constructs the mourning as a form of moral resentment. In this regard, *Graves* follows Panh's *The Missing Picture* (2013), a film that represents his autobiography, in which he says that mourning is impossible: this is embodied in the repeated image of the figurine representing his father being

FIGURE 10.2. Ants eating the sculptures of the dead

buried, though after each burial his head remains uncovered. This repetitiveness of the "time of the dead" as a reflection of moral resentment is realized in the commentary and imagery of *Graves*.

In Rithy Panh's perpetrator cinema, resentment transcends its earlier philosophical definitions as an embodiment of a damaged morality and—based on the survivors' reclaiming their subjectivity vis-à-vis the perpetrators'—becomes a major perspective for addressing the Cambodian genocide. Under the specific uniqueness of the Cambodian autogenocide, in which the Khmer Rouge murdered their own people, and under the cinematic-cultural phenomenon of post–Khmer Rouge perpetrator cinema, Panh's perpetrator cinema stresses the unvindictive resentment as unavoidable, crucial, epistemology.

In his memoir, Rithy Panh says: "I think about those four years, which aren't a nightmare, which are neither dream nor nightmare, even though I still have plenty of nightmares. Let's call it a complicated chapter in my life. And one which I'll never forgive. For me, forgiveness is something very private. Only politicians arrogate to themselves the right to grant reprieves or pardons in the name of all—a right unimaginable when mass crimes or genocides are concerned. I don't believe in reconciliation by decree. And whatever's too quickly resolved scares me. It's peace of soul that brings about reconciliation and not the reverse."[42] This new approach, which I call "moral resentment," has implications for cinema's ability to forge nonhegemonic and nonconsensual ethics. I suggest delaying what is considered an urgent need for prevention in favor of the ethics embodied in moral resentment that puts forth both the survivors and the victims, the dead. Rithy Panh's moral resentment becomes, thus, a way to distinguish how evil might be experienced, symbolized, judged, and finally incorporated into a system of ethics.[43]

NOTES

1. This scholarship includes Ervin Staub, "Genocide and Mass Killing: Origins, Prevention, Healing and Reconciliation," *Political Psychology* 21, no. 2 (2000): 367–382; John Borneman, "Reconciliation after Ethnic Cleansing: Listening, Retribution, Affiliation," *Public Culture* 14, no. 2 (2002): 281–304; Ernesto Verdeja, "Derrida and the Impossibility of Forgiveness," *Contemporary Political Theory* 3, no. 1 (2004): 23–47; Damien Short, "Reconciliation and the Problem of Internal Colonialism," *Journal of Intercultural Studies* 26, no. 3 (2005): 267–282; Andrew Schaap, "Reconciliation as Ideology and Politics," *Constellations* 15, no. 3 (2008): 249–264; Jens Meierhenrich, "Varieties of Reconciliation," *Law and Social Inquiry* 33, no. 1 (2008): 195–231; Jeffrey K. Olick, "Time for Forgiveness: A Historical Perspective," in *Considering Forgiveness*, ed. Aleksandra Wagner with Carin Kuoni and Matthew Buckingham (New York: Vera List Center for Art and Politics, 2009), 85–92; Ann Rigney, "Reconciliation and Remembering: (How) Does it Work?," *Memory Studies* 5, no. 3 (2012): 251–258; and Eve Monique Zucker, "Trauma and Its Aftermath: Local Configurations of Reconciliation in Cambodia and the Khmer Rouge Tribunal," *Journal of Asian Studies* 72, no. 4 (2013): 793–800. The TRC was established in South Africa in 1995 and began its work in 1996. It continued through 1998 and then was extended until 2002. The complete name for the ECCC is the Extraordinary Chambers in the Courts of Cambodia for the Prosecution of Crimes Committed during the Period of Democratic Kampuchea.
2. Jacques Derrida, "On Forgiveness," in *On Cosmopolitanism and Forgiveness*, trans. Mark Dooley and Michael Hughes (New York: Routledge, 2001), 29.
3. Hannah Arendt, *The Human Condition*, 2nd ed. (Chicago: University of Chicago Press, 1998).
4. Derrida, "On Forgiveness," 32–33.
5. Derrida, 31–32 (emphasis in the original).
6. Derrida, 39.
7. Derrida, 35–36.
8. Derrida, 28 (emphasis in the original).
9. Derrida, 30.
10. Derrida, 42.
11. Derrida, 44.
12. The Third is the dead, the meaningful Other.
13. Derrida, 52 (emphasis in the original).

14. Derrida, 49–50. See Verdeja's critique of Derrida in "Derrida and the Impossibility of Forgiveness."

15. Much of the scholarly work on Cambodian cinema and Rithy Panh's cinema deals with questions of reconciliation and healing. See recent essays by, e.g., Annette Hamilton, "Witness and Recuperation: Cambodia's New Documentary Cinema," *Concentric: Literary and Cultural Studies* 39, no. 1 (2013): 7–30; Leshu Torchin, "Mediation and Remediation: La parole filmée in Rithy Panh's *The Missing Picture* (*L'image manquante*)," *Film Quarterly* 68, no. 1 (2014): 32–41; and Vicente Sánchez-Biosca, "Challenging Old and New Images Representing the Cambodian Genocide: *The Missing Picture* (Rithy Panh, 2013)," *Genocide Studies and Prevention: An International Journal* 12, no. 2 (2018): 140–164.

16. Jean Améry, *At the Mind's Limits: Contemplations by a Survivor on Auschwitz and Its Realities*, trans. Sidney Rosenfeld and Stella P. Rosenfeld (Bloomington: Indiana University Press, 1980).

17. Améry, 62–81; Jean Améry, *Radical Humanism: Selected Essays*, ed. and trans. Sidney Rosenfeld and Stella P. Rosenfeld (Bloomington: Indiana University Press, 1984).

18. Kaing Guek Eav, nicknamed Duch, was the first Khmer Rouge leader to be tried by the ECCC. He was convicted of crimes against humanity, murder, and torture and sentenced to thirty years' imprisonment. On February 2, 2012, the ECCC extended his sentence to life imprisonment. He died on September 2, 2020.

19. Rithy Panh with Christophe Bataille, *The Elimination: A Survivor of the Khmer Rouge Confronts His Past and the Commandant of the Killing Fields*, trans. John Cullen (New York: Other Press, 2013).

20. "New People" was the Khmer Rouge term describing the new class of civilian Cambodians, including anyone from an urban area and thus corrupted by Western ideas, in contrast to the privileged class of peasants from rural areas, the Old People (Base/Ancient People).

21. Panh, *The Elimination*, 97.

22. Améry, *At the Mind's Limits*, xxiii.

23. See David Myers, "Jean Améry: A Biographical Introduction," in *Holocaust Literature: An Encyclopedia of Writers and Their Work*, ed. S. Lillian Kremer (New York: Routledge, 2002), 24. During his lifetime, Améry published more than twenty works and novels. On October 17, 1978, he took his own life and was subsequently buried in Vienna.

24. Améry, *At the Mind's Limits*, xxi.

25. Friedrich Wilhelm Nietzsche, *On the Genealogy of Morals*, trans. Douglas Smith (New York: Oxford University Press, 2009); Max Scheler, *Ressentiment*, trans. Lewis B. Coser and William W. Holdheim (Milwaukee: Marquette University Press, 2010). *Ressentiment* is the French word for "resentment" (from the Latin intensive prefix *re*, and *sentir*, "to feel"—*resentir* means "to re-sent," to feel again). Manfred S. Frings says that "the French word possesses a peculiar strong nuance of a lingering hate that our English word 'resentment' does not always carry." See, "Introduction," in Scheler, *Ressentiment*, 4.

26. Aleida Assmann, "Two Forms of Resentment: Jean Améry, Martin Walser and German Memorial Culture," *New German Critique* 90 (Autumn 2003): 123–133; Arne Johan Vetlesen, "A Case for Resentment: Jean Améry versus Primo Levi," *Journal of Human Rights* 5 (2006): 27–44; Jeffrey K. Olick, "From Theodicy to *Ressentiment*: Trauma and the Ages of Compensation," in *The Politics of Regret: On Collective Memory and Historical Responsibility* (New York: Routledge, 2007), 153–173; Magdalena Zolkos, "Jean Améry's Concept of Resentment at the Crossroads of Ethics and Politics," *European Legacy* 12, no. 1 (2007): 23–38; Thomas Brudholm, *Resentment's Virtue: Jean Améry and the Refusal to Forgive* (Philadelphia: Temple University Press, 2008).

27. Améry, *At the Mind's Limits*, 72.

28. Assmann, "Two Forms of Resentment," 124–125.
29. In the opening scene of Panh's *Exile* (2016), an extreme close-up of the director's eyes reveals that the Khmer Rouge propagandistic image of hundreds of women carrying baskets full of sand is engraved onto his eyes, and—shown twice—looks as if it is part of the vitreous.
30. See Deirdre Boyle, "Trauma, Memory, Documentary: Re-enactment in Two Films by Rithy Panh (Cambodia) and Garin Nugroho (Indonesia)," in *Documentary Testimonies: Archives of Suffering*, ed. Janet Walker and Bhaskar Sarkar (New York: Routledge, 2010), 155–172.
31. Panh, *The Elimination*, 261. For a closer stylistic reading of the role of the photograph of the victim in Duch's evasiveness, see Vicente Sánchez-Biosca's chapter in this volume.
32. Leo Kuper, *The Prevention of Genocide* (New Haven, CT: Yale University Press, 1985); Israel W. Charny, "A Classification of Denials of the Holocaust and Other Genocides," in *The Genocide Studies Reader*, ed. Samuel Totten and Paul R. Bartrop (New York: Routledge, 2009), 518–537.
33. Améry, *At the Mind's Limits*, 77.
34. Stanley Cohen, *States of Denial: Knowing about Atrocities and Suffering* (Cambridge, UK: Polity Press, 2001), 80.
35. Améry, *At the Mind's Limits*, 68.
36. Améry, 68–69.
37. See Pascale-Anne Brault and Michael Naas, "To Reckon with the Dead: Jacques Derrida's Politics of Mourning," in Jacques Derrida, *The Work of Mourning*, ed. and trans. Pascale-Anne Brault and Michael Naas (Chicago: University of Chicago Press, 2001), 3 (emphasis in the original).
38. Necromancy is a practice of magic involving communication with the dead. Derrida, *The Work of Mourning*, 159.
39. Derrida, 42.
40. Derrida, 160 (emphasis in the original).
41. Jacques Derrida, *The Gift of Death*, trans. David Wills (Chicago: University of Chicago Press, 1995), 41.
42. Panh, *The Elimination*, 245–246.
43. See my book, Raya Morag, *Perpetrator Cinema Confronting Genocide in Cambodian Documentary* (New York: Columbia University Press, 2020).

PART 4 MEMORY, VOICE, AND CINEMATIC PRACTICE

11 • LOOKING BACK AND PROJECTING FORWARD FROM *SITE 2*

LINDSAY FRENCH

Rithy Panh's work famously includes documentary, fiction film, animation, historical essay, and autobiography, as well as artistic collaborations with painters, musicians, choreographers, writers, and other filmmakers and the establishment of an important center for archiving, teaching, and learning about film for a new generation of film professionals in Phnom Penh. Many have commented that Panh's work constitutes an extended exploration of the fact and experience of genocide in Cambodia, in different artistic modes. Longtime collaborators have said that working with Rithy Panh is like working on one continuous film.[1]

Site 2 (1989), Panh's first feature-length film, is a documentary about one of several refugee camps still operating in the late 1980s on the Thai-Cambodian border, an ongoing legacy of the Khmer Rouge revolution that, ten years after its technical demise, was still playing out in a protracted guerrilla war along the border. *Site 2* was shot less than ten years after Panh himself had passed through some much grimmer camps on his way to resettlement in France, having lost his parents, several siblings, and numerous in-laws, nieces, and nephews to starvation and brutality under the Khmer Rouge. Panh, born in 1964, was eleven when the Khmer Rouge took over his country, fifteen when the Khmer Rouge were overthrown by the Vietnamese army, sixteen when he got to France, and twenty-four when he graduated from the prestigious Institute des Hautes Etudes Cinématographiques (IDHEC, La Fémis). That same year he returned to the border camps to make his first feature film. He had yet to return to Cambodia.

Panh writes at the end of his autobiographical book *The Elimination*, "I've evoked the world of yesterday so that the bad part of it may not come back again. . . . As for the good part of that former world . . . , that part can't be erased. It's not a bygone day, it's an effort and a work in progress; it's the human world."[2]

This essay looks back at *Site 2* as the first step in Rithy Panh's ongoing, immensely rich and varied "work in progress" to understand the destruction in his past and his efforts to continue to make and remake the human world. It considers who Panh was when he made his first film, and what complex issues faced the Cambodian people in general at that time. It looks at the cinematic choices he made (among those that were open to him) filming in Site 2 and the concerns that animate this documentary. And it projects forward into his evolving filmography, in light of the constantly changing political situation in Cambodia and an evolving collective process of coming to terms with such a violent history. It is informed by my own ethnographic work of more than twenty months in Site 2, beginning just as Panh's film was being completed, and an ongoing ethnographic project in Cambodia since then. *Site 2* began an exploration in film for Panh that continued over the next thirty years and is continuing today.

DOCUMENTING "LIFE AS IT IS" IN SITE 2

Site 2 was filmed when Rithy Panh was twenty-four, just barely out of film school, returning to a fraught period in his own life, without a framework yet for understanding what had happened to him. It was also his first encounter with an entire population of people like himself, who had managed to survive the Khmer Rouge revolution but were struggling with the memory of it, albeit under very different circumstances than he, who had spent the previous ten years in France largely alone with his memories and his loss. In Site 2 he found 180,000 people who had lived through similar experiences but had spent the years since 1979 (or some significant part of them) stuck in the miserable limbo of a series of refugee camps in Cambodia and Thailand, struggling to maintain their humanity in the midst of an ongoing, dehumanizing situation.

As Panh writes in "La parole filmée: Pour vaincre la terreur" ("Filmed speech: To vanquish terror"): "At that time people were only talking about the Khmer Rouge guerrillas and the occupying Vietnamese. People spoke of the political and military situation, of war and peace, but never about the everyday life of the displaced populations. Nobody talked about the kids who had never seen rice fields, who did not know where rice came from. In Site 2, children under ten years old only knew barbed wire, and thought that rice came from trucks."[3] Panh was not especially interested in political talk at this time. He was interested in the experiences of people living in Site 2, and in their thoughts and memories.

With only a three-day pass from the Thai military, which controlled access to and egress from Site 2, Panh did not have a lot of time to find a story in this sprawling bamboo and thatch slum located in a corner of Thai territory where nobody else wanted to live. He spent the first two days immersing himself in the life of the camp; he did not shoot. On the third day, walking door to door in the residential sections looking for a character ("un personage"), he found Yim Om. She was asleep; he woke her up. But very quickly there grew a sympathetic rapport between the two of them, as she began to recount her life story. She made a profound impression on Panh, and with her permission he began to film her. (These first images of Yim Om, when she had just met Panh, constitute the opening sequence of the film.) Panh went back to the Thai military and secured two more weeks in the camp for his small French film crew, which he used to follow Yim Om through her days, recording her speaking about her life and shooting at close range the motions of her daily living: cooking, cleaning, and keeping her small bamboo and thatch house organized, feeding her family, bathing at the back of her house by the water jar, rushing to collect water daily and rice and fish in the weekly distributions, trading extra rations in the market for vegetables and clothes for her five children, and, importantly, remembering her past.

I have spent some time trying to imagine what it might have been like for Rithy Panh to enter Site 2 in 1988 with the goal of making a documentary film about it. I was working in Site 2 myself right after Panh made his film, doing ethnographic research for a doctoral dissertation in social anthropology. In a very basic way, I was trying to do something similar to Panh: to understand how people were living their postholocaust lives in this camp, to come up with a framework that would enable me to represent this powerfully to others. What Panh presents in *Site 2* is familiar to me, and yet his focus and his emphasis were very different from mine. I was trying to understand the international politics of the border camps, and the local politics and social organization within the camp itself—because this helped me to understand the circumstances within which people experienced and understood their lives in Site 2. I was writing for a Western academic audience that, for the most part, had no idea why a camp like this existed, why an enormous population of Cambodians had become, essentially, hostages to a complicated international political and military impasse. I wanted to understand what it was like to survive the Khmer Rouge genocide and be stuck ten years later in this camp under these circumstances. I called this the political economy of experience in Site 2 in my dissertation.[4]

What Panh focused on, however, was something much more personal, primal, and inchoate: the embodied experience of Cambodian survivors living in the camp, and one woman's reflections on this. What must this experience have been like for him, encountering for the first time a whole population of Cambodians struggling as he was with their memories of the past? As he recounts in the autobiographical portions of *The Elimination*, although he was living with family members in France, they had not spent the previous decade in Cambodia, and he had kept his memories of the 1970s to himself. He was struggling to make his way as a teenager in a new language and found few opportunities to address his memories directly. An early encounter with a bully showed him how much violence he was capable of when his sense of self was pushed to the limits, an unbidden but explosive response to the violence he had internalized in the 1970s. He took up drawing and painting, then ventured into woodworking. It seems clear he was searching for a means of artistic expression. He believed deeply in the power of images, but words seemed too important to exclude. Ultimately, he chose film as his medium in art school because, as he wrote, it "shows the world, presents beauty, but also deals in words." And, he figured, it kept his fists in his pockets.[5]

Rithy Panh wrote later that the goal of the documentary atelier he developed in Phnom Penh in the 1990s was to look at Cambodia "as it is today," that is, right then. He was determined to create such an atelier when he returned to Cambodia a year after *Site 2* was released, which he did in part by working to train a new generation of film professionals and establishing Bophana, an important audiovisual resource center for film students and others, in 2006. But this atelier did not exist when he arrived at Site 2 in 1988; he was on his own with his experiences, his feelings, and his newly minted university training in film. His work with Yim Om in Site 2 can be seen as a first pass at that effort to document life "as it is."[6]

"LIFE AND MEMORY": EMBODIED EXPERIENCE

Yim Om's words and Rithy Panh's camera attend to the details of her daily life in Site 2: the spaces and places in her house; the few objects there, and how she acquired and used them; how she and her daughter worked around each other in that small space to kindle a fire in the stove and prepare a meal; how she used her own bucket shower to bathe one of her small children as well. He shows the humiliation of squatting in a long line at the distribution field waiting to receive her family's weekly ration of rice and dry, salty fish. He records the loud music playing at the distribution field, which reminded him of the music the Khmer Rouge played when they took people away to be executed.

Panh writes about how he filmed in Site 2: "I very much insisted on everyday life, and the reality of the camp from day to day. . . . I wanted to register the details, the everyday gestures, all the little resistances without which a human being becomes an animal in a cage—because that is what life in a refugee camp is."[7] Yim Om confirms this animal imagery in the film, saying, "Our life is without effect, like a crab at the bottom of his hole. We are stuck here, we can't dig any further. This is the end."[8] People said similar things to me in Site 2: "I feel like a frog in a well here." Or: "We have lived in this camp in the forest so long we have become monkeys." Or: "We are like a dog that has been chained for so long it becomes mean and vicious, and finally begins to bite people. Like the dog, a man becomes mean, almost crazy from being in this camp too long."

What I did not see, though, was the way the routines and gestures of daily life could constitute a bulwark against total despair, a determination to remain human. Perhaps this was visible to Panh from his own experience, watching his mother struggle to hold together her family as his father, several siblings, a niece, and a nephew died one by one under the Khmer Rouge: feeding her children what she could, refusing to weep when his father died, refusing to break down or give in to the dehumanization.[9] Panh writes:

> I like very much when we see [Yim Om] sweeping, and also the moment when she shows how she attaches a mosquito net over the bed, and when she says, "my rice I put here, and there the salt. . . ." Her resistance is in these daily gestures. . . . [Yim Om] seemed to say, "In spite of everything, I have a place to sleep, I have a place to eat, even if it is far from my homeland." It is not human to park people in such a crowded, miserable place, where they cannot budge. . . . She showed these conditions in the smallest details—there wasn't even enough space to dig a new latrine.
>
> Her recitation is a political act. She has no need to accuse anyone—not the U.N., not the Thais, not the different Khmer factions fighting with one another. She doesn't denounce anybody. Simply, she shows how she has protected her personality and her dignity in spite of all she was submitting to.[10]

What Yim Om was submitting to was "the grand administrative machinery of the U.N.,"[11] the humiliation of the distributions, the meagerness of her confined existence, the demoralization of dependence. And the endlessness of this situation. As Panh writes, this was very difficult for Cambodian peasants who are proud, dignified people and know how to take care of themselves.[12] I understood this from the way people talked to me about their lives before the Khmer Rouge revolution and how they spoke about their life in the camp. Panh understood it and expressed it through peoples' bodily gestures.

Rithy Panh wrote later that in his documentary practice in Cambodia he focuses on daily life and memory, on "la vie et la mémoire."[13] Memories of the past were a constant part of Yim Om's days and nights. Her dreams of the past were as real to her as her waking life in the camp. She says, "Only my body is here. My thoughts and my heart are in my country." She dreams of a time before the Khmer Rouge controlled Cambodia, which makes her homesick and sad: "I dreamed I was in my village in the big house where I lived with my parents. I saw all my belongings: hundreds of sacks of rice. I had clothes, and money to spend. I saw my mother and father and myself as I used to be. Then I woke up and found myself here, and I wanted to cry."[14]

Yim Om talks about how her family were forced from their village as early as 1970 by the Khmer Rouge; about how their village was "liberated" by the Khmer Rouge, and they were forced to work collectively; about how her father was killed *before* 1975, and her two brothers later. She talks about the decision to flee to the border when "everything was confused," and the many camps that she and her family moved between as each one came under attack; she talks about the death of a small son in one of these camps, run over by a truck. She does not speak directly about Pol Pot time, the worst period between 1975 and 1979, or if she did, Panh chose not to include this in his film. He focuses on her nostalgia for her life before the war and her accounts of the difficulty of life on the border.

And yet, the effects of these unspoken memories on survivors are exactly what Rithy Panh was interested in, what he could immediately connect to and I could not. He wrote that his efforts to set up a documentary atelier after *Site 2* was released were shaped by the desire to address these memories: "In Cambodia, memory has been profoundly destroyed. Beyond the massacres and the suffering, the Khmer Rouge have put in place a machine for effacing memory, a machine of total delirium. . . . We, who have survived that period, and the youth who came after, have no more memory."[15] Panh was committed to recovering memories of the past, both the good and the bad, and understanding their effects on the present. This effort, it seems, began with Yim Om.

About documentary film, Panh writes, "I do not believe in naturalism. . . . I try instead to give a sense of the facts. The evident phenomena certainly, but I dig until I find a situation that I did not know about, that provides a new clarity to things."[16] For Panh in 1988, Yim Om provided that clarity about Site 2. He does not give us an overview or *explain* what is going on in Site 2 (that is what I was trying to do); he simply shows us Site 2 through the daily repetitions and especially the words of one very depressed Khmer woman. Yim Om is not "representative"; she seemed to me almost catatonic in her lack of expression, and not typical of the women in Site 2, or those I got to know anyway. But Panh takes us deep into her experience, showing us the numbing repetition of her days, the intrusion of her memories, and her inability to dig herself out of the hole of her depression.

Site 2 feels longer than its eighty-six minutes. It is repetitive. The camera takes its time. The shots are long, and the camera remains on people for several seconds after they have stopped speaking. Yim Om, from whom we hear the most, speaks with very little expression and rarely smiles. At a certain point her commentary begins to seem like an endless litany of complaints. I remember this from Site 2. Eventually I came to understand that these "complaints" were one way people could tell me, "I am not the person you see before you. I would not be living this way if I did not have to be. I worked in Cambodia, I cared for my family, I went to the temple, I respected the monks. I do not accept the way I am forced to live here."

But also, it seems to me these editing choices may have been one way to reinforce the viewer's understanding of the demoralizing and deadening effect of living in such a miserable place for so long, with no way of knowing when it all would be over and little hope that it ever would be. As one community leader said to me in Site 2: "Nothing changes. Ten years in the same place, the same situation: same, same, same! People have no spirit left. They begin to despair." In a small way, Rithy Panh forces us to recognize this through our own experience of the film.

SITUATED PERSPECTIVES

Some of the most despairing monologues in *Site 2* are followed by scenes of children in the camp: usually boys (the girls typically had domestic chores) pitching pebbles, swimming in the reservoir, making and flying kites. Panh shows us kids lining up for school and reciting their lessons in unison, girls on one side of the room and boys on the other. And we see a dynamic teacher working to engage his class. People often said to me, as Yim Om said, "I have no hope for my life now, I think only about the future for my kids." Yim Om made sure her children went to school and studied at night, in spite of the constant interruptions in their education: "I can't give them land or money, but I push them to study. This will be their wealth." Panh too seemed fascinated by these children and their irrepressible energy. The scene in which a group of boys prance about in the costume of an elephant they have fashioned out of a plastic sheet is one of the truly delightful and happy scenes in the film. I see this as a kind of acknowledgment of the damage suffered by those who lived through Pol Pot time and a desire to focus on the children who, although they will eventually bear different burdens, do not carry this particular scar. Rithy Panh was certainly aware of the difference between these children and the children who had lived through the Pol Pot years, like himself.

We also see poor children who do not go to school, who spend their days collecting and washing discarded plastic bags to sell for a few Thai baht. Projecting forward, they remind us of scenes of trash pickers on the outskirts of Phnom Penh that Rithy Panh films in *The Burnt Theatre* (2005). These are children whose parents cannot support them or who have no parents at all, and learn to take care of themselves at too young an age. In some ways they are analogous to the children who grew up under the Khmer Rouge regime, having to fend for themselves.

Site 2 does not explore differences in wealth within the camp, but it is clear they exist. Yim Om mentions this herself when she says, "Rich people have relatives abroad who send them money. The rich are very rich, and can eat what they want. The poor can barely survive on the rations provided." In fact, Yim Om's family, while not rich, were among the relatively privileged. Her husband worked for the Khmer administration in the camp, in the Agriculture Department. This gave him extra rations, the opportunity to do agricultural work that he knew and loved, and no doubt gave him access to some fresh vegetables.[17] They lived in the center of camp on a well-swept street, which, although crowded, was preferable to living at the edge of the camp, where the houses were much more vulnerable to theft.

It took me some time to recognize differences of wealth and status in Site 2, and these differences would not be obvious to the ordinary viewer, although Panh would have understood them immediately. But this was not his focus in the film. His establishing shots do not dwell on these distinctions: between people relaxing at the reservoir and walking along the dike, and those leaving and returning to camps with loads of firewood on their shoulders, for example. (Only the poorest risked the danger of land mines to forage for wood outside the camp.) Instead, he shows us the distributions, in which everyone participates, the women leaving with heavy loads on their heads. He shows us the Thai market in the center of the camp, and the smaller Khmer markets in the sections. He provides several long tracking shots from a main access road looking across a ditch into the residential sections. In general, these scenes all seem equally miserable.

It *was* striking to me that Panh managed not to show any images of the United Nations or nongovernmental organization (NGO) presence in the camp, however. (The one exception is on International Human Rights Day, when we hear a voice in English announcing the presence of a "strong and patient" elephant, the day's mascot, and see the U.N. logo on the banner on the elephant's back as it walks slowly through a crowd of people.)[18] The U.N. and NGOs provided the resources through which the camp operated, and we are shown some of the effects of their presence in the film at the distribution fields. But we do not see their large offices or the agency trucks emblazoned with logos, nor do we see any of the small army of international staff that was in the camp six days a week, working in schools, hospitals, and distributions and on the camp infrastructure.[19]

In part this is because most of the international activity was focused along the main roads of the camp accessible by trucks, while most Cambodian activity took place in the residential sections where the roads were narrow and trucks could not travel. This is where Panh did much of his shooting. But, beyond that, in this camp of 180,000, the 200 foreigners were scarcely visible to the inhabitants, most of whom had little or no contact with us. The machinery of the U.N. administration was significant; individually we were not. With a few exceptions, we had virtually nothing to do with their experience, and the experience of living in the camp was the focus of the film.

We do hear several comments in the film about UNBRO (the U.N. structure created to provide assistance to the camp): the fact that international staff left the camp at the first sign of danger, and did not stay overnight, which was the most dangerous time. This was true; it was the result of a complicated arrangement between the U.N., the Thai government, and the Khmer leadership in the camp that restricted the international presence to daylight hours and required international staff to leave if there was any serious danger. Site 2 functioned as the civilian base for an armed political faction that was fighting with Thailand's support against the Vietnamese-backed army of the Cambodian government. The very existence of this and other U.N.-supported "refugee" camps on Thai soil was contingent upon maintaining this arrangement: the U.N. would not interfere with interactions between the civilian and military leadership of the population as long as it took place out of sight, after the U.N. representatives had left the camp.[20] Thus Site 2 was controlled by civilians during the day, and by the military at night. And the U.N. was responsible for the safety of its own staff first.

For me, the most powerful scene in *Site 2* was the final one, shot at night, in the dark; the camera moves through a residential section. Figures seated outside their houses materialize in the gloom and eye the camera warily. Children dart into the frame and run ahead into the dark. A solitary young woman appears standing beside her doorway, dressed in a white blouse and sarong; probably a prostitute. There is an overwhelming sense of foreboding, to which the music contributes. This scene feels completely different from the rest of the film, which was shot entirely in the daytime.

Nighttime *was* the most dangerous time in Site 2, when the international staff were gone and soldiers, both Khmer and Thai, were in control of the camp. In this city of 180,000 there was no electrical power, and the nights were dark and threatening. This was when the guerrilla soldiers recruited from this population came into Site 2 to visit their families, to drink and carouse. Weapons were abundant, and robberies were common, as was abuse by the Thai guards.

Perhaps this scene struck me so powerfully because it resonated strongly with one of my own most memorable experiences in the camp. After months of lobbying U.N. security, I was finally granted permission to spend one night in Site 2 with an UNBRO protection officer, the sole international staff allowed to remain in camp overnight. In theory he was patrolling the camp in a truck and checking in at the hospitals and police headquarters. Mainly he stayed tuned to his radio handset, with which he could communicate with the hospitals, the Thai guards, and UNBRO offices outside the camp.

In our hour-long drive around the camp that night, we encountered frightened-looking Khmer police guarding the perimeter of residential sections with small bonfires, Thai guards bristling with weapons patrolling the camp in their own truck, and an emergency in one of the hospitals: a family walking into the camp that night from Cambodia had encountered a land mine, and the foot of a young girl had been blown off. This one night in the camp made abundantly clear what was not always obvious during the day: Site 2 was a dangerous place to live. The final shot of *Site 2*, looking into an all-enveloping darkness, suggests that this darkness could simply go on and on.

It did not, though. Two years after *Site 2* was released, a political agreement was reached between all the interested parties, the guerrilla war ended, and the residents of Site 2 were repatriated to Cambodia to participate in a U.N.-monitored election between the four previously warring factions. By the time I left Site 2 in 1991, people were making plans to go home. But in 1988, when Rithy Panh was filming, there was no light at the end of the tunnel.

HISTORY, MEMORY: WORK IN PROGRESS

This is a reminder that each of Rithy Panh's films has been made at a particular moment in Cambodia's recent and rapidly evolving history, and a particular moment in his own evolving understanding of that history. We can follow his filmography as a record of the issues facing Cambodians at the time the films were made, and of his own exploration of the effects of genocide on the population over time. They also record his developing talent as a filmmaker. *Site 2* was his first effort, in 1988, when it was not possible to film in Cambodia. The border camp was as close as he could get.

Later films address the fraught political climate at the time of the first national election (*Cambodia, Between War and Peace*, 1991); Cambodia's acceleration into the globalized world of the twenty-first century, even as most of the population remained embedded in very local poverty (*The Land of the Wandering Souls*, 2000); and memories embedded in the archives at S-21, the Khmer Rouge central detention and torture center, and in the bodies of the guards who worked there (*Bophana: A Cambodian Tragedy*, 1996; *S21: The Khmer Rouge Killing Machine*, 2003). Panh explores growing urban poverty in *Paper Cannot Wrap Ember* (2007) and takes a deep dive into the mind of an executioner at the time of the Khmer Rouge Tribunal. This resulted in both *Duch, Master of the Forges of Hell* (2011) and *The Elimination* (2012 for the original French version; 2013 for the English translation), his written reflection on this experience. Eventually he focuses his camera directly on his own experiences, in the innovative and affecting *The Missing Picture* (2013) and *Graves without a Name* (2018), his most personal and intimate film to date. Interspersed with these documentaries are essay films and fictional dramas that explore aspects of Cambodia's history, both recent and colonial.

Panh has said that documentary demands accountability to the facts, but fiction gives him greater freedom to express his own opinions.[21] So it is striking that his next major film after *Site 2*, *Rice People* (1994), an adaptation of a Malaysian novel that he sets in Cambodia, portrays a rural farming family in the aftermath of the Khmer Rouge genocide, struggling with poverty and misfortune. The main character, a rice farmer whom he calls Yim Om, ultimately loses her mind when her husband dies of infection from a snakebite. Clearly the real Yim Om had stayed with him.

It would be hard to say that *Site 2* contains the germ of all that came after. We can say that this project was the beginning of a deep personal engagement with *specific* Cambodian experiences. Rithy Panh's focus on memory, the erasure of memory under the Khmer Rouge, and the recovery of memory as a means of understanding the past and one's place in it in the present is a project that has informed all the films and artistic collaborations that have followed. Panh's work over the last thirty years takes us through increasingly sophisticated artistic and cinematic renderings of a profoundly disturbing period of history. It is a personal undertaking to remember, think about, and try to understand his own experiences of genocide through art.

But it also participates in and helps to facilitate a collective process of digging, discovering, questioning, remembering, reenacting, contemplating together with others, and working to develop a shared understanding of that history. Panh has an obsession with learning, with knowing, with understanding what fueled the cruelty of the Khmer Rouge, and how this has shaped the experiences of Cambodians since that time. As he writes in his autobiographical book, this requires work: "the work of research, of understanding, of explication. This isn't some sad obsession; it is a struggle against elimination."[22] In what is now once again a one-party state, where the prime minister (in office since 1986) is a former Khmer Rouge cadre who does not hesitate to threaten violence, and free expression is by no means guaranteed, this takes a great deal of courage as well as tremendous artistic talent.[23]

NOTES

1. Rithy Panh, "Confronting Images of Ideology: An Interview with Rithy Panh," interview by Deirdre Boyle, *Cineaste* 39, no. 3 (2014): 34.
2. Rithy Panh with Christophe Bataille, *The Elimination*, trans. John Cullen (New York: Other Press, 2013), 268.
3. Rithy Panh, "La parole filmée: Pour vaincre la terreur," *Communication* 71 (2001): 375. All translations are mine.
4. I spent twenty months doing ethnographic research in Site 2 between June 1989 and July 1991. I was working as a volunteer for the International Rescue Committee, an American NGO, collecting life stories for a book about Site 2 published by IRC, called *Displaced Lives*. This work constituted the research for a 1994 PhD dissertation in social anthropology from Harvard University, entitled "Enduring Holocaust, Surviving History: Displaced Cambodians on the Thai-Cambodian Border, 1989–1991."
5. Panh, *The Elimination*, 5–6.
6. Panh, "La parole filmeé," 373.
7. Panh, 375.
8. Panh, 376.
9. See Panh, *The Elimination*, 100.
10. Panh, "La parole filmée," 375.
11. Panh, 375
12. Panh, 375–376.
13. Panh, 373.
14. Panh, 376.
15. Panh, 373.
16. Panh, 377.
17. The majority of the people in Site 2 were farmers, and the lack of agricultural work for farmers led to all sorts of problems in the camp. As Yim Om's husband put it, "When a man doesn't work, he doesn't think he is worth anything." He has lost the ability to support his family. Demoralization, frustration, and shame, along with ready access to weapons of war, contributed to high levels of violence in the camp.

18. The elephant was the most memorable part of that day, which inspired the kids' hilarious imitation mentioned earlier. When a cluster of balloons was released that day attached to a sign proclaiming human rights, a voice can be heard in the film calling out, with typical sardonic Khmer humor: "There go our human rights—they are flying away!"

19. As part of this small army I was, needless to say, very aware of this international presence.

20. The arrangements between the Khmers, the Thais, and the United Nations changed over the twelve years that Cambodians were living on the border. By 1988 there was only one camp in Thailand where Cambodians were recognized and treated as statutory refugees, under the terms of the United Nations High Commission for Refugees conventions. In all other border camps (Site 2 was one of six), Cambodians were treated as "displaced persons," without those statutory protections.

21. Deirdre Boyle, "Finding the Missing Picture: The Films of Rithy Panh," *Cineaste* 39, no. 3 (2014): 29.

22. Panh, *The Elimination*, 162.

23. Hun Sen, who has been prime minister since 1986, has gradually consolidated power in the hands of the Cambodian Peoples Party, most recently outlawing the one opposition party capable of challenging his control in the polls, jailing its leaders, and forcing other prominent party members to leave the country to avoid arrest.

12 • BOPHANA'S IMAGE AND NARRATIVE

Tragedy, Accusatory Gaze, and Hidden Treasure

VICENTE SÁNCHEZ-BIOSCA

If the public and collective image of the genocide in Cambodia could be condensed into visual representations, two contenders would be perpetrator images, or icons of affliction:[1] two mug shots taken of prisoners upon their arrival at the detention and torture center code-named S-21. These are two snapshots that, given the absence of law courts in the Khmer Rouge regime, condemned all those put on file to an inevitable death. These deaths, preceded by torture sessions, hunger, and humiliating treatment, were destined to be forgotten. The photographs portray two women who personify the defenselessness and fragility of the victims before the violence of this destructive machine, which began with this "trial by camera."[2] The first of these photographs represents Chan Kim Srun, wife of Sek Sat, a Khmer Rouge cadre and secretary of Region 25; the woman is holding her baby on her lap while her face expresses resignation awaiting a fate she knows is already sealed. The second photograph is of Hout Bophana, the young wife of Ly Sitha, a former Buddhist monk converted into a cadre after the revolution. Her love letters were replete with literary and mythological references, which would lead to her undoing, since they revealed how the authors were, according to the Khmer Rouge worldview, corrupted by Western culture.

From very early on and for various reasons, the image of Chan Kim Srun enjoyed a privileged status. First, her photograph had been among the seventy-eight pictures chosen to be restored by the photographers Douglas Niven and Chris Riley for their book, *The Killing Fields* (1996), which was the basis of a series of international exhibitions, beginning with the Museum of Modern Art in New York in spring 1997.[3] Second, a greatly enlarged version of this mug shot occupies a prominent position in the permanent exhibition at the Tuol Sleng Genocide Museum. Since the discovery of the chair for measuring crania used by those responsible for the repression, the side view mug shot of Chan Kim Srun was even associated with this device, thus bestowing it with a new distinction. Third, the composition of the photograph according to the original negative alone (the version stapled to the "biography" was cropped and did not show the baby in her lap) was endowed with a narrative and emotional intensity capable of immediately shaking viewers, without their needing to know anything about the figure portrayed. Chan Kim Srun's facial expression was interpreted as the fatal premonition of what awaited her and her son.[4]

In contrast, Bophana's headshot is less evocative from a narrative perspective: her gesture before the camera is so contained and severe that it appears to be emotionally impenetrable, perhaps conveying a meaningful resistance. However, with the passing of time, Bophana's story has grown in prominence—it began with written documents as her mug shot was only unearthed in 1994. The significance of both icons has distinct origins: the powerful image of Chan Kim Srun does not rest on her confession (which would be the story of a falsified life); Bophana's, in contrast, hinges on a narrative. Moreover, the significance of both images has changed as they have traveled the iconosphere: Chan Kim Srun's image evolved until 2011, when her biography was reconstructed by inscribing it in her family tree, while Bophana's became more and more endearing, and her vulnerability managed to defy the authority of the dystopian revolutionary society.[5] The person mainly responsible for this challenge is the filmmaker Rithy Panh, in whose films the young Bophana has come to epitomize the heroic fight for dignity and love in the dehumanized hell of the Khmer Rouge. In addition, the iconic photographs of Bophana and Chan Kim Srun have been decoded according to a double framework, local and Western: Bophana, because of her knowledge of French and English and her emotional refuge in the *Reamker*, the Khmer version of the Ramayana; and Chan Kim Srun, insofar as her frozen posture before the camera has been interpreted as an Asian pietà.

In 1996, Rithy Panh released his documentary *Bophana: A Cambodian Tragedy*. This film was the fruit of his research inspired by the *Washington Post* journalist Elizabeth Becker, in the mid-1980s, who discovered the love story of "Comrade Deth." In contrast to Becker, Panh shifted the focus from Deth to Bophana and turned her story into an allegory for the country's fate. He reconstructed the lovers' ordeal in the hell that was Democratic Kampuchea. After discovering the repression file kept in the Tuol Sleng archives, which included love letters, a biography, and the final confession and photocopies of three photographs, Panh traveled to the scenes of the drama and filmed interviews with witnesses. However, Bophana cannot be reduced to one of the stages in the filmmaker's work; instead, from the moment he discovered her, she became an emotionally charged figure who runs through almost all his films in such a subtle manner that she has reached a kind of subliminal presence. Vestiges of Bophana's story inhabit Rithy Panh's filmography in the form of brief commentaries, the embedding of her figure in details of the scenography, or the sudden appearance of her mug shot in the hands of the perpetrators.

This chapter attempts to trace the presence, migration, and functions of the Bophana image in Rithy Panh's films. Since her presence is sometimes disguised, this analysis requires a careful look at the technical-expressive resources of filmmaking, such as frame composition, editing, montage, use of archival footage, and sound effects. These forms of expression illustrate the hypothesis proposed here that Panh sees cinema in terms of a performative enunciation: his images attempt to produce changes in reality (including mental reality) and not just represent it. The same is true of Bophana's incursions into his films: far from constituting mere traces of style, the references function as performative acts: giving testimony, grieving, indicting the perpetrator, providing a sentimental attachment in which the filmmaker finds refuge. I would suggest that Bophana is an instigating voice that drives Rithy Panh. This figure of affliction becomes a metaphor for the "missing picture," which the filmmaker claims to follow and which names a promise of personal deliverance, a protest, and a crystallization of insurmountable sorrow.[6] Bophana becomes, then, a symptom of Rithy Panh's films and perhaps of Rithy Panh tout court.

FORGING AN ICONOGRAPHY, TELLING A NARRATIVE

Elizabeth Becker's account of Bophana's story appears in a chapter of her book *When the War Was Over*, entitled "The Romance of Comrade Deth." It contains almost all the elements that would be used in Rithy Panh's film: a young, urban woman, educated during the enlightened reign of Prince Sihanouk, sees her life plummet toward grave misfortune with the outbreak of civil war after the Lon Nol coup in 1970. She is then raped by a soldier, attempts suicide, gives birth in extremis, abandons her baby, and ekes out an existence working strenuous hours selling rice in Phnom Penh's Central Market. A reencounter with a distant first cousin (Ly Sitha), with whom she grew up, offers the fleeting illusion of love and happiness. But then the Khmer Rouge take power, the city is evacuated, and she is deported to an oppressive rural commune, all of which hastens her along the path of desperation. Then, just as Comrade Deth's initiatives seem to give hope that the lovers will be reunited, the fall of his superior, Koy Thourn, proves catastrophic for it entails Deth's arrest.[7]

Becker's is a very powerful account: it works with premonitions, tragic irony (an about-face when their destiny appears to be heading in the right direction), the parallels between the history of the party and the private lives of the lovers, the turning points, Deth's gestures of hubris, and the allegorical references to the

Reamker. In short, Becker resorts to typical elements of a tragedy to give coherence to her account and concede agency to destiny. So, what does Rithy Panh's documentary contribute to this story?

At this point, some historical context is necessary. While *Bophana: A Cambodian Tragedy* was circulating, there were a number of historical, artistic, and media events that had a bearing on the legacy of the Khmer Rouge genocide, and from the visual perspective, the S-21 mug shots, restored by Niven and Riley, began a life beyond the walls of the Tuol Sleng detention center. Moreover, *Bophana: A Cambodian Tragedy* is a turning point because it sketches out many of the elements that would become indispensable in the director's subsequent films. First, there is a historical focus on the civil war (1970–1975), the Khmer Rouge evacuation of Phnom Penh, and the deportation of the city's inhabitants to rural communes. It also confronts violent acts of repression, including the purges, the interrogations, the confessions, and the executions at Choeung Ek. These elements return unrelentingly throughout Panh's films, obsessively expressed through repetitive use of archival footage. Second, the film composes a symbolic iconography to represent Bophana, based on her dossier and ID mug shot. Panh then deconstructs these objects, inserting them into unexpected contexts. Third, it combines the testimonies of the victims and perpetrators, the latter taking on a decisive role in the task; this in turn requires the director to maintain a nonintrusive distance from them. Finally, there is the role assigned to embodied memory, which is expressed through reenacting the past, since in totalitarian regimes the rigidly disciplined body language outlives the word. *Bophana* becomes a kind of ethical-aesthetic catalyst for the filmmaker and an experimental laboratory at the same time. Let us dig a little deeper.

The documentary opens in the Tuol Sleng archives, where the archivists take out the dossiers of Bophana and Comrade Deth: letters, photographs, and confessions. Immediately afterward, the camera enters one of the museum exhibition rooms accompanying a member of her family, M. Thoeut, who identifies the mug shot of the young Bophana on one of the panels of faces on display. Then, through sobs, he conjures up her farewell in the turbulent Phnom Penh taken by the Khmer Rouge on April 17, 1975. We then go to one of the workshop rooms, where Vann Nath is working on a diptych depicting Bophana. Each of the two parts is based on a photograph. On the left is a young woman with everything before her. She wears a pearl necklace, as if for a social event. In the angle at which she is shown, her eyes shy away from direct contact, and her expression is discreet and confers a slightly melancholic air, transmitted through a palette of bright, almost naïve, colors. It is based on a photocopy of a photograph on file in her prison dossier and was probably found along with the objects confiscated from her husband when he was arrested.

On the right, Nath is working on a version of the mug shot on record: only the face has been painted, while the rest is just an outline of her silhouette

FIGURE 12.1. Vann Nath repainting the mug shot in his Bophana diptych

(figure 12.1). In the image and likeness of his model, it stands in stark contrast to the other painting: an interrogatory direct view and expression of visual violence that the snapshot captured when she was arrested. Given the diptych layout, this second image projects the shadow of a fateful destiny over the other. However, by restoring the image of the young woman with the colors that were wrested from Bophana, Vann Nath (and Rithy Panh with him) somehow frees the image of Bophana from the disciplinary frame in which the file-destruction device imprisoned her.[8]

These three iconic-narrative moments constitute a condensation of the unfortunate love story, the persecution, the repression, and the torture on one and the same stage—S-21/Tuol Sleng—albeit set in three microspaces: the archives room dedicated to research, the permanent exhibition open to the general public, and the workshop where Vann Nath had translated the sculptures of Pol Pot onto canvas in 1978 and where, after November 1979, the first canonical iconography of the Khmer Rouge crimes took shape.[9] But, above all, they confer upon the figure of Bophana an image of conflict: the youthful look in the prime of her life is opposed to the imaginary prison cell represented by the mug shot and the black pajamas associated with incarceration. Once this dialectic has been shown, the filmmaker introduces a new resource: a voice-over that returns to Bophana's childhood and explores the places of her misfortune, gathering testimony from those who knew her or who lived through similar experiences. In this manner, a narrative path opens up with two interactive voices, one feminine and the other masculine, which take the reins of this story through the exchange of letters between Bophana and Deth. Evoking images of the *Reamker* that re-create the imaginary universe—at the same time refuge and allegory—of the young woman, Panh submerges the viewer in the legendary world of the Khmer Rouge.

So, where Becker saw a "romance," Panh steers toward a tragedy, turns Bophana into the protagonist, and underlines her tragic virtue, namely, what the ancient Greeks called *areté*: the dignity of the hero or heroine in the face of the inescapable forces of destiny, which here are represented by the Khmer Rouge. Fifteen years later, Becker would come back to Bophana, who had then become a "national figure." She would highlight the female agency, evoking sisterhood with the three archivists who discovered the dossier for her (Lim Bun Chou, Chea Sam Aun, and Lach Voleak Kalyann), who were fully aware that "only Bophana's story captured how the Khmer Rouge had torn apart the very soul of Cambodia."[10] Following Rithy Panh as an authority on Bophana, Becker vindicates the message of resistance, courage, and dignity for her personification, which she associates with Anne Frank, the Virgin Mary, and Shakespeare's Juliet.[11]

After endless days of torture and the loss of her identity in S-21, the film closes with Bophana being transported and executed in the killing fields of Choeung Ek. The camera returns to the cells of Tuol Sleng, advancing until it focuses on the mug shot of the victim. The person responsible for the convoys to Choeung Ek, Him Huy, tells how the prisoners were transported blindfolded in the middle of the night to the open graves, where they were killed. Huy reenacts the method of execution in front of the camera, which endows his body with a paradoxical function. While his spoken account figures him as a witness, with his gestures he assumes the leading role in this reenactment: he crouches down and imitates the position the victims adopted as they advanced toward the edge, the mortal blow to the head, and then their throats cut as they fell into the open mass grave.[12] This was the fate awaiting Bophana. In this surprising act we see an outline of the mechanisms used by the filmmaker to portray the perpetrators in his later film *S21: The Khmer Rouge Killing Machine*. Significantly, Rithy Panh will end *Bophana: A Cambodian Tragedy* by rescuing two photographs: one of the young woman, the other of her husband, joined together on-screen. Whereas the first reproduces the photograph that precedes the catastrophic events to come, the second shows Ly Sitha dressed in the monk's habit he abandoned when he joined the revolution.

Bophana, the protagonist in this film matrix, was never again to be absent from Rithy Panh's films. Though she did not play such a leading role in subsequent films, she became a catalyst for Panh's successive approaches to the Cambodian genocide: Bophana counters the perspective of the ordinary perpetrators in *S21*; she slips surreptitiously into the interview with Duch, the man responsible for the machinery of repression; her presence evokes the experience of exile and the memory of the dead. Bophana-icon, Bophana-symbol, Bophana–affective image: in order to address these three modulations, we have to move from a direct narrative and iconographic discourse to a symptomatic reading.

FROM COVERT CAMEO TO ACCUSATION

S21: The Khmer Rouge Killing Machine is a choreographic and perspectivist film. Gathered around Vann Nath and under Rithy Panh's direction, the ordinary perpetrators who performed their tasks in this torture center (record keepers, guards, interrogators, those in charge of transport, a photographer) transform the now deserted prison-museum cells into a theater where the specter of past crimes comes to life through reenactment. They thus allow us to see something which has hardly left a trace beyond a fragmentary collection of photographs that illustrate only some of the consequences. These facts are the mechanisms of the detentions, the lives of those detained, chained to each other, the blind logic of torture, or the forced handwritten confessions. The figure of Bophana plays a role in these reconstructions. About a third of the way into the film, the former torturer Prak Khân reads instructions from a mysterious book found in S-21, to which historians and archivists have given the title *The Interrogators' Manual*, namely, some notes probably taken by the torturer Chan based on sessions dictated by Duch to his juniors.[13] These are some of the premises: torture is not devised "for amusement," but rather to extract information; you have to terrify the detainee and make them suffer so they confess; before beating, it is necessary to examine their state of health, because if the prisoner dies then the document is lost. After this, Khân reviews one of the documents that bears his signature, identifies four interrogators from that time in a photograph, and names the three units to which they were assigned to work: the soft, the hot, and the chewing unit. The image cuts to the reaction of Him Huy and another guard, both silent, as Khân goes on with his explanation about the suffering prisoners underwent. The camera then spins around to Khân, who continues with his description as he gazes down at the document. From where Khân is positioned, the camera descends, and he falls from view at the same time that a typewriter appears on-screen and then a series of enlarged mug shots spread out on a table (figure 12.2). One of them stands out because of its size, Bophana's. Throughout this fragment, Khân's voice is ever present. When the image returns to the torturer, he regrets his former arrogance before the enemy, an animal that had to be eliminated. So, riding on the unbroken spoken word, the editing associates the current scene with the past: the typewriter refers to drawing up the confession and the photos of those souls whose bodies were torture fodder. In this context, Bophana embodies the quintessential role of the victim, symbolically and discretely, since it is highly likely that the viewer does not know who she is.

FIGURE 12.2. The typewriter, Bophana's mug shot, and the shackles

Later on, we find ourselves watching a similar scene. The perpetrators discuss among themselves the way they fabricated evidence against the detainees and the process of undoing their memory. Suddenly, Rithy Panh embeds a surprising composition in an extremely elaborate depth of field shot: in the foreground, placed on the same table, is the dust-covered typewriter; next to it is an empty chair, which alludes to the act of confession; a little farther back we see one of the perpetrators motionless, as if petrified. Just a few steps back, various documents lie in a pile, and on top of them a blown-up version of Bophana's mug shot catches the eye, upon which two shackles lie, like those that clasped the feet of the prisoners. In the background, the group of former perpetrators talk about how they drained the prisoners' memory. This shot is followed by a reverse shot that purges the surroundings to leave only the typewriter, Bophana's photograph, and the shackles in the field of view. If any image could synthesize the experiences of the victims in S-21, it is condensed in this composition. Bophana thus becomes an icon and a symbol at the same time.

Her mug shot appears on two other occasions, playing a more discrete, almost subliminal role as if trying to interpellate with her gaze the perpetrators who tortured, maybe raped, and executed her. Her photograph first appears in the hands of Prak Khân while he is talking with his former comrades; the second time, the mug shot seems to be spying on Him Huy from the table. These are a prelude to Bophana's presence in another film before the man who commanded the interrogations and killings at S-21, Duch.

The documentary *Duch, Master of the Forges of Hell* entails a change of style as regards the status given to the perpetrator: the protagonist here is the man to whom Son Sen, the minister for interior affairs, handed over the repression apparatus of S-21. On this occasion there is neither choreography nor multiperspectivism; this is a face-to-face encounter between the filmmaker and the master of torture.[14] Significantly, in this context, through shot composition and editing, Panh slips in the figure of Bophana before the demigod in S-21 who decided that she was to be eliminated. Panh thus converts the subliminal into a staged pattern: Bophana will be present through her photograph and the documents from her dossier on Duch's desk, with him hardly aware of it. One could say that Bophana is the support that Rithy Panh needs in his single combat with Duch.

The filmmaker challenges the commander of S-21, presenting him with the victim's dossier, a dossier that is associated with one of the first purges within the ranks of the party and that brought about the downfall of Koy Thourn. Conscious of the performative power of the photographs and the documents, Panh films Duch's hands meticulously manipulating the documents with utmost care like the zealous administrator he was, almost caressing each sheet. Later, Duch places these repression-forged images next to those that portray Bophana from earlier on when she was happy. Finally, Duch acknowledges his own handwriting and signature next to the date that signaled the end of her life. From the point of view of Duch's narrative itinerary as the final editing presents it, the structure appears as a process of *anagnorisis* (agnition), in which the protagonist is driven to recognize his true identity, even if Duch's agnition fails in the end.

Moreover, the itinerary Rithy Panh imposes on his interviewee symbolically closes the distance between Bophana and Duch: instead of using the classical structure of shot reverse shot, the filmmaker seeks copresence in the space, incorporating Bophana's photograph and Duch's body in the same frame. This space sharing is a kind of monstrosity in itself, since it suggests the destructive power of the gaze as leading to elimination. At the end of this process, Duch, a careful exegete of documents, points with his finger at Bophana's signature, the one that sealed her destiny. He does so as he must have done the day on which he resolved her execution, extending his forefinger to the very spot where Bophana's thumbprint had been stamped. It seems as if Duch is revisiting the process of her destruction. Outrageously, the scene suggests physical contact with the victim through this old sheet of paper: a downright desecration. Rithy Panh ends Bophana's case by using a collage shot of all the symbolic ingredients like a condensation of the plot: the shot described earlier in the analysis of *S21: The Khmer Rouge Killing Machine.*

Thus, the disjunctive effect of Duch's gaze is pondered in an inverted manner by Panh, who does not hesitate to make this clear in his interview: "Duch asks me why I'm always showing him photographs. 'What's the point?' he asks, in that tone of his. I answer, 'But the thing is . . . they're listening to you. Koy Thourn is here. Bophana's here. Taing Siv Leang too. I believe they're listening to you.'"[15]

SPECTRALITY: FROM ADOPTION TO REENCOUNTER

In Rithy Panh's intimist account *The Missing Picture* (2013), Bophana makes a strategic cameo appearance when the narrator reflects on the iconic lack: "And, all said and done . . . what does an image of death show? I prefer the one of the unknown young woman who defies the camera and the eye of the perpetrator, and she still looks at us." The camera did not flinch from showing us how young she was: it heads toward Bophana's mug shot, lost in a Tuol Sleng panel, as if this photograph were the reverse side of the missing picture around which the film is organized. In that moment of uncertainty and fragility of recalling his childhood, Rithy Panh acknowledges that this snapshot is his ally and bestows it with a role of resistance that helps him to structure his own identity, as he sees in her an almost unbelievable defiance faced with an all-encompassing power.

However, it falls to *Exile* (2016), a lyrical documentary about forced displacement and the theater of memory, to propose an intimate and almost religious metaphor for the place the filmmaker assigns to this young woman in his work: in his own words, that of a sister.[16] Inside the cabin where the protagonist lives, on some occasions bleakly empty, on others crowded like an imaginary museum with memories, dreams, objects, and photographs, the character embodied by the actor Sang Man appeals to Bophana twice.[17] The first time takes place in a sequence preceded by archival images that show an Apsara dancer followed by some chickens that lay eggs. Panh cuts to a handwritten letter that the protagonist reads. At the foot of the same figure, a recognizable name: Sédadeth. It is one of the love letters written by Bophana's husband, which Panh used in his 1996 film. Among the documents that accompany this precious treasure there is a diploma from a language school, a photograph of Panh's mother, and next to it, another of Bophana. It is a never before used snapshot of the young woman that was given to Rithy Panh in France by a friend. In this photograph, Bophana dons a low-cut dress, wearing a necklace—which we saw in that photocopy kept among her detention documents—as well as earrings and a Western hairstyle (figure 12.3). Bophana, smiling, poses with her body half turned to the camera. It embodies the "movie star–like" style which Becker mentioned as typical of the 1970s. The two photographs remain side by side in the hands of the protagonist while the voice-over recites: "Pages, pages, words, words. Each page is a journal, each word an instant. Pages, words to bring you back from death, you and yours, innocent wonder, then torn apart, violated by the masters, deprived of bread, deprived of meaning. Words, alas, to find your miseries, to once again dig up

FIGURE 12.3. Snapshot of a young Bophana

your suffering and the end. Words, only words, to erase the death which erases them. Pages, pages, words, words."

With great care, the silent being who inhabits the cabin does up the small packet, protects it with a paper wrapping, ties it with a bow, digs a hollow in the middle of the cabin floor, and places this treasure inside. Immediately afterward, he covers the hole with earth, flattens it with his hands, and places a small stone over the spot. At this very moment a clap of thunder rips though the soundtrack, and a storm is unleashed.

These figures reappear near the end of the film. The ground is covered with reeds, but no object is placed on them. In the background, the man is sitting, motionless. A tapestry of family photographs unfolds on the front and right-hand walls. Among them, the photograph of Rithy Panh as a child that we have seen lit up by the flame of a match at the beginning of the film. Above this image stand out those already mentioned of his mother and Bophana. On the right, a greatly enlarged photograph catches our eye. It is Bophana. The young man gets up and goes over these snapshots from memory while music plays in the background. His left hand follows his eyes and caresses Bophana's face. Then he turns on his heels and looks at the opposite side. Meanwhile, another figure gets up from the place where the filmmaker was at the beginning and in turn examines the same photographs, as if in a circle of unfolding and reencounter. Finally, both bodies dissolve, the scene remains deserted, and the photographs progressively disappear wall by wall until only two of them remain on the back wall: one of Bophana and the other of Panh's mother. After fading to black, these two photographs appear as if by a spell, enlarged to full screen, appealing to a shared affection.

In the moments that immediately follow, the filmmaker shows the protagonist caressing the photograph of his lost mother, dwelling on her oval-shaped face and drawing out a smile. It is to her that he addresses his words. In the reverse shot, the young man sits down, and in a superimposed image, his face is in turn caressed by the protecting hands of his mother. *Exile* is a moving film about the lost mother. It is precisely for this reason that Panh's inclusion of Bophana in this moment of emotional exchange is so meaningful. By doing so, he adopts her into his family and turns her into an affective image.

Rithy Panh's more recent film—*Graves without a Name* (2018)—constitutes a ritualist reencounter with his family, disappeared during the deportation, and a ceremonial laying of their souls to rest. In the midst of a landscape that is difficult to recognize, where these "new people" found death, Panh, with the help of monks and seers, tries to find the site where the bodies of his own family were discarded, to put their remains together and reunite himself once more with them, as if he himself had died. Given the Khmer Rouge's dehumanizing of the "new people" and total disregard for their bodies after death, this is an impossible task. For their souls to rest in peace requires reviving testimonies, summoning the dead, and performing rituals on the landscape, which is in sum what we could call, following Maria Tumarkin, a traumascape (a landscape that condenses trauma).[18] Rithy Panh's family, with his mother and father at the head, is represented by the photographs and other material objects that remain from the past. Scattered over the natural surroundings that saw these people suffer and die, they allow the filmmaker to summon the people, recover them, feel them and, finally, cremate them. Among the photographs of his father, photographed as an enlightened schoolteacher, and his mother in the same foreground as it appeared in *Exile*, Rithy Panh includes the image of Bophana as if she were a sister who had disappeared. Panh rescues this photograph, free from suffering and prior to her fall into a world of pain and misfortune, in which she is dressed in her evening gown. It is not the criminal look of the Khmer Rouge that the filmmaker invokes but, rather, a snapshot that does not contain any vestige of her destruction. The landscape where his relatives died and where their souls wander is a scene replete with signs of appeasement. The trees, the mass graves, the clearings in the forest, and the voices of the monks and the elderly are filled with signs from the Buddhist ritual. Then, Rithy Panh himself, concealed by deliberately out-of-focus shots, camera distances, and oblique shots, finally enters to consummate this encounter.

Bophana will appear like this on five occasions, since although she did not die in this landscape, she nonetheless experienced the same deportation as those who perished there. The first appearance happens amid an invocation by an elderly woman to identify the place where the body of a woman was thrown, most likely Panh's mother. The following shots pass over some photographs that identify family members, among which Bophana has been added. In the second, the voice-over mentions the search for traces of Rithy Panh's family and the impossibility of destroying the memory of a man. On the remains of corrugated iron covered in dust a pile of photographs is spread out, one on top of the other, as if someone had just thrown them there. Bophana is invoked a third time later on, at the foot of the tree that symbolizes the scene where the murder was committed.

Two final appearances complete this adoption of the young woman: in a small model that maps out the territory with small mounds of earth that, along with the hedges, mark the graves, photographs of members of Rithy Panh's family are raised. Bophana has been chosen among them, in a place of honor, exposed to the wind on a branch of the chosen tree and shot against the sky in a low-angle shot. This person invoked is a condensation of an emotion that offers shelter. The filmmaker has appropriated her, turned her into a sister; as such, joining his family, Bophana also joins Panh in his attempt to find ultimate salvation.

CONCLUSION

In 2006, Rithy Panh, in collaboration with Ieu Pannakar, founded an institution whose purpose is to recover, restore, disseminate, and ultimately, for new generations, use the audiovisual heritage of Cambodia. It was a way of reconstructing the visual foundations for the memory of this country that had been disfigured. This manner of appropriating (the images of) history was baptized with a meaningful name: Bophana Audiovisual Resource Center. In the projects undertaken since, the center has confirmed what Panh proposes with his cinematography: a conception of cinema as a performative act that aspires to transform reality through films. In some respects, this principle is included in the figure, account, and affective image of Bophana, as if this small lever represented the most original and lasting gesture of the filmmaker, at least since his 1996 film. The image of Bophana is as changeable as the work of Rithy Panh: it expresses her love and misfortune; it observes from the wings the drama of Cambodia's ordeal; it accuses those who determined her annihilation; it defies her captors from its spot on the crowded Tuol Sleng walls; it is preserved as a treasure and adopted by the filmmaker, who offers the young woman a burial place alongside his beloved mother. In all of this, Bophana, as a narrative, emotion, or fetish, embodies that which Rithy Panh produces with each of his films. This *innocente merveille* is more than just an image; she turns into a motor driving Panh's cinema.

But, as we have seen, the image of Bophana is never alone. It appears interlocked with other images. Her iconography is the product of Vann Nath and is a collection of the effects this painter had on the work of Rithy Panh. Nath survived S-21 and acted as a mediator of its memory, goading the reaction of the perpetrators and observing their reenactment. For this reason, Rithy Panh commissioned Nath to paint the diptych that represents Bophana and, thus, the vicissitudes of S-21. This diptych renders Bophana in two incompatible yet inseparable images: the first, the young woman associated with the cosmopolitanism of Cambodia, the Apsara dance, and the 1960s ("new people," as she would be called by the Khmer Rouge), and, the second, the mug shot that condemned her. Since Vann Nath's death in 2011, his oil painting of Bophana can be found hanging on the staircase that leads to the second floor of the Bophana Center in Phnom Penh. From there, she gazes at the visitors and perhaps watches over the recovery of the country's battered images.

NOTES

Chapter title: This chapter was written in the framework of the research projects "Contemporary Representations of Mass Violence Perpetrators: Concepts, Narratives, and Images" (HAR2017-83519-P) and "Figures of Perpetrators of Mass Violence: Narratives and Images" (AICO/2018/136).

1. Marianne Hirsch uses the term "perpetrator photographs" to refer to those photographs taken by the Wehrmacht soldiers in the East for their own consumption, adding that they "illustrate the quality of the perpetrator's look as well as its connection to the perpetrator's deed."(Marianne Hirsch, "Surviving Images: Holocaust Photographs and the Work of Postmemory," *Yale Journal of Criticism* 14, no. 1 (Spring 2001): 26. We have expanded the concept of "perpetrator images" to name those "photographic, cinematographic, or other types of images made by those who commit criminal acts. In a sense, then, they may be considered as elements of the apparatus of destruction since they incarnate the gaze of executioners or their accomplices before, during, or after carrying out the crime." See Vicente Sánchez-Biosca, "Perpetrator Images: Quel destin pour les images prises par les criminels?," *Mémoires en jeu/Memories at Stake*, no. 8 (2018–2019): 131. Assuredly, this is the role played by the mug shots of the prisoners registered at S-21 in the Khmer Rouge machine of destruction.

2. Nic Dunlop, *The Lost Executioner: The Story of Comrade Duch and the Khmer Rouge* (London: Bloomsbury, 2005), 148.

3. Douglas Niven and Chris Riley, *The Killing Fields* (Santa Fe, NM: Twin Palms, 1996), n.p. This mug shot is among the twenty-two chosen by Adrienne Williams for the exhibition *Photographs from S-21: 1975–1979* held between May 15 and October 7, 1997, in the museum's Gallery Three (https://www.moma.org/calendar/exhibitions/247?installationimageindex=3).

4. Before Niven and Riley brought this photography to a broader audience, Dominique Mérigard had photographed it in the museum in 1994. When he published his book fourteen years later, he described it as "a deeply troubling expression of courage mixed with resignation." See Dominique Mérigard, *Témoin S-21: Face au genocide des Cambodgiens* (Manosque: Le Bec en l'air, 2008), n.p.

5. Beth Van Schaack, Daryn Reicherter, and Youk Chhang, eds., *Cambodia's Hidden Scars: Trauma Psychology in the Wake of the Khmer Rouge* (Phnom Penh: DC-Cam, 2011). The book is dedicated to treating and healing post-traumatic stress disorder in general. However, the chapters are headed with color photographs of children, particularly girls, with their faces covered by the mug shot of Chan Kim Srun. The authors stress the transmission of trauma through the genealogy of this victim, connecting it to Marianne Hirsch's notion of "postmemory," as the memory legacy received by the generation that did not directly suffer the violence in question. See Marianne Hirsch, *The Generation of Postmemory: Writing and Visual Culture after the Holocaust* (New York: Columbia University Press, 2012).

6. For further reading on this, see Vicente Sánchez-Biosca, "Challenging Old and New Images Representing the Cambodian Genocide: *The Missing Picture* (Rithy Panh, 2013)," *Genocide Studies and Prevention: An International Journal* 18, no. 2 (2018): 140–164.
7. Elizabeth Becker, *When the War Was Over: Cambodia and the Khmer Rouge Revolution* (New York: Public Affairs, 1986), 212–225.
8. The term "disciplinary frame" comes from John Tagg and refers to a study of photography in the Foucauldian tradition of surveillance and what Tagg terms the "violence of meaning." In this sense, capturing the enemies in a photographic frame as the basis for interrogation, torture, and final execution could be understood as the ultimate expression of this use of photography as a means of domination. John Tagg, *The Disciplinary Frame: Photographic Truths and the Capture of Meaning* (Minneapolis: University of Minnesota Press, 2009).
9. Vann Nath, *A Cambodian Prison Portrait: One Year in the Khmer Rouge's S-21*, trans. Moeun Chhean Nariddh (Bangkok: White Lotus, 1998), 100.
10. Elizabeth Becker, *Bophana* (Phnom Penh: Cambodia Daily Press, 2010), 79.
11. Becker, 79.
12. Ashley Thompson, "Mnemotechnical Politics: Rithy Panh's Cinematic Archive and the Return of Cambodia's Past," in *Modern and Contemporary Southeast Asian Art: An Anthology*, ed. Nora A. Taylor and Boreth Ly (Ithaca, NY: Cornell University Press, 2012), 237.
13. See, among others, David Chandler, *Voices from S-21: Terror and History in Pol Pot's Secret Prison* (Berkeley: University of California Press, 1999), 108; Dunlop, *The Lost Executioner*, 125–140.
14. A long analysis from this point of view can be found in Vicente Sánchez-Biosca, "The Perpetrator's *Mise-en-scène*: Language, Body, and Memory in the Cambodian Genocide," *Journal of Perpetrator Research* 2, no. 1 (2018): 65–94.
15. Rithy Panh with Christophe Bataille, *The Elimination* (New York: Other Press, 2013), 261. For a framing of these scenes through the theme of nonvindictive resentment, see Raya Morag's chapter in this volume.
16. Rithy Panh, e-mail to author, September 28, 2017.
17. Deirdre Boyle, "Exile, within and Without: New York in Two Modes from Rithy Panh," *Film Quarterly* 71, no. 1 (2017): 12.
18. See Maria Tumarkin, *Traumascapes: The Power and Fate of Places Transformed by Tragedy* (Melbourne: Melbourne University Publishing, 2005).

13 • MEMORY TRANSLATION

Rithy Panh's Provocations to the Primacy and Virtues of the Documentary Sound/Image Index

DAVID LAROCCA

Rithy Panh's *The Missing Picture* (*L'image manquante*, 2013) provides a unique and vital contribution to our ongoing reflection upon the meaning of the documentary audiovisual index. In what follows, I highlight some of the heuristic effects of Panh's achievement in *The Missing Picture* for the ontological, epistemological, and ethical principles that are, and have been, at work in mainstream studies of documentary sound and moving images. I hope to focalize some ways in which Panh's cinematic innovations challenge presumptions in the making, viewing, and categorizing of documentary films, a challenge in turn that may help us achieve a new degree of clarity about the personal and historical content he addresses in *The Missing Picture* (and elsewhere in his work), while also productively isolating formal issues in the broader cinema of documentation.

To begin, consider what could be called the methodological "purity" of a work such as *Shoah* (1985, dir. Claude Lanzmann), a film that is defiant in its dismissal of archival footage from "the time of"—what theorists describe as the profilmic register of events; Lanzmann's point of address is, instead, squarely and securely on his present-day witnesses. In stark contrast, Panh is not a purist in this sense but someone who *mixes* the personal with the public, imposes private memory upon the coursing of history. He transforms found footage through montage and collage, and often goes further by replacing or displacing the archive altogether (whether of private relic or public artifact) with scenes of figurines made of clay (indeed, in *The Missing Picture*, we are even privy to the *making* of the proxies, not just their finished presence, "performance," or "reenactment"). Panh's additive, layered style—of photo-filmic archive in company with voice-over, clay, collage, and so on—provides a provocation to various models and methods of documentary purity, including those that "save" the photo-filmic archive/index until the end of the running time, as if to shock us out of our inurement to documentary "reality." We see this now-generic move, for example, at the conclusion of *Waltz with Bashir* (2008, dir. Ari Folman), when animation is forgone in favor of an unveiled confrontation with the traditional photo-realistic index (in both graphic images and terrifying sounds). Panh, again, by contrast with Lanzmann and now Folman, avoids further extremes—say, the over-presentation of the wounded, dying, and dead (as we find them, arguably, in *Night and Fog* [*Nuit et brouillard*, 1956, dir. Alain Resnais]) or their nonpresentation (as in *Shoah* and *The Maelstrom: A Family Chronicle* [1997, dir. Péter Forgács]).

Rather than these prominent and influential (indeed, now canonical) approaches, Panh introduces us to a novel methodology, and a further category in the taxonomy of documentary filmmaking: a mixed style characterized by a shifting terrain of nonlinear translation of the private and public. For Panh, the available public archive of sonic and visual indexes is a resource for giving shape to personal history; the figurine is installed as a representative of or for personal memory (often paired or layered with other audiovisual resources); autobiographical voice-over creates narrative coherence in the face of gaps, fissures, and lacunae. In turn, as is illustrated by *The Missing Picture* itself, the privately generated work of art becomes a potent presence and force for a shared public history, including as a new kind of "evidence" for renewed juridical proceedings. As if borrowing from ancient mythologies that allow the gods to draw life from raw earth—to make humans from clay—Panh becomes a maker of worlds and the attendant memories that give rise to personal experience and the coursings of history.

To help articulate this mixed category of documentary, I consider *The Missing Picture* in the context of documentary efforts to remember human catastrophes, such as wars, genocides, and other traumas. Through a series of comparisons with documentary modes of address and depiction, we are given a chance to recognize Panh's adjacent artistic proposals. Moreover, I wish to place Panh's film beside what may be called companionable work by others. Though these illustrative contemporary examples lie beyond the purview of filmic expressions of genocide and mass atrocity—perhaps for that difference, they illuminate something of Panh's methods and effects, namely: Sarah Polley's *Stories We Tell* (2013) and Charlie Kaufman and Duke Johnson's *Anomalisa* (2015). These films, when coupled with *The Missing Picture*, provide an occasion to recover remarks by György Lukács (1885–1971), ones that take us first to the nature and form of the essay and, by extension, the essay film. With Lukács, we approach anew the essay film as we find it in Panh's distinctive contribution, not least as a way of thinking about the film's ethical and existential import and the manner in which it does not forestall the act of judgment but invites it, and, indeed, compels it to continue.

MEMORY AND DOCUMENT: PRIVATE HISTORY AND PUBLIC HISTORY

There is something of a paradox—or at least a meaningful provocation—at the heart of Panh's project: to generate a public history from a private memory. By making images *of* memories (or *from* memory)—as if in compensation or surrogacy for the images that were never made, or that were destroyed or silenced—Panh's *The Missing Picture* makes a bold claim to the work, meaning, and constitutive powers of documentary filmmaking. In this way, a "missing picture" is both a trope and a figure of "missing memory," which obscures an enthymeme, namely, that an image is not a memory or, more elaborately: that an archival image (still or in a series, accompanied by sound, or silent) does not yield a memory. Maybe such media can be called "historical," maybe not, for even Panh says that the extant film footage made by the Khmer Rouge is merely propaganda (understood as a form of "selective memory," having retained only those images perceived to glorify the revolution while destroying the rest, so that the revolution, as Panh says, "only exists on film"). Does this distinction between memory and history help us think about Panh's film as an essay film that shifts back and forth between *private* memory (as personal history) and *public* history? To what end might this alternation—and translation—be instructive to us at a time increasingly troubled by the crisis of the documentary index (e.g., as represented most evocatively by the rise of deepfakes and the generative adversarial network [GAN])?

The invocation to remember (indeed, in the case of genocides, near in time and long ago, which may involve an incumbent *moral obligation*) is not the same thing as providing (a public or shared) history. One can glean this distinction readily in witness-based documentaries, such as *Shoah*, and even in later innovations of documentary form that unsettle our reliance on the indexical sound/image, such as the mostly animated *Waltz with Bashir*. Because abundant audiovisual documentary proof of the Holocaust exists—in film, audio, photographs, and so forth—one can use the interviews with survivors in Lanzmann's documentary as a *supplement* to the archive of indexes. What of Panh's work, then, where the archival picture (and sound) is largely missing or misidentified? Aside from the available, limited archive he employs, Panh offers—indeed, creates—instead, the supplement. Consequently, Panh's memories—as embodied by clay figurines, as photo-audio montages and compilations—are made to *stand in* for public histories that were lost or never made (histories that would otherwise have relied on the audiovisual archive as elements of empirical proof).

For a further point of medial comparison, consider the techniques Panh uses in *The Missing Picture* with those deployed by Péter Forgács in *The Maelstrom: A Family Chronicle*, the latter of which is *entirely* composed from archival amateur film footage—every frame. Forgács manipulates the color, frame rate, and direction of film, includes nondiegetic sound and music, adds emphasis with freeze frames, and so on, but the film is still, we want to say, archive-based. The underlying image is indexical, and yet there is copious and overt manipulation of the mise-en-scène. We ask, then, does *The Maelstrom* (as a work of art) *also* become history? If Forgács's work makes this transition, this translation, I would like to say that movement—from one state or status to another—can help us think about Panh's *The Missing Picture*, asking first, does Panh's film also make the passage? If not, why not? And why does the distinction between these works of artist-archivists matter? For one thing, we see how our continued negotiations over the status of the documentary sound/image index often imply, though occasionally explicitly state, what counts and what does not—what is or becomes archive and what "remains" art.

In these negotiations, not surprisingly, further questions arise: Given the malleability, distortions, fallibility, and losses of personal memory, the peculiarities of subjective recollection, and so on, how are we to think about personal accounts as a form of *public* history? How can an autobiographical reminiscence, such as Panh offers—and constitutes, in part, by means of clay figures—achieve a measure of recognition as impersonal, for example, in the way a home movie can, at times, rise to the level of collective significance (such as in *The Maelstrom*, when a domestic archive inadvertently presents a glimpse of history)? Are we not better off circumscribing private or personal history so it remains, as it were, (merely?) personal? For example, we seldom seem to make the leap from a literary memoir or autobiography (as works of art, say) to public history, so why allow this transition for traumatic events such as wars, genocides, social unrest, and natural catastrophes? As part of a reply to such queries, we can turn to film historian Scott MacDonald, who has remarked: "One of the fascinations with memory is the way it can reflect lived experience in ways that actual documents of the remembered experiences cannot (of course, documents can often tell us what memory cannot)."[1] Thus, if we have before us two realms—one of memory, one of document—we are left to wonder if they can overlap, and how we would adjudicate that overlap if given a chance. The metaphor of "overlap," to be sure, is meant to account for what I am describing as a form of translation—in this context, a way of describing the movement of a memory *into the realm of* the document (and vice versa). In the case of audiovisual artifacts, we are driven to ask peculiar questions, such as: "Does your memory accord with the photograph?" But then we would have to be *shown* the photograph, which would affect/inform one's memory. Thus, a project of a "missing picture"—much less *the* missing picture—would require a reliance on memory as the sole realm of historical reference. We watch as Panh generates a series of material creations—figurines, composite/collage images—to, as it were, conjure an archive where there once was one, or never was one.

FIGURING HISTORY, MAKING THE ART-ARCHIVE

Despite the impressions of one's first encounters with *The Missing Picture*, the predominant mode of artistic innovation is not animation. Rather, it is more accurate, and fitting, to say that "still lives" are filmed; they are filmed, indeed, the way that clay, marble, or metal statuary is often filmed by the movie camera. (To be careful and consistent, though, there is one scene—when a clay figurine flies—that calls out for qualification as animation.) Instead of the exposure (defeat, or delay) of the archive, with Panh we see something like its invention—and the possibility of an indirect exploration of history, by way of personal memory, in place of the vigorous demand for indexical representations, verifiable facts, testifying witnesses, and so forth. Again, godlike, Panh and his team of clay sculptors achieve a kind of cinematic legerdemain: by handiwork, they hand us a new realm in which we are meant to see and hear the mingling of historical events with personal thoughts. A child might recognize a register of this activity as "playing with dolls," and while that practice of the imagination is no epithet in the present context, we can be sure to appreciate how Panh enriches the theatrical stage by means of cinematography, editing, intercutting, superimposition, music, voice-over, and much else. Hence the so-called child's play, even as it is advanced by a kind of folk (or outsider) art and craft, takes a further step into art object and conceptual art; Panh finds the cleave point where such play and handiwork assume world-historical meaning—the very making of personal identity, which in turn may come to inform national identity and human understanding.

Other films contribute occasions for complementary and clarifying insights. Take, for example, Sarah Polley's *Stories We Tell*. Like Panh, Polley would appear to "make figurines" as well, or film them, insofar as she employs actors to tell her story. Part of the intelligence of Polley's movie is the revelation of how easily we are lulled by our familiarity with film to think of these dreamed-up reenactments *as* indexical (i.e., indexical of Polley's 1970s youth instead of as present-day reenactments). Polley's Super 8 creations made to look like home movies are a variant of a hoax, one that is demurely revealed during the film's running time.[2] When invoking a past that has no indexical images—as is the case for Panh and Polley—how can we use their different approaches to think further through why the indexical remains an inherited default for claims to truth and, by consequence, claims to legitimacy in the archive and restitution in the courtroom? One way is to consider that translating private history (based on memory) into public history involves *archive creation that courts its status as art*. The further question for our time is whether we are comfortable with such a dual or blended status. Can we speak intelligently about the art-archive—especially when the documentary sound/image index remains under assault?

Scholars have helped us with Panh's other work,[3] and these and related investigations are especially pertinent to thinking about the relationship between re-creating via proxies (clay, multimedia, etc.) and the cinematic forms of reenactment usually reserved for humans, and thus experienced by viewers *as* human(s). For example, Jennifer Cazenave's attention to the geologic turn in media studies underscores what she calls the "materiality of mourning"—hence an emphasis on the way Panh's figurines are made from Cambodian earth, where so much innocent blood was spilled, and thus calls to mind the continuity between the lives (and deaths) of the executed and the rather inert, relatively anonymous clay statuettes we encounter on film.[4]

I should like to extend my invocation of Polley's film for the way it helps us investigate figure-based characterization: in her film, as noted, she uses actors. But there are other models to consider, ones that draw us back closer to Panh's methods, such as in the stop-motion work employed by Charlie Kaufman and Duke Johnson in *Anomalisa*—a film that may provide another vector for thinking through the embodiment of memory, thought, and history. Consider a productive interaction between Panh's practice in *The Missing Picture* and Kaufman's in *Anomalisa*, for example, where the two works, in tandem, reveal novel responses to philosophical skepticism (as we find it addressed in the work of Stanley Cavell): that is, of finding ways to, as Cavell writes, "live one's skepticism," which is to say to find a world *beyond* one's own mind and memory.[5] We are said to do or achieve this not by feats of knowledge but by way of acknowledgment, and much of Panh's core motivation seems to be just that: to manifest a world of lost others in order to pay them homage, to see them again in order to honor them; instead of animation, we are faced with reanimation. Memory and clay have made revenants.

In the context of the two films, the discovery of a world outside of oneself is—tragically in Panh, comically in Kaufman, but perhaps paradoxically in both works—achieved via surrogate. Contrast this approach with variants of the autobiographical essay-film style of Ross McElwee and Agnès Varda; the faux home movie aesthetic of Polley and Casey Affleck; and the poetic-existential mode of Alain Resnais.[6] Instead, Kaufman's *Anomalisa* uses plastic figurines and stop-motion methodologies to animate certain existential conundrums; in the process, the film illustrates how the figuration of thought and memory with figurines can profitably act as a proxy for our customary reliance on indexical sounds and images. Kaufman has consistently, in film after film, articulated a series of robust representations of doubles and doppelgängers along with the functions of pseudonyms, masks, puppets, and other proxies.[7] In *Anomalisa* the decision to create a film composed *entirely* of puppets provides a specific kind of move away from, or confrontation with, the indexical—especially visual—attributes of the film medium; recall that in *Being John Malkovich* (1999, dir. Spike Jonze), puppets were present but also functioned as a trope for thinking about the human lives at stake. Whatever human expression Kaufman manages to achieve through his puppets in *Anomalisa*, it must be conveyed through (or again, translated by) these figures, and the illusions created by stop-motion techniques.

With Polley's and Kaufman's separate (and distinctively different) contributions to the art form at hand, we return to Panh with new questions: In *The Missing Picture*, are we speaking of a distinction between a true index versus false index? For example, the fabrication of an index "out of" memory, from memory, as if we (or Panh, at least) were capable of building an index—sculpting it out of clay, summoning memories from the mud. Panh quite movingly shows the making of a clay figurine; he then says, as if calling a person out of obscurity and into existence: "He is my father." This kind of totemism (which does seem to deserve the name animation, but perhaps, again, reanimation) becomes an engaging invitation to think through the nature of "true" representation. Panh's lament about his lost father—"His suit is white, his tie is dark. I want to hold him close"—is spoken plaintively by the narrators.[8] The sincerity of that moment—seeing the father, as if already "in hand"—and the son's desire to hug him would appear to transcend the habitual bounds of our thinking (and feeling) about the index. Indeed, Panh pushes us to consider that our familiar reliance on the signifying power of the (conventional?) photographical image is but one mode in which memory or history may be made, preserved, and subsequently come to inhabit space and time. For instance, in the absence of a photochemical trace, Panh's use of clay-as-medium would appear to have achieved the transformation of clay into an ontologically rich site of meaning—a veritable transubstantiation.

Would our affective and moral sensibilities have been as moved by a photograph of Panh's father, were one to exist? Or perhaps a few seconds of home movie footage? What can we say about our reliance on photographs—and the photorealistic affordances of moving pictures—for doing the work of memory, imagination, public history, and private storytelling, especially when an artist compels us to enter a different (competing?) realm of representation? And shifting from ontology to epistemology, let us ask, finally, at the end of *The Missing Picture*, are we prepared to say the photograph is not just true but "truer" than the figurine? The fact that we speak with comparative evaluation of truth (viz., where one kind of object is "more true" than another) shows that we have much yet to consider and to explain. Among the further questions Panh's creative work agitates: Have we entered a language game—or exited one? Have the well-worn grooves of our thinking about the index—say, in photographic or photo-filmic terms—obscured (or elided) the ways in which nonphotographic representation may be constitutive of truths of a similar (or at least of a competing) caliber?

THOUGHTS ON THE FORMS OF THE ESSAY FILM

As I have appealed to categories such as art and archive (and typographically recommended their intimacy in the "art-archive"), I continue by thinking about how Panh's *The Missing Picture* also figures as an essay film. Contemporary film theorists Timothy Corrigan, Nora Alter, Laura Rascaroli, Elizabeth A. Papazian, and Caroline Eades, among others, have written compellingly about the attributes and virtues of the essayistic qualities of cinematic creation.[9] I would like, at this point, with their scholarship in mind, to add an earlier but still vital voice on the characteristics of the essay as such, namely that of György Lukács. In "On the Nature and Form of the Essay," Lukács speaks adjacent to the dawn of cinema—circa 1910—and yet the development of cinema that is essayistic, in his terms, appears not just discernible but also credible. This double register is fiercely prominent in works of essay films that aim to bridge a certain divide between epistemology and axiology: that is, to propose a moral insight in the midst of some instance of aesthetic and medial representation. With Panh's *The Missing Picture* as our point of reference, as well as his other films that rethink and remake art and archive—consider these remarks by Lukács collected in a volume fittingly titled (for our purposes here) *Soul and Form*:

> Thus the essay seems justified as a necessary means to the ultimate end, the penultimate step in this hierarchy. This, however, is only the value of what it *does*; the fact of what it *is* has yet another, more independent value. . . . Therefore [the longing, which is "a fact of the soul"] needs not only to be satisfied (and thus abolished) but also to be given form which will redeem and release its most essential and now indivisible substance into eternal value. That is what the essay does. . . . This "application" creates both that which judges and that which is judged, it encompasses a whole world in order to raise to eternity, in all its uniqueness, something that was once there. The essay is a judgment, but the essential, the value-determining thing about it is not the verdict (as is the case with the system) but the process of judging.[10]

These selections may do a disservice to the coherence of Lukács's point, since there are allusions to concepts (such as "the hierarchy," "the system") that he had earlier developed. But several important notions can be gleaned for immediate relevance here: first, the identity of a given work (what it *is*) is bound up with its effects (what it *does*). Such a performative notion of art should find kindred support from the linguistic theorizing and ordinary language philosophy of J. L. Austin, as well as contributions of avant-garde and experimental sound, cinema, theater, and dance. Second, that essayistic artwork is especially well-positioned to "redeem and release"—that is, reveal—the value at the heart of a given project, indeed, to underscore the canny Panhian appreciation for the way form and soul interact. Third, Lukács contends that art becomes a locus for thinking through a *series* of judgments (rather than confirming a settled verdict).

Instead of hoping for the emergence of stable criteria for judging the indexical validity of a given audiovisual creation, the call to an endless series of judgments seems especially poignant and necessary. Panh's *The Missing Picture*, as a distinctive member of the film form known as the essay film, offers a notable contribution to—and reminder of—the need to attend to each instance of the archive, each encounter with the art that contributes to it. The archive is not a static entity, but—as clay in the hands of the artisans who craft figurines for Panh—it is a medium up for negotiation and thereafter perpetual renegotiation. History and moral assessment are not set in stone but remain malleable—acquiescent to input and adjustment by those who work them, who model and mold them over time. We, the inheritors of history, are charged not just with determining what is *in* the archive, but also are involved, ethically, with its generation and regeneration (as well as our evolving judgments about what we catalogue and compare). Importantly, such ongoing reconsideration does not forestall the possibility of establishing reliable principals, beliefs, and commitments, but instead forces us to articulate what such positions are or might be. I will close with remarks that aim to illustrate the iterative nature of interpreting Panh's film—here *The Missing Picture* but also reaching out to other works, such as *S21: The Khmer Killing Machine* (2003).

In light of the commentary invoked earlier (by Corrigan, Alter, Rascaroli, and others), we should be able to claim, uncontroversially, that *The Missing Picture* is an essay film, but at the same time, we want to remember that the essay film is not a monolithic concept with a predesignated or predigested set of qualities and characteristics (after all, Phillip Lopate described his project to do so as a "search"[11]). Indeed, if we hold fast to the etymology of "essay" (*essai*, Fr.), then we are in close company with the experimental—and appropriately, the trial. Panh's film is not one thing but the trying out of many: a repository for the representation of existing historical photo-filmic archives (scores of them suppressed and therefore not widely known); a document of figurative sculptures made for the occasion and for the purposes of dramatic storytelling; a locus for narrativizing public and private history via autobiographical voice-over; and an intriguing variant of a home movie. On this last point, consider how Panh begins the film.

The opening image is arresting for it is motion picture coverage of film (i.e., celluloid) that can no longer be set in motion. It is footage of a morgue for movies, where viewers are faced with the corpses of film. We are confronted with inert materiality and no animation, forced to confront what has been "stilled," and so, lost—without having much, if any, sense of what was, in fact, lost. How can one make such assessments (of loss) abstractly? For we do not see the people who were killed, but (merely?) the images of the dead—and now the dying images themselves. Panh, by contrast, having lived within and then survived the Khmer regime, prompts us to consider an intimate relationship—almost at times a correspondence—between the private memory of the man (the voice) offering the scripted, disembodied remarks and the room of historical documents now lost to history. The room, under this aspect, appears to be an image of a deteriorating mind and its memory; with each new phase of degradation, the "memory of history" is further effaced. Panh (like his kin and community) suffers a double loss: of human life *and* of filmic accounts of those lives. How does Panh respond to this double register of carnage—such violence against people and against film, against art, against the archive that would preserve and protect? By making something anew, by reconstituting the world from personal and shared memories, by working Zeus-like to summon spirits from the earth, molding men, women, and children from clay and then filming the figures: the first time as figure, the second time as film.

Panh, then, is not "creating history," for example, by constituting realities from the past that have been lost, so much as he is "re-creating stories" *of* or *from* that history—the only kinds of creation that are available to him in the wake of lost indexical sounds and images; of course, *access* to the past itself (and all the losses it contains) is something that underwrites the credibility of his autobiographical claims to veridicality. We can return again, at this junction, to MacDonald's earlier observation that "documents can often tell us what memory cannot." By re-creating stories, Panh does not vie with history (as if to place *The Missing Picture* in competition with whatever audiovisual index does or might exist), but instead sidesteps it: creates a document that subverts the habitual fallacy of equating indexicality with assured truth. Panh's twist on MacDonald's claim, however, makes it possible for us to take seriously the way that memory may become—by artistic translation—a document unto itself. In short, art fit for the historical archive.

The Missing Picture becomes an artifact testifying to the intersection of the home movie, essay film, and the re-created story,—when Panh's artful conjuring of "his story" from private memory finds embodiment in the presentness, and representativeness, of his motion picture. The iconicity of Panh's father-in-clay allows for both the specificity of his lost father and the general category of all lost fathers. History in *The Missing Picture* does not return isomorphically (as we often naively assume it does when we watch archival film footage) but distorted and refracted in a many-layered, experimental home movie essay film (full as it is of voice-over narration, manipulated found footage, collage, clay figurines, and much else).

Tracing, as I have been, the various provocations Panh achieves in *The Missing Picture*, we approach a potentially productive cleave point—namely, where his notion of re-creating stories intersects with the work of other filmmakers who describe their work (or find their work described) as involving "reenactment." Among many salient cases worthy of comparison and contrast, consider anew Sarah Polley's *Stories We Tell* (the title of which reads differently in the wake of Panh's re-creating stories) and several works by Errol Morris, but famously *The Thin Blue Line* (1988, in which a reenactment led to legal exculpation—as if it were not reenacted at all but, in fact, functioned as forensic evidence made at "the time of" the incident in question). With Morris, the "trials" of his essay films mount (e.g., with *The Fog of War* [2003] and *Standard Operating Procedure* [2008]). Even more proximate to Panh's film, consider Joshua Oppenheimer's *The Act of Killing* (2012) and its companion film, *The Look of Silence* (2014), that, like *The Missing Picture*, attempt to address a Southeast Asian genocide by what we could describe as "indirect" means. That is, Oppenheimer (who admires Panh's work and clearly also his methods) eschews a reliance on, or indeed any use of, stock, found, or other archetypal documentary footage (assuming that some did or might still exist) in favor of present-day interviews and reenactments. *The Act of Killing*, for example, involves the idiosyncratic approach of having perpetrators "act out" their crimes in the guise of making B-level genre pictures, such as the gangster movies that they loved and emulated to catastrophic effect.

Standing in the company of the aforementioned films, there is a beguiling realization that Polley, Morris, and Oppenheimer, each in their own way, have undertaken challenges to and reconfigurations of the sound/image index (Polley through ersatz home movie footage; Morris through historical reenactments, stylization, and moral interrogation; and Oppenheimer by empowering his prospective interviewees to make films of their own). In an unsettling way—again, in an insight prompted by Panh—Polley, Morris, and Oppenheimer would seem to have used "dolls" for their own productions: Polley enlisting family members, Morris actors, and Oppenheimer murderers who also happen to be movie lovers. As a group of filmmakers, then, they have helped us recognize the problems and limitations of the (still) prevailing affection and regard so many have for the authority and authenticity of the documentary sound/image index. In their work, they have shocked us into considering that we have been trained to relate to these images and sounds with deference—with a trust or faith bordering on the totemic and occult—while we should rather be more circumspect.

Among the various lessons on offer, we can take up *The Missing Picture* as a testament to the vitality of film for the human confrontation with—and thus consideration of—the ethical. When Timothy Corrigan writes about the essay film, and specifically the nature of reenactment in essays films, he has Lukács' essays on essayism in mind. In Corrigan's reading, we are reminded that *The Missing Picture* is a kind of trial or judicial proceeding, similar to other refractive essay films (such as Abbas Kiarostami's *Close-Up* [1990], which should also figure in our thoughts). We know that for Errol Morris, reenactment becomes "expressionistic rather than realistic," and as such "works in the service of ideas rather than facts."[12] Here we could draw on Werner Herzog's notion of "ecstatic truth," which serves to underwrite films as agitations to the "accountant's truth."[13] But with Corrigan's direction, and earlier work by Bill Nichols and Ivone Margulies, we may approach Panh's unique take on reenactment's claim to juridical status, in particular, its demand upon viewers (again, after Lukács), to occupy a state of judgment rather than to declare a verdict.[14] "As in a judicial trial," writes Corrigan, "in which reenactments are also standard strategies, there are two layers of cinematic reenactment, one that illustrates the event or subject reenacted and the other that demands rethinking that event or subject through its adaptive framework."[15] As such, according to Corrigan, "reenactments construct ethical stages requiring a kind of evaluative judgment."[16] History remains wet clay.

Unlike standard reenactment scenarios, *The Missing Picture* features mostly inert clay figures. Consequently, the "desubjectivization" that Nichols and Corrigan highlight in essay films, especially of a refractive or metacinematic kind, achieves a new degree of expression—one that may complicate our reading of reenactment by actors (as opposed to dolls).[17] Nichols would describe the move to representative proxies (such as dolls and figurines) as one in which we face "a gap between the objectivity/subjectivity binary and the workings of the fantasmatic," but what happens specifically to the interstitial space in *The Missing Picture*?[18] Is it widened or collapsed? As Nichols continues: "Facts remain facts, but the iterative effort of going through the motions of reenacting them imbues such facts with the lived stuff of immediate and situated experience."[19] More crucially for our purposes here, reenactment "complicates the literal, linear, and binary logic of the judicial system" and "reinscribes the ambiguity of perspective, and voice, that separates such judicial determinations from the plain of fantasy."[20] We have already seen how this separation may dissolve, as when Morris's *The Thin Blue Line* is used as evidence—and exculpatory evidence at that. What, then, of Oppenheimer's *The Act of Killing* or Panh's *The Missing Picture*: Are these personal testimonies (involving distinctive and divergent modes of reenactment) that can also find the gap between fact and fantasy foreshortened or closed? With *The Missing Picture*, we have one man's imaginative ("fantasmatic") take on his personal history, which, in turn, becomes an art-artifact for the consideration of the public—including what Cathy J. Schlund-Vials calls "juridical belatedness," as well as the ongoing judgment of viewers beyond the courts (namely, viewers in cinemas and at home across the globe and across time).[21]

As a concluding thought, could we productively adopt the trope of "adaptation" (familiar as it is to cinema studies) as a way of considering what it is Panh is up to? I have been using "translation," drawn more from studies of language, as a suitable cognate metaphor. Partly I do so because the business at hand is a form of or variation on the process of transit—*metaphora* (to transfer); *trephein* (to turn). Panh lays before us in *The Missing Picture*, in frame after frame, the notion that some kind of *adaptation* or *translation* is necessary when we move from the scene of history to the filmed scene, from the empirical world to mind and its memories—and back again. Panh's contribution, in this film and more generally in his work, is to have us contend with the historical significance and artistic pertinence of personal memory. We are reliably forced to ask how it is that we go from an inner experience to an outward *representation* of that inner experience.

Do we fake it (like Polley), stage it (like Morris), invent it (like Herzog), act it out (like Oppenheimer) or, as Panh does, draw from the extant record (say, found footage) as a complement to scale models, dioramas, and folk art deployed in the service of cinema? We hear much about the "magic of the movies," how the medium, or some films more than others, "cast a spell," so we should be cognizant of the way Panh's memory translations afford this uncanny achievement. The waves crashing near the film's start now seem like a gentle hypnosis, calling us forth to enter an alternate realm—a realm in which the spirits of the dead are alive and well, not on film but in the world that film finds (for instance, in Panh's autobiographical remarks [spoken by others]; in the clay figurines; in the work of collage that gives *The Missing Picture* its distinctive tone, texture, and narrative shape). Indeed, it is the missing picture—the destruction of the archive that might have been—that makes *The Missing Picture* possible. Soon after the waves subside, the spell has been cast, and we stop asking after the "true" or "real" sound/image index; we enter a new realm "beyond document," a world of sensation unlike the standard-bearers of the genre.[22] Documentary film as we have known it would seem, like the souls of the dead, like the dissolving celluloid, to have transcended itself at last.

NOTES

1. Scott MacDonald, *Binghamton Babylon: Voices from the Cinema Department, 1967–1977* (Albany: State University of New York Press, 2015), xviii.
2. This differs from Casey Affleck's *I'm Still Here* (2010), which deliberately covets its fictions and thereby contributes to a subgenre we could call hoax vérité. See my "A Reality Rescinded: The Transformative Effects of Fraud in *I'm Still Here*" (537–576), and the section "Film as Lie as Truth" in the introduction, "Representative Qualities and Questions of Documentary Film" (7–23), in *The Philosophy of Documentary Film: Image, Sound, Fiction, Truth*, ed. David LaRocca (Lanham, MD: Lexington Books, 2017).
3. I have in mind especially Deirdre Boyle's "Shattering Silence: Traumatic Memory and Reenactment in Rithy Panh's *S-21: The Khmer Rouge Killing Machine*," *Framework* 50, no. 1/2 (Spring and Fall 2009): 95–106. Regarding the film under consideration here, for example, Jennifer Cazenave's "Earth as Archive: Reframing Memory and Mourning in *The Missing Picture*," *Cinema Journal* 57, no. 2 (2018): 44–65, is essential.
4. Cazenave, "Earth as Archive."
5. See Stanley Cavell, *The Claim of Reason: Wittgenstein, Skepticism, Morality, and Tragedy* (Oxford: Oxford University Press, 1979), 440.
6. I have noted earlier the films I have in mind for Polley, Affleck, and Resnais, but let me add points of reference for McElwee and Varda. For McElwee: *Sherman's March* (1985), *Time Indefinite* (1993), *Bright Leaves* (2003), and *Photographic Memory* (2011); for Varda: *Jane B. for Agnès V* (1988), *The Gleaners and I* (2000), *The Beaches of Agnès* (2008), *Faces Place* (2017), and *Varda by Agnès* (2019).
7. See my chapters "Unauthorized Autobiography: Truth and Fact in *Confessions of a Dangerous Mind*" (89–110) and "Inconclusive Scientific Postscript: Late Remarks on Kierkegaard and Kaufman" (269–294), and the new preface (2019) in *The Philosophy of Charlie Kaufman*, ed. David LaRocca (Lexington: University Press of Kentucky, 2011).

8. *The Missing Picture*'s listed narrators are Randall Douc (Fr.) and Jean-Baptiste Phou (Eng.).
9. Timothy Corrigan, *The Essay Film: From Montaigne, after Marker* (Oxford: Oxford University Press, 2011); Nora Alter and Timothy Corrigan, eds., *Essays on the Essay Film* (New York: Columbia University Press, 2017); Laura Rascaroli, *The Personal Camera: Subjective Cinema and the Essay Film* (New York: Columbia University Press, 2009); Laura Rascaroli, *How the Essay Film Thinks* (Oxford: Oxford University Press, 2017); Elizabeth A. Papazian and Caroline Eades, eds., *The Essay Film: Dialogue, Politics, Utopia* (New York: Columbia University Press, 2016).
10. György Lukács, "On the Nature and Form of the Essay," in *Soul and Form*, ed., John T. Sanders and Katie Terezakis, trans. Anna Bostock (New York: Columbia University Press, 2010), 33–34.
11. Phillip Lopate, "In Search of the Centaur: The Essay-Film," *Beyond Document: Essays on Nonfiction Film*, ed. Charles Warren (Middletown, CT: Wesleyan University Press, 1996), 243–270.
12. Royt Grundmann and Cynthia Rockwell, "Truth Is Not Subjective: An Interview with Errol Morris," *Cineaste* 24, no. 3 (2000): 8.
13. See note 2 and also my "'Profoundly Unreconciled to Nature': Ecstatic Truth and the Humanistic Sublime in Werner Herzog's War Films," in *The Philosophy of War Films*, ed. David LaRocca (Lexington: University Press of Kentucky, 2014), 437–482; and Werner Herzog, "Minnesota Declaration," *The Philosophy of Documentary Film: Image, Sound, Fiction, Truth*, ed. David LaRocca (Lanham, MD: Lexington Books, 2017), 379–380.
14. See Bill Nichols, "Documentary Reenactment and the Fantasmatic Subject," *Critical Inquiry* 35, no. 1 (Autumn 2008): 72–89, and *Rites of Realism: Essays on Corporeal Cinema*, ed. Ivone Margulies (Durham, NC: Duke University Press, 2002), esp. Margulies's "Exemplary Bodies: Reenactment in *Love in the City, Sons*, and *Close Up*" (217–244), and more recently her *In Person: Reenactment in Postwar and Contemporary Cinema* (Oxford: Oxford University Press, 2018); Corrigan, *The Essay Film*, 197.
15. Corrigan, *The Essay Film*, 196.
16. Corrigan, 197.
17. Corrigan, 196.
18. Nichols, "Documentary Reenactment," 77.
19. Nichols, 77–78.
20. Nichols, 77.
21. Cathy J. Schlund-Vials, "Evincing Cambodia's Genocide: Juridical Belatedness, Historical Indictment, and Rithy Panh's *The Missing Picture*," *Contemporary French and Francophone Studies* 20, no. 2 (2016): 287–296.
22. See Warren, ed., *Beyond Document*.

14 • RITHY PANH

Storyteller of the Extreme

SOKO PHAY

Translated from French by James Grieve

If one thing explains why Rithy Panh's career as a filmmaker began early, it was his need to make sense of the appalling trauma inflicted on him by the extermination of his close family and the Cambodian people. His entire life has been permanently marked by the moment that broke it in two: forced exile and the deaths of several members of his family. The life he has made for himself and his whole view of the world have been irremediably structured by that founding calamity of a sundered existence. As a survivor, nothing has been more essential for him than to knit together the unraveled life, even after four decades of trying.

From his first documentary, *Site 2* (1989), to the recent *Graves without a Name* (2018), he has kept asking the same unchanging question: How can we go on outliving together our dear dead? This attempt to give back to the dead the history and the identity they deserve also shows that for Rithy Panh his belief in filmmaking and the power of words is an act of faith. Before he could tell in words and images of the deaths of his nearest and dearest, he had to examine the workings of genocide and listen to both the survivors and the killers in *Bophana: A Cambodian Tragedy* (1996), *S21: The Khmer Rouge Killing Machine* (2003), and *Duch, Master of the Forges of Hell* (2011). After a harrowing encounter with Duch, who had been in charge of the S-21 extermination center, and the depression it brought on, the writing of *The Elimination* with Christophe Bataille enabled Panh to take charge of his memory and identity, and to tell, for the first time, his autobiography.

This gripping account is extended in the film *The Missing Picture* (*L'image manquante,* 2013), which shows his own experience as an adolescent who has been through deportation and witnessed the deaths of his loved ones. He himself had come close to death several times and had been subjected to forced labor in the camps and in their communal graves. Thus *The Missing Picture* marks a turning point in his filmography. It was in this film that Panh found a new way to tell of the Cambodian genocide, which he took further in *Exile* (2016) and *Graves without a Name*. What is striking in all three works is the "I" of the autobiographer, who speaks on his own behalf and presents himself as a "witness-as-survivor."

THE WITNESS IN THE FIRST PERSON

Bearing witness is a speech act, a performative act, which turns the spectator into an "indirect witness" through the ordeal of experiencing an event via its recounting. The filmmaker tells of what he saw and heard, but also of what he had to endure in order to survive, like staving off hunger by eating a rat, an insect, or a bit of leather. The "I" of the witness is always a "we"; bearing witness is always, consciously or unconsciously, done for others. Through this interplay of "I" and "we," the past and the present are linked, as are the dead and the community of the living. By telling it in film form, Panh is both an eyewitness (*testis*) attesting to things seen and heard and a survivor (*superstes*), someone who has come back from among the dead—literally as well as metaphorically, for the Khmer Rouge forced him to carry and bury the dead bodies when he was a mere teenager. He is back from the dead to convey to the living, insofar as it is within his power, what the dead cannot speak or express for themselves: the unspeakableness of genocide.

Panh is more than a witness; he is a great storyteller, as famously defined by Walter Benjamin: "The storyteller takes what he tells from experience—his own or that reported by others. And he in turn makes it the experience of those who are listening to his tale."[1] That "the art of story-telling is coming to an end" Benjamin links to the fact that "experience has fallen in value" since the Great War. As he puts it in another well-known passage: "With the World war, a process began to become apparent which has not halted since then. Was it not noticeable at the end of the war that men returned from the battlefield had grown silent—not richer, but poorer in communicable experience?"[2]

Furthermore, our word "experience" derives from the Latin *experior*, which means "to feel," "to test," or "to suffer." The root of the word, *-perior*, can also be seen in *periculum* (peril, danger). The calamity that Panh seeks to convey to us via his documentary art was life-endangering for him. He says in *The Missing Picture*: "There are many things that man should not see or know; and should he see them, he would be better off dead. But should any of us see or know these things, then he must live to tell of them."[3]

However, to be able to enrich and transmit to others such extreme experience, it took Panh thirty-eight years of laboring with it within himself and studying the

Cambodian genocide. His approach is neither that of the historian nor that of the lawyer, but that of the survivor who relies on the resources of art to investigate the strange ways in which those who have survived relate to memory and to the fact of their own survival. How can he convey the extreme experience that he went through? How can others be brought to share in memories that are at constant risk of being forgotten, when mass murder itself is at risk of being erased?

Whereas genocide is a group experience, suffering always remains an individual one. Behind the mass crime, there is the trace of a personal story. So it is that each and every personal account turns into a symbolic itinerary. The three works *The Missing Picture*, *Exile*, and the more recent *Graves without a Name* serve as stimuli to thought on how images can come together in "works as archives,"[4] providing evidence of genocide and a "resting place" for the dead. To reconstruct a memory that is both individual and collective, it is essential to find the lost meaning of what is left. Obviously, Panh's films cannot assuage the grief for the loss; but for the viewer, who is the person they are ultimately intended for, they can sharpen awareness of such things and prick the conscience. As the essential third party in this transaction, the viewer becomes even more of a "witness-cum-relayer."

THE MISSING ARCHIVES OF GENOCIDE

"In the middle of life, childhood returns. The water is sweet and bitter. I seek my childhood like a lost picture. Or rather it seeks me. Is it because I am fifty years old? Because I have known troubled times when fear alternates with hope?"[5] These are Panh's poignant words at the beginning of *The Missing Picture*. If he was ever to find his proper place in the life he led as a man, he had to find the images of his childhood, as he tried to find the family house that he had seen for the last time on April 17, 1975. And when he did locate it, it had been transformed beyond recognition. He decided to make a model of the villa as it had once been, as it stood in his memories. So that the scale would be right, he modeled a little clay figure to represent himself as a child. It was from this that the film grew.

For survivors of genocide, the lasting effects are profound and continue to haunt their lives long after. If such a witness is obsessed by a form of "truth," it is because life cannot be lived without the return of reality. The fact is that denial of genocide, which happens through the double disappearance of people and of evidence that they lived, entails the necessary destruction of what was real. For deniers, a mass crime that has left no trace is a crime that never took place. Thus, the absence of truth haunts the survivor. Panh, having learned of the confession of a cameraman killed at S-21 who said he had photographed scenes of execution, set about locating this documentary evidence.[6]

For years he looked high and low for this evidence. As he explained: "Clearly, no single image can suffice to prove there was mass crime; but it can be thought-provoking, it can start a mental process leading to the building of history."[7] By now, he knows that the image *must be missing*, which is why he decided to *construct it*. With the reconstituted miniature settings and the strikingly expressive little clay figures, he brings the viewer into their world. Though they are inanimate, they seem to be given *soul* via the many slow and delicate movements of the camera. This impression of their psychology is furthered by the framing and the close-ups.

Filmmaking, lying between the real and the fictional, between document and imagination, brings to life scenes that attest to the reality experienced by the victims, yet which are to be found in no archive. To illustrate his childhood memories of Phnom Penh before the onset of the Khmer Rouge regime, Panh uses extracts from audiovisual archives, especially black-and-white images from the 1960s. Into these he inserts color figurines—a loving couple, for instance, amid the busy streets of the capital—as though to bring the dead past alive. He says in *The Missing Picture*: "I remember that world, imperfect but human. According to Pol Pot, it was '2000 years of slavery.'" These words are a comment on two almost identical shots of Phnom Penh at two different periods: one is full of the bustle of city life; the other, filmed by the Khmer Rouge, gives a panoramic view of the same streets utterly deserted during the fall of the city. The uncanny difference between fullness and emptiness leaps from the pictures.

Filmmaking enabled Panh not only to restore his personal memory but also to reveal the inner workings of genocide as practiced by the Khmer Rouge, by deconstructing the lies of their images. In their desire to obliterate the former time, which they saw as impure and imperialistic, they went so far as to fabricate false memory: in their propaganda films, we see the comings and goings of human beings on work sites, all busy digging and carrying loads of stone and soil to and fro. But Panh's account uncovers the hidden face of Democratic Kampuchea: "For months I dug a water reservoir in the middle of arid plains. I never saw a drop of water. Not one" (figure 14.1).[8]

What the Khmer Rouge images conceal is the physical and psychological exhaustion of the "new people" in the labor camps under open skies, the hunger in the collective canteens—while the Khmer Rouge took their meals in secret—the illness and death in the paltry hospitals, the terror and the hunt for imaginary enemies during the self-criticism sessions. Democratic Kampuchea became the place where a large-scale falsehood was fabricated. This was one reason why Panh projects pictures from the Khmer Rouge archives on the walls of his miniature house, as a voice-over comments: "There is no such thing as truth. All there is is films. The revolution is cinema." This remark is meant to be provocative. As pictures, Pol Pot's revolution seems ideal; seen against reality, it is deadly, having killed a quarter of the Cambodian people.

FIGURE 14.1. Digging the reservoir, but no water

EXILE AS DESOLATION AND RESISTANCE

Having recounted in *The Missing Picture* the appalling conditions in which his family had lived and died, Panh continued his introspection via the core of Khmer Rouge ideology in his second autobiographical film, *Exile*. It reflects on the absence, loss, and disintegration of self wrought in a person by extreme violence. Panh cast an actor in his own role and set the action in a hut, which is the locus of all the metamorphoses. The title of the film refers to his status as survivor and exile. As a survivor, he is forever rootless, living twice over in a state of not belonging. At one level, he experienced the emptying of Phnom Penh in April 1975, which was his first exile, inside his own country.[9] At the second level, he came to know exile outside it, through spending some time in a refugee camp on the border with Thailand, then living in France. Exiles, who remain outsiders, internalize the experience of decentering, as Edward Said put it when he defined exile as "fundamentally a discontinuous state of being."[10]

Figuratively, exile means experiencing one's total and utter exclusion from the human community. As an onlooker, one witnesses one's own extreme aloneness, one's dehumanization. As Jean Améry describes it: "To be amputated of our dignity was implicitly life-threatening."[11] Hannah Arendt saw desolation as the aloneness of individuals uprooted both physically and psychologically by totalitarian systems.[12] Desolation deprives one of the slightest possibility of engaging in an exchange. One is as though abandoned by all others and by oneself. In such a state, one becomes superfluous, one is no one, one is dispensable. This feeling of not belonging in the world is one of the most desperately hopeless and radical that there can be.

FIGURE 14.2. Framed photographs hanging in the hut

Nevertheless, even in the grip of famine or reduced to nothing but a tatter of the Khmer Rouge's future refuse, Rithy Panh asserts paradoxically that he is undefeatable. As Robert Antelme says in *L'espèce humaine*, the act of seeking food is also an act of radical resistance.[13] To stand upright and keep one's dignity, despite the extreme nakedness of one's being, is the other exile. For, as Panh sees it, exile can have a positive connotation, as a form of protection in the face of the reign of terror of the Khmer Rouge who observed everything and controlled everything. This can be seen in a sequence from *Exile* in which he shows his hut gradually turning into a room full of shelves of books and objects from the former life, through the imaginative power of cinema. A woman's wistful voice, that of a singer from the past, takes the viewer back to a lost time that is still alive. Even in such total isolation and bereft of all but himself, he can recall times of happiness. Black-and-white films from the 1960s show the bustling streets, the buses, and the places near the markets.

Sometimes, sleeping or dreaming can be the exile's last resort, the ultimate psychic refuge. According to Panh: "If you can recite in secret some lines by Robert Desnos, or remember a song, even one that you don't know the words to, if you can imagine yourself in color when everyone else is in black, that is a poetic mode of resistance."[14] To possess some images of one's own; to be able to imagine colored clothing or see oneself wearing a favorite garment amid everyone forced by the Khmer Rouge to dress in black; to fancy that your hut has got plants growing in it or contains paper birds, moons, clouds made of cotton, or a huge nest; or to see it as hung with a great many framed photographs—especially a picture of his mother, to whom he pays moving homage—is ultimately to safeguard one's memory and one's human truth (figure 14.2).

THE LANDSCAPES OF GRIEF

To give dignity back to the dead is the task that Rithy Panh sets for himself in all his films, in particular *Graves without a Name.* The opening shot is of the filmmaker's back, as he sits on a stool draped in the orange cloth favored by Buddhist monks; a young bonze shaves off all his hair. A shaven head symbolizes detachment and the renunciation of the world of material things that is necessary for access to the spiritual way and to mourning. The voice-over speaks the words that express the dilemma of every survivor: "Let us say I was dead. Yes, dead. My eyes were downcast, as they are now. I had already seen many things that no one should ever have to experience. My hands and feet were black with dust or scattered ashes. Death can be such a gently reposeful wind."

Panh bears witness to unending grief and the impossibility of mourning, to being on the border between life and death. This is exactly the agonizing "survivor paradox" identified by Richard Rechtman: "In fact, whenever the survivors spoke of being alive, the risk they ran was that this would make their dear dead disappear. This made them immediately fear that, in so doing, they were fulfilling the macabre desire of their torturers by erasing the last traces of their existence. But whenever they spoke on behalf of the dead, they felt that the absent ones were themselves; and they were confronted with the fact that they were made of the same undifferentiated substance, as though the destinies of the dead and of the living were one and the same."[15] This dialogue with the dead is the core of the film, bringing to visibility the importance of place and the landscapes of memory.

In this film, Panh is shown as himself, unlike the two earlier autobiographical films in which his part is played primarily by a clay figurine (*The Missing Picture*) or by an actor (*Exile*). In this he took the advice of the Buddhist priests and the masters of ceremonies: "If you wish to find the souls of your family and grieve fully, it must be done by you, not by an actor."[16] And yet, as in *The Missing Picture,* the first of his films in which he appears in front of the camera, albeit briefly, he is always shown as less than fully present, seen from behind, at an angle, in the distance, or out of focus.

He goes back to the scene of the crime, the province of Battambang in northwest Cambodia, to show in particular the landscape of Trum, the village from which his family was deported. "To begin with," he says, "I did not dare even to venture out behind the village, beyond it, into the landscape. It is so full of other things. This is the place where our family lost its center of gravity. Trum was our center of gravity. When that disappears, you start to lose yourself bit by bit."[17]

One thing that is striking in this film is the majestic beauty of the landscapes, whether seen from the air (as filmed by drone), in front view, or in close-up. Nature in all its splendor restores us to something timeless and deep in a lost paradise. It seems to have remained intact. This place where it all began, which is indelibly marked by the dead, becomes an enigma, a lost secret: what remains stubbornly inaudible is the main thing, the reasons for all the dying. Nature becomes the speechless witness to tragedy: in Cambodia, more than forty years after the Khmer Rouge, the traces of the massacres are rarely visible in the landscape, apart from the few official memorials such as S-21 or Choeung Ek, which were paradoxically the main centers for purging their own ranks. The other 189 places of execution, most of which lie in remote hinterlands, still go unrecognized.

Nature has thus reasserted itself over the evidence of extermination. Even today, the filmmaker finds it hard to visit such places, all overgrown as they are. And he never stays for long, for fear of treading on the bones of his family, as they lie buried alongside other victims of the Khmer Rouge. The whole landscape, which has become their shroud, continues to haunt the world of the living. *Graves without a Name* enables us to sense the extent of the destruction and the erasure of the locations, though none of them give any sign of disturbance, any hint of being so appallingly upturned. Nature here is a paradox, at times revealing the scars of destruction (for instance, the crevasses at Choeung Ek), at others covering up all traces of the violence inflicted.

In his attempt to decipher these landscapes ravaged by genocide, Panh sees himself as a filmmaker-as-archaeologist seeking vestiges: "I needed to film those souls, to show the landscape and the marks left by the massacres."[18] Although he has never been able to find the places where his family died, he goes on looking for them, with the help of animist rituals, and by asking mediums and elders to make contact with their spirits. He questions witnesses, including two former members of the Khmer Rouge who agree to speak of the past, and in so doing to take a step toward humanity by acknowledging long after the event that they had been so misguided by their ideology. He searches without rest, noting the slightest sign in the ghost villages, the merest rustle of a breeze among trees or reflections on the surface of a stream. As he scrapes at the ground, he finds scraps of cloth and traces of human beings such as a tooth held in clay. There is a vestige of humanity in this DNA: despite the Khmer Rouge and their efforts to cover up what had taken place, evidence is still there. In this "archaeology of ghosts,"[19] by turning up *the evidence of the suppression of evidence*, Panh exhumes a buried past and "reaches out" to the wandering souls.

UNFINISHED BURIAL

Panh, who has been haunted for decades by the deaths of his family, because he still does not know where their bodies lie, never stops trying to save their souls, condemned to wander because they have died violent deaths and had no proper burial. For, in Cambodia, the most hallowed rite is the one for the dead, whom it helps to become reincarnated in a better life. According to Buddhist belief, those who have died a violent death are forever prevented from enjoying that new life cycle. Such persons, who are known by different words in different cultures (ghosts, spirits, shades, etc.) and whose behaviors are subject to a complexity of classifications, are known as *khmoc chau* (literally "uncooked dead").[20] They are distinct from the *khmoc chen* (the cooked dead), who have died of natural causes and been given the proper funeral rites, carried in procession by the community, the family, and the priests in broad daylight.

So the *khmoc chau* are people who have died tragically, by being murdered, say, or drowned. This has prevented them from being cremated or even at times being buried in a cemetery; if a ceremony is actually held for them, it is done as discreetly as possible, to avoid some misfortune befalling the community. The untimely dead are in fact not benevolent beings. Because they have no resting place, they visit the living, especially at night, whom they terrify by their appearance and the hideous faces they pull. Such apparitions often happen at the very spot where they died; there is barely a village where one of these ghosts does not haunt a certain path, which the locals stay well away from. The spirits of the uncooked dead, the most feared and hated of all, can only be kept away by exorcism.

By depriving the 2 million who died in the Cambodian genocide of proper burial, the Khmer Rouge made them *khmoc chau*, that is, restless beings who terrify the population and haunt the survivors with guilt. In this way, they inverted the symbolic and religious systems, turning the rites for victims of problem deaths into an everyday reality and thoroughly perverting the relation with the dead. They also destroyed people's humanity on both planes of its existence, the plane of life and the plane of death. This is perceptible in the word *kamtech* (to turn into dust), which epitomizes the essence of the Cambodian genocide. By forbidding funeral rites, the Khmer Rouge brought "madness" upon the survivors and their descendants, who are thus prevented from engaging in the proper mourning that enables people to get on with their lives. Panh believes that by giving answers to these people, thinking of them, and pacifying memory through respect for them, it may be possible to free them one day. The mission that he is undertaking is to give them back their dignity.

In this sense, *The Missing Picture* is a funeral monument dedicated to his parents, an homage to the act of resistance they undertook: to his father, who chose to stop eating animal food because "I am a man," and to his mother, who recounted the funeral ceremony that her husband ought to have had in accordance with tradition. It was the symbolic and image-producing power of such a burial in words that gave Panh his faith in creation through cinema: "I believe my faith in cinema was born that day. I believe in the image, even if it's staged, interpreted, worked on. In spite of dictatorship one can film a true image."[21] By filming an imaginary funeral and recounting the dignified beauty of the Buddhist procession, he gives his father a symbolic burial. Cinema as a device combining fiction and reality creates a "representational space" in which, oddly, the nearest and dearest can be honored.

In the same way, at the end of *Exile* we see graves made of dirt with incense sticks burning on them. Framed pictures of loved ones, notably his mother and Bophana, are there, set against a great tree.[22] In the following sequence, the same mounds are covered in white roses—white being the color of mourning in Asia—each and every one of them planted by Rithy the child, played by an actor. With these symbolic rites, he hopes their souls can find peace and thus be able to leave the limbo where they languish.

In *Graves without a Name*, Panh comes back to this burying of his dear ones, but this time with actions of greater precision. He films himself taking full part in the ancestral ritual. At the crime scenes, he collects the pebbles in which the missing bodies of the dead are incarnated; with great delicacy, he washes them one by one, then wraps each of them in a piece of spotless fabric and puts it into one of the little paper coffins. Each of the members of his dead family is identified by a photograph standing in front of each of their ten graves: his parents, his brothers and sisters, his niece and his nephews, and Bophana, who was also part of the family.

The procession of the dead is accompanied by the slow chanting of the priests. Panh stands there among the few participants, with his head shaven as tradition requires for anyone in mourning; in his hands he holds a little coffin, which will be set on twigs for the cremation (figure 14.3). When the incineration is complete, the master of ceremonies says a prayer for the dead, as he sprinkles holy water on the ashes. Panh then washes the blackened pebbles before placing them in a stupa, the domed funerary monument of Buddhism, whose function it is to preserve memory. In *Graves without a Name* he says: "Confronted by these images, I weep incessantly. I cannot stop. I am not a grave, just the voice that hoped. Lying among you, I smile at you, I traverse you. I open my hand without fear and let myself be tempted by the wind." By making their presence felt among us, he translates into words and pictures a past that keeps on recurring, as though the souls were inviting us to travel with them.

CONCLUSION

Although Panh has been constantly at work, especially in *The Missing Picture*, *Exile*, and *Graves without a Name*, building his symbolic burial site, offering his dead a "garment of peace," this has not afforded any repose. At times deliverance seems to be out of reach: "I imagined that, if I kept on making films, their wandering souls would stop visiting me at night, that they would free themselves from me. But the more films I make, the more I see them. I wonder sometimes whether my work as a filmmaker has not imprisoned them. Yet I long for their

FIGURE 14.3. A funeral ritual for Panh's lost loved ones

souls to be free and to be at peace as well. The relation between pictures, the souls, and me is rather complicated."[23]

Indeed, the past floods in, like a breaker that is too strong, a leitmotif in *The Missing Picture*. The grief is not assuaged; its movement becomes keener, like a surf full of the past breaking on the present: "Amid this chaos of waves flooding over me, I must keep my head above water. Art, creation and cinema are a breather for the soul. I am dead, I come back to life, but I come back with death. At the same time, it is this death that has remade me."[24] Although part of him died with his family at the hands of the Khmer Rouge, he sees his exile in France as a new departure, and creation through filmmaking as a rebirth. Besides, in Buddhist belief, death is never definitive but only ever a death-as-rebirth.

In a sense, Panh creates so as not to die a second time. In *Graves without a Name* he says: "I did not want to be part of the image. But it got the better of me. I have made so many images to forget that I was dead, I denuded myself." Through these three films of his, which amount to a composite reflection on the long-drawn-out and difficult reconstruction of self, Panh, who has experienced such a disintegration of his own being, has divulged his past, his aloneness, and his infinite sorrow as never before. By means of this *gift* to everybody, he has fulfilled the task of transmitting the missing images of genocide and made us reflect upon the place of the dead in our present.

Beyond the tragedy of Cambodia, this storyteller of the extreme shows that creativity can allow us to think what is unthinkable about genocide, while at the same time revealing the irreducibility of human beings. His films bear constant witness that nothing and no one has been forgotten. One meaning that we can give to what wandering souls do is "living on."

NOTES

1. Walter Benjamin, "The Storyteller: Reflections on the Work of Nicolas Leskov," in *Illuminations,* ed. Hannah Arendt, trans. Harry Zohn (New York: Schocken Books, 1969), 87. All translations provided by James Grieve unless otherwise noted.
2. Benjamin, 84.
3. Rithy Panh with Christophe Bataille, *L'image manquante* (Paris: Grasset, 2013), 68.
4. See my essay "Les archives manquantes du génocide cambodgien," in *Archives au présent,* ed. Patrick Nardin, Catherine Perret, Soko Phay, and Anna Seiderer (Saint-Denis: Presses Universitaires de Vincennes, 2017), 167–168.
5. Panh, *L'image manquante,* 9.
6. At S-21, confessions by victims, obtained mainly through torture, were seen by the Khmer Rouge as proof of treason justifying their being put to death.
7. See the press kit for *L'image manquante.*
8. Panh, *L'image manquante,* 20.
9. The purpose of the wholesale deportation of all the urban populations of Cambodia was to uproot town dwellers from their milieu. Because they had been born or lived in towns, which were seen as places of imperialistic contamination, they were considered to be impure, in need of ideological reeducation, and subject to the policy of land collectivization.
10. Edward W. Said, *Reflections on Exile and Other Essays* (Cambridge, MA: Harvard University Press, 2000), 177.
11. Jean Améry, *Par-delà le crime et le châtiment: Essai pour surmonter l'insurmontable* (1966; Arles: Actes Sud, 1995), 143.
12. See Hannah Arendt, *Les origines du totalitarisme, suivi de Eichmann à Jérusalem,* trans. Jean-Loup Bourget, Robert Davreu, Anne Guérin, Martine Leiris, Patrick Lévy, and Micheline Pouteau (Paris: Gallimard, 2002), 834.
13. See Marie Bornand, *Témoignage et fiction* (Droz: Genève, 2004), 8–10.
14. Rithy Panh, "Rithy Panh: 'Une fois qu'on est exilé, apatride ou réfugié, on le porte toute sa vie,'" interview by Elisabeth Cardon, *Le Temps,* March 10, 2017, https://www.letemps.ch/culture/rithy-panh-une-quon-exile-apatride-refugie-on-porte-toute-vie.
15. Rechtman, "L'empreinte des morts: Remarques sur l'intentionnalité génocidaire," in *Cambodge, l'atelier de la mémoire,* ed. Soko Phay-Vakalis (Battambang: Sonleuk Thmey, 2010), 137.
16. Rithy Panh, "Avec *les Tombeaux sans noms,* Rithy Panh rend leur dignité aux victimes des Khmers rouges," interview by François Ekchajzer, *Télérama,* June 27, 2019, https://www.telerama.fr/television/avec-les-tombeaux-sans-noms,-rithy-panh-rend-leur-dignite-aux-victimes-des-khmers-rouges,n6299078.php.
17. Rithy Panh, "Rithy Panh: 'Je n'ai pas envie d'arriver à la conclusion que l'homme est mauvais,'" interview by Arnaud Vaulerin, *Libération,* January 4, 2019, https://www.liberation.fr/debats/2019/01/04/rithy-panh-je-n-ai-pas-envie-d-arriver-a-la-conclusion-que-l-homme-est-mauvais_1701054.
18. Panh, interview by Arnaud Vaulerin.
19. See my article "Fictions mortifères et esthétisation de la mort," *NAQD,* no. 33–34 (December 2016): 47.
20. See the work of Ang Choulean, in particular "La notion de mort et la notion d'esprits," in *Les êtres surnaturels dans la religion populaire khmère* (Paris: Cedorek, 1986), 97–114.
21. Rithy Panh with Christophe Bataille, *The Elimination: A Survivor of the Khmer Rouge Confronts His Past and the Commandant of the Killing Fields,* trans. John Cullen (New York: Other Press, 2013), 105.

22. Bophana was one of the victims of the S-21 extermination center.
23. Panh, interview by François Ekchajzer.
24. Rithy Panh, "Rithy Panh: 'Comment parler de cette mort en nous?,'" interview by Jean-Claude Raspiengeas, *La Croix*, October 8, 2013, http://www.la-croix.com/Culture/Cinema/Rithy-Panh-Comment-parler-de-cette-mort-en-nous-2013-10-08-1036456.

ACKNOWLEDGMENTS

It would not have been possible to complete this volume without the institutional and financial support of our home universities, Clemson University and the Australian National University (ANU). At Clemson, we express our gratitude to the Humanities Hub, the Department of Languages, and the College of Arts, Architecture, and Humanities. At the ANU, we must thank the Research School of the Humanities and the Arts, the Humanities Research Centre, and the Screen Studies Reading Group in the School of Literature, Languages and Linguistics. We also wish to acknowledge the late James Grieve for his translation of chapter 14 from the original French.

We are especially grateful to staff at the Bophana Center for their consummate skill and warm hospitality, in Phnom Penh and virtually: Piseth Tieng, Sopheaktra An, Ratana Cheng, Ratana Lach, Kazumi Arai, and most of all Sopheap Chea, the center's executive director, who kindly facilitated communication and provided prompt and critical assistance and access to films. The volume benefited immensely from a daylong symposium, uniting more than half of the contributors, held at the Bophana Center in July 2019.

Finally, we would like to express our deepest gratitude to Rithy Panh, whose example of generosity, talent, and perseverance has inspired each of us. We further thank the contributors to this volume, who have demonstrated much of the same care and respect for Rithy's work that he cultivates in every project.

BIBLIOGRAPHY

Adler, Laure. *Marguerite Duras*. Paris: Gallimard, 1998.

Agamben, Giorgio. "Notes on Gesture." In *Means without End: Notes on Politics,* translated by Vincenzo Binetti and Cesare Casarino, 49–62. Minneapolis: University of Minnesota Press, 2000.

Alpers, Svetlana. *The Art of Describing: Dutch Art in the Seventeenth Century*. Chicago: University of Chicago Press, 1984.

Amad, Paula. "Between the 'Familiar Text' and the 'Book of the World.'" In *Virtual Voyages: Cinema and Travel,* edited by Jeffrey Ruoff, 99–116. Durham, NC: Duke University Press, 2006.

———. *Counter-archive: Film, the Everyday, and Albert Kahn's Archives de la Planète*. New York: Columbia University Press, 2010.

———. "Visual Riposte: Looking Back at the Return of the Gaze as Postcolonial Theory's Gift to Film Studies." *Cinema Journal* 52, no. 3 (Spring 2013): 49–74.

Améry, Jean. *At the Mind's Limits: Contemplations by a Survivor on Auschwitz and Its Realities*. Translated by Sidney Rosenfeld and Stella P. Rosenfeld. Bloomington: Indiana University Press, 1980.

———. *Par-delà le crime et le châtiment: Essai pour surmonter l'insurmontable*. Arles: Actes Sud, 1995.

———. *Radical Humanism: Selected Essays*. Edited and translated by Sidney Rosenfeld and Stella P. Rosenfeld. Bloomington: Indiana University Press, 1984.

Anderson, Benedict. *Imagined Communities: Reflections on the Origins and Spread of Nationalism*. Revised ed. London: Verso, 2006.

Ang Choulean. *Les êtres surnaturels dans la religion populaire khmère*. Paris: Cedorek, 1986.

Arendt, Hannah. *The Human Condition*. 2nd ed. Chicago: University of Chicago Press, 1998.

Assmann, Aleida. "Two Forms of Resentment: Jean Améry, Martin Walser and German Memorial Culture." *New German Critique* 90 (Autumn 2003): 123–133.

Assmann, Jan. "Communicative and Cultural Memory." In *Cultural Memory Studies: An International and Interdisciplinary Handbook,* edited by Astrid Erll and Ansgar Nünning, 109–118. Berlin: De Gruyter, 2008.

Barbour, John. "Edward Said and the Space of Exile." *Literature and Theology* 21, no. 3 (2007): 293–301.

Barnes, Leslie. "Objects of Pleasure: Epistephilia and the Sex Worker in Rithy Panh's *Le papier ne peut pas envelopper la braise*." *French Cultural Studies* 5, no. 2 (2015): 56–65.

———. *Vietnam and the Colonial Condition of French Literature*. Lincoln: University of Nebraska Press, 2014.

Becker, Elizabeth. *Bophana*. Phnom Penh: Cambodia Daily Press, 2010.

———. *When the War Was Over: Cambodia and the Khmer Rouge Revolution*. New York: Simon and Schuster, 1986.

Benjamin, Walter. "The Storyteller: Reflections on the Works of Nicolai Leskov." In *Illuminations,* edited by Hannah Arendt, translated by Harry Zohn, 83–109. New York: Schocken Books, 1969.

Bernath, Julie. "'Complex Political Victims' in the Aftermath of Mass Atrocity: Reflections on the Khmer Rouge Tribunal in Cambodia." *International Journal of Transitional Justice* 10, no. 1 (2016): 46–66.

Bhabha, Homi. *The Location of Culture*. London: Routledge, 1994.

Bizot, François. *Facing the Torturer*. Translated by Charlotte Mandell and Antoine Audouard. New York: Knopf, 2012.

———. *The Gate*. Translated by Ewan Cameron. New York: Random House, 2003.

———. "Préface." In David Chandler, *S-21 ou Le crime impuni des Khmers rouges*, 5–11. Paris: Autrement, 2002.

———. *Le saut du Varan* Paris: Flammarion, 2006.

Blanchard, Pascal. "Un musée sur l'histoire coloniale: Il est temps." *Libération*, May 29, 2019. https://www.liberation.fr/debats/2019/05/29/un-musee-sur-l-histoire-coloniale-il-est-temps_1730468.

Blanchard, Pascal, Nicolas Bancel, Gilles Boëtsch, Christelle Taraud, and Dominic Thomas. *Sexe, race & colonies: La domination des corps du XVe siècle à nos jours*. Paris: Editions La Découverte, 2018.

Bloom, Peter J. *French Colonial Documentary: Mythologies of Humanitarianism*. Minneapolis: University of Minnesota Press, 2008.

Blum-Reid, Sylvie. *East-West Encounters: Franco-Asian Cinema and Literature*. New York: Wallflower Press, 2003.

———. "Khmer Memories or Filming with Cambodia." *Inter-Asia Cultural Studies* 4, no.1 (2003): 126–138.

Bornand, Marie. *Témoignage et fiction*. Droz: Genève, 2004.

Borneman, John. "Reconciliation after Ethnic Cleansing: Listening, Retribution, Affiliation." *Public Culture* 14, no. 2 (2002): 281–304.

Boyle, Deirdre. "Exile within and Without: New Work in Two Modes from Rithy Panh." *Film Quarterly* 71, no. 1 (2017): 10–17.

———. "Finding the Missing Picture: The Films of Rithy Panh." *Cineaste* 39, no. 3 (2014): 28–32.

———. "Interviewing the Devil: Interrogating Masters of the Cambodian Genocide." In *A Companion to Contemporary Documentary Film*, edited by Alexandra Juhasz and Alisa Lebow, 506–523. West Sussex, UK: Wiley Blackwell, 2015.

———. "Shattering Silence: Traumatic Memory and Reenactment in Rithy Panh's *S21: The Khmer Rouge Killing Machine*." *Framework* 50, no. 1/2 (Spring and Fall 2009): 95–106.

———. "Trauma, Memory, Documentary: Re-enactment in Two Films by Rithy Panh (Cambodia) and Garin Nugroho (Indonesia)." In *Documentary Testimonies: Archives of Suffering*, edited by Janet Walker and Bhaskar Sarkar, 155–172. New York: Routledge, 2010.

Brault, Pascale-Anne, and Michael Naas. "To Reckon with the Dead: Jacques Derrida's Politics of Mourning." In Jacques Derrida, *The Work of Mourning*, edited and translated by Pascale-Anne Brault and Michael Naas, 1–30. Chicago: University of Chicago Press, 2001.

Brudholm, Thomas. *Resentment's Virtue: Jean Améry and the Refusal to Forgive*. Philadelphia: Temple University Press, 2008.

"Building Construction Site in Cambodia Collapses, Killing at Least 13 and Trapping Dozens." ABC News, June 23, 2019. https://www.abc.net.au/news/2019-06-22/cambodia-building-collapse-kills-and-injures-workers/11238284.

Burgler, Roel. *The Eyes of the Pineapple: Revolutionary Intellectuals and Terror in Democratic Kampuchea*. Saarbrucken: Verlag Breitenbach, 1990.

Camacho, Lisa Marie. *Social Death*. New York: New York University Press, 2012.

Camus, Albert. *The Myth of Sisyphus*. Translated by Justin O'Brien. New York: Vintage, 1959.

Card, Claudia. "Genocide and Social Death." *Hypatia* 18, no. 1 (2003): 63–79.

Carmichael, Robert. *When Clouds Fell from the Sky: A Disappearance, a Daughter's Search and Cambodia's First War Criminal*. London: Mason-McDonald Press, 2015.

Cavell, Stanley. *The Claim of Reason: Wittgenstein, Skepticism, Morality, and Tragedy*. Oxford: Oxford University Press, 1979.

Cazenave, Jennifer. "Earth as Archive: Reframing Memory and Mourning in *The Missing Picture*." *Cinéma Journal* 57, no. 2 (2018): 44–65.

Césaire, Aimé. *Discours sur le colonialisme*. Paris: Présence Africaine, 1955. *Discourse on Colonialism*. Translated by Joan Pinkham. New York: Monthly Review Press, 1972.

Chandler, David. *A History of Cambodia*, 4th ed. New York: Routledge, 2018.

———. "Songs at the Edge of the Forest: Perceptions of Order in Three Cambodian Texts." In *At the Edge of the Forest: Essays on Cambodia, History and Narrative in Honor of David Chandler*, edited by Anne Ruth Hansen and Judy Ledgerwood, 31–46. Ithaca, NY: Cornell University Press, 2008.

———. *Voices from S-21: Terror and History in Pol Pot's Secret Prison*. Berkeley: University of California Press, 1999.

Charny, Israel W. "A Classification of Denials of the Holocaust and Other Genocides." In *The Genocide Studies Reader*, edited by Samuel Totten and Paul R. Bartrop, 518–537. New York: Routledge, 2009.

Chartier, Christine. "Que la barque se brise, que le jonque s'entrouve." *Arte France*, October 2001. http://download.pro.arte.tv/archives/fichiers/01676247.pdf.

Chhim, Sotheara. "*Baksbat* (Broken Courage): A Trauma-Based Syndrome in Cambodia." *Medical Anthropology* 32 (2013): 160–173.

Chon, Gina, and Thet Sambath. *Behind the Killing Fields: A Khmer Rouge Leader and One of His Victims*. Philadelphia: University of Pennsylvania Press, 2010.

Chow, Rey. *Primitive Passions: Visuality, Sexuality, Ethnography, and Contemporary Chinese Cinema*. New York: Columbia University Press, 1995.

Chy, Terith. *When the Criminal Laughs*. Phnom Penh: Documentation Center of Cambodia, 2014.

Cohen, Stanley. *States of Denial: Knowing about Atrocities and Suffering*. Cambridge, UK: Polity Press, 2001.

Conklin, Alice. *A Mission to Civilize: The Republican Idea of Empire in France and West Africa, 1895–1930*. Stanford, CA: Stanford University Press, 1997.

Corrigan, Timothy. *The Essay Film: From Montaigne, after Marker*. Oxford: Oxford University Press, 2011.

Corrigan, Timothy, and Nora Alter, eds. *Essays on the Essay Film*. New York: Columbia University Press, 2017.

"Construction." *Open Development Cambodia*, May 12, 2016. https://opendevelopmentcambodia.net/topics/construction/.

Creed, Barbara, and Jeanette Hoorn. "Memory and History: Early Film, Colonialism, and the French Civilizing Mission in Indochina." *French History and Civilization* 4 (2011): 223–236.

Cruvellier, Thierry. *The Master of Confessions: The Making of a Khmer Rouge Torturer*. Translated by Alex Gilly. New York: HarperCollins, 2014.

Das, Veena. *Life and Words: Violence and the Descent into the Ordinary*. Berkeley: University of California Press, 2007.

Derrida, Jacques. *The Gift of Death*. Translated by David Wills. Chicago: University of Chicago Press, 1995.

———. *On Cosmopolitanism and Forgiveness*. Translated by Mark Dooley and Michael Hughes. New York: Routledge, 2001.

———. *The Work of Mourning*. Edited and translated by Pascale-Anne Brault and Michael Nass. Chicago: University of Chicago Press, 2001.

De Swaan, Abram. *The Killing Compartments: The Mentality of Mass Murder*. New Haven, CT: Yale University Press, 2014.

Diderot, Denis. *Diderot on Art II*. Edited and translated by John Goodman. New Haven, CT: Yale University Press, 1995.

Dirlik, Arif. "Rethinking Colonialism: Globalization, Postcolonialism, and the Nation." *Interventions* 4, no. 3 (2002): 428-448.

Dunlop, Nic. *The Lost Executioner: The Story of Comrade Duch and the Khmer Rouge*. London: Bloomsbury, 2005.

Duras, Marguerite *L'amant*. Paris: Minuit, 1984. *The Lover*. Translated by Barbara Bray. New York: Pantheon, 1985.

———. *L'amant de la Chine du nord*. Paris: Gallimard, 1991. *The North China Lover*. Translated by Leigh Hafrey. New York: New Press, 1992.

———. "Chant du caporal," Fonds Duras, Institut Mémoires de l'Edition Contemporaine, DRS 30.10, "*Un barrage contre le Pacifique*, textes préparatoires."

———. *Un barrage contre le Pacifique*. Paris: Gallimard (Folio), 1950. *The Sea Wall*. Translated by Herma Briffault. New York: Harper and Row, 1952.

Ea, Meng-Try, and Sorya Sim. *Victims and Perpetrators? Testimony of Young Khmer Rouge Comrades*. Phnom Penh: Documentation Center of Cambodia, 2001.

Edgerton, Samuel E. *The Mirror, the Window and the Telescope: How Renaissance Perspective Changed Our Vision of the Universe*. Ithaca, NY: Cornell University Press, 2009.

Eisenstein, Sergei. *The Eisenstein Reader*. Edited by Richard Taylor. Translated by Richard Taylor and William Powell. London: British Film Institute, 1998.

Federici, Silvia. *Revolution at Point Zero: Housework, Reproduction, and Feminist Struggle*. New York: PM Press, 2012.

Ferguson, James G. "Of Mimicry and Membership: Africans and the 'New World Society.'" *Cultural Anthropology* 17, no. 4 (2002): 551–569.

Fernandes, Marie-Pierre. *Un barrage contre le Pacifique hier et aujourd'hui: De Prey Nop à Sadec avec Marguerite Duras*. La Compagnie du Caillou, 2011.

Foucault, Michel. *Language, Madness, and Desire: On Literature*. Edited by Philippe Artières, Jean-François Bert, Mathieu Potte-Bonneville, and Judith Revel. Translated by Roberto Bononno. Minneapolis: University of Minnesota Press, 2015.

French, Lindsay. *Displaced Lives*. IRC Oral History Project. Bangkok: International Rescue Committee, 1991.

———. "Enduring Holocaust, Surviving History: Displaced Cambodians on the Thai Cambodian Border 1989–1991." PhD diss., Harvard University, 1994.

———. "Exhibiting Terror." In *Truth Claims: Representation and Human Rights*, edited by Mark Philip Bradley and Patrice Petro, 131–155. New Brunswick, NJ: Rutgers University Press, 2002.

Frings, Manfred S. "Introduction." In Max Scheler, *Ressentiment*, translated by Lewis B. Coser and William W. Holdheim, 1–18. Milwaukee, WI: Marquette University Press, 2010.

Gemignani, Marco. "The Past If Past: The Use of Memories and Self-Healing Narratives in Refugees from the Former Yugoslavia." *Journal of Refugee Studies* 24, no. 1 (2011): 132–156.

Griffiths, Alison. *Wondrous Difference: Cinema, Anthropology, and Turn-of-the-Century Visual Culture*. New York: Columbia University Press, 2002.

Grundmann, Royt, and Cynthia Rockwell. "Truth Is Not Subjective: An Interview with Errol Morris." *Cineaste* 24, no. 3 (2000): 4–9.

Gunning, Tom. "Before Documentary: Early Nonfiction Films and the 'View' Aesthetic." In *Uncharted Territory: Essays on Early Nonfiction Film*, edited by Daan Hertogs and Nico de Klerk, 9–24. Amsterdam: Stichting Nederlands Filmmuseum, 1997.

———. "'The Whole World within Reach': Travel Images without Borders." In *Virtual Voyages: Cinema and Travel*, edited by Jeffrey Ruoff, 25–41. Durham, NC: Duke University Press, 2006.

Hamilton, Annette. "Witness and Recuperation: Cambodia's New Documentary Cinema." *Concentric: Literary and Cultural Studies* 39, no. 1 (2013): 7–30.

Hansen, Anne Ruth, and Judy Ledgerwood, eds. *At the Edge of the Forest: Essays on Cambodia, History and Narrative in Honor of David Chandler*. Ithaca, NY: Cornell University Press, 2008.

Harvey, Graham. *Animism: Respecting the Living World*. 2nd ed. London: Hurst, 2017.

Heijmans, Philip. "Chinese Money Is Driving One of Asia's Fastest Property Booms." *Bloomberg*, September 11, 2018. https://www.bloomberg.com/news/features/2018-09-10/chinese-money-is-driving-a-property-boom-in-cambodia.

Herzog, Werner. "Minnesota Declaration." In *The Philosophy of Documentary Film: Image, Sound, Fiction, Truth*, edited by David LaRocca, 379–380. Lanham, MD: Lexington Books, 2017.

Hinton, Alexander Laban. *Man or Monster? The Trial of a Khmer Rouge Torturer*. Durham, NC: Duke University Press, 2016.

———. *Why Did They Kill? Cambodia in the Shadow of Genocide*. Berkeley: University of California Press, 2005.

Hirsch, Marianne. *The Generation of Postmemory: Writing and Visual Culture after the Holocaust*. New York: Columbia University Press, 2012.

———."Surviving Images: Holocaust Photographs and the Work of Postmemory." *Yale Journal of Criticism* 14, no. 1 (Spring 2001): 5–37.

Hoven, Elisa. "Civil Party Participation in Trials of Mass Crimes: A Qualitative Study at the Extraordinary Chambers in the Courts of Cambodia." *Journal of International Criminal Justice* 12, no. 1 (2014): 81–107.

Hoven, Elisa, Mareike Feiler, and Saskia Scheibel. "Victims in Trials of Mass Crimes: A Multi-perspective Study of Civil Party Participation at the Extraordinary Chambers in the Courts of Cambodia." *Cologne Occasional Papers on International Peace and Security Law*, no. 3. Cologne: Cologne University Press, 2013.

Hruby, Denis. "Cambodia Suffers from an Appalling Mental Health Crisis." *Global Post*. June 17, 2014. http://www.globalpost.com/dispatch/news/regions/asia-pacific/cambodia/140616/cambodia-suffers-appalling-mental-health-crisis.

Huppert, Isabelle. "Interview." *Cinémoi*. Included as a special feature on the DVD release, 2008.

International Labour Organization. "Enhancing Occupational Safety and Health Standards in Construction Sector in Cambodia." Accessed December 9, 2020. https://www.ilo.org/asia/projects/WCMS_577102/lang--ja/index.htm.

Ith, Sarin. "Life in the Bureaus (Offices) of the Khmer Rouge." In *Communist Party Power in Kampuchea (Cambodia): Documents and Discussion*, compiled and edited by Timothy Michael Carney, 42–55. Data paper no. 106, Southeast Asia Program, Department of Asian Studies, Cornell University, January 1977.

Jackson, Karl, ed. *Cambodia 1975–1978*. Princeton, NJ: Princeton University Press, 1992.

Jennings, Eric T. "*The Sea Wall.*" *Fiction and Film for Scholars of France: A Cultural Bulletin* 4 (2009). http://h-france.net/ffth/classics/indochine-and-the-sea-wall/.

Kaplan, Caren. *Aerial Aftermaths: War from Above*. Durham, NC: Duke University Press, 2018.

Khieu Samphan. *L'histoire récente du Cambodge et mes prises de position*. Paris: L'Harmattan, 2004.

Kiernan, Ben. *How Pol Pot Came to Power: Colonialism, Nationalism, and Communism in Cambodia, 1930–1975*. New Haven, CT: Yale University Press, 2004.

———. *The Pol Pot Regime: Race, Power, and Genocide in Cambodia under the Khmer Rouge, 1975–79*. New Haven, CT: Yale University Press, 1996.

Krogsgaard, Jan, and Thomas Weber Carlsen. "Voices of the Khmer Rouge." Austro Sino Art Program. Accessed November 7, 2019. http://www.austrosinoartsprogram.org/blog/jan-krogsgaard-thomas-weber-carlsen-voices-khmer-rouge.

Kuper, Leo. *The Prevention of Genocide*. New Haven, CT: Yale University Press, 1985.

Langford, Jean M. *Consoling Ghosts: Stories of Medicine and Mourning from Southeast Asians in Exile*. Minneapolis: University of Minnesota Press, 2013.

LaRocca, David. "Inconclusive Scientific Postscript: Late Remarks on Kierkegaard and Kaufman." In *The Philosophy of Charlie Kaufman*, edited by David LaRocca, 269–294. Lexington: University Press of Kentucky, 2011.

———. "'Profoundly Unreconciled to Nature': Ecstatic Truth and the Humanistic Sublime in Werner Herzog's War Films." In *The Philosophy of War Films*, edited by David LaRocca, 437–482. Lexington: University Press of Kentucky, 2014.

———. "A Reality Rescinded: The Transformative Effects of Fraud in *I'm Still Here*." In *The Philosophy of Documentary Film: Image, Sound, Fiction, Truth*, edited by David LaRocca, 537–576. Lanham, MD: Lexington Books, 2017.

———. "Representative Qualities and Questions of Documentary Film." In *The Philosophy of Documentary Film: Image, Sound, Fiction, Truth*, edited by David LaRocca, 1–54. Lanham, MD: Lexington Books, 2017.

———. "Unauthorized Autobiography: Truth and Fact in *Confessions of a Dangerous Mind*." In *The Philosophy of Charlie Kaufman*, edited by David LaRocca, 89–110. Lexington: University Press of Kentucky, 2011.

Le Corbusier. *The Modulor*. Translated by Peter de Francia and Anna Bostock. Basel: Birkhäuser, 2000.

———. *Toward an Architecture (Texts and Documents)*. Translated by John Goodman. Los Angeles: Getty Research Institute, 2008.

Ledgerwood, Judy. "Khmer Kinship: The Matriliny/Matriarchy Myth." *Journal of Anthropological Research* 53, no. 1 (Autumn 1995): 247–261.

Legendre, Aimé-François. *Le far-west chinois: Deux années au Setchouen*. Paris: Plon, 1905.

Lemonde, Marcel. *Un juge face aux Khmers Rouges*. Paris: Le Seuil, 2013.

Lim, Alvin. *Cambodia and the Politics of Aesthetics*. New York: Routledge, 2013.

Locard, Henri. *Le "Petit Livre Rouge" de Pol Pot ou les paroles de l'Angkar entendues dans le Cambodge des Khmers Rouges du 17 avril 1975 au 7 janvier 1979*. Paris: L'Harmattan, 1997.

Lopate, Philip. "In Search of the Centaur: The Essay-Film." In *Beyond Document: Essays on Nonfiction Film*, edited by Charles Warren, 243-270. Middletown: Wesleyan University Press, 1996.

Lukács, György. "On the Nature and Form of the Essay." In *Soul and Form*, edited by John T. Sanders and Katie Terezakis and translated by Anna Bostock, 16–34. New York: Columbia University Press, 2010.

Ly, Boreth. "Screening the Crisis of Monetary Masculinity in Rithy Panh's *One Night after the War* and *Burnt Theatre*." In *Film in Contemporary Southeast Asia: Cultural Interpretation and Social Intervention*, edited by David C. L. Lim and Hiroyuki Yamamoto, 53–72. London: Routledge, 2012.

———. *Traces of Trauma: Cambodian Visual Culture and National Identity in the Aftermath of Genocide*. Honolulu: University of Hawai'i Press, 2020.

Ly Daravuth, and Ingrid Muan. *Cultures of Independence*. Phnom Penh: Reyum, 2001.

Lyotard, Jean-François. *The Differend*. Translated by George Van den Abbeele. Minneapolis: University of Minnesota Press, 1989.

MacDonald, Scott. *Binghamton Babylon: Voices from the Cinema Department, 1967–1977*. Albany: State University of New York Press, 2015.

———. *A Critical Cinema 3: Interviews with Independent Filmmakers*. Berkeley: University of California Press, 1998.

Mai, Joseph. "*Site 2*: Style and Encounter in Rithy Panh's Cinéma-monde." In *Cinéma-monde: Decentred Perspectives on Global Filmmaking in French*, edited by Michael Gott and Thibaut Schilt, 25–44. Edinburgh: Edinburgh University Press, 2018.

Mangeot, Philippe, Jean-Philippe Renouard, and Isabelle Saint-Saëns. "La parole des tueurs: Une mémoire des corps: Entretien avec Jean Hatzfeld et Rithy Panh." *Vacarme* 2, no. 27 (2004): 31–36.

Margulies, Ivone. "Exemplary Bodies: Reenactment in *Love in the City, Sons*, and *Close Up*." In *Rites of Realism: Essays on Corporeal Cinema*, edited by Ivone Margulies, 217–244. Durham, NC: Duke University Press, 2002.

———. *In Person: Reenactment in Postwar and Contemporary Cinema*. Oxford: Oxford University Press, 2018.

Marx, Karl. "Estranged Labour." In The Economic and Philosophical Manuscripts, in The Marx-Engels Reader, edited by by Robert C. Tucker, 70–81. 2nd ed. New York: W. W. Norton, 1978.

———. "Wage Labour and Capital." In *The Marx-Engels Reader*, edited by Robert C. Tucker, 203–217. 2nd ed. New York: W. W. Norton, 1978.

Meas, Roth. "KR Soldiers Voice Views on Film." *Phnom Penh Post*, February 28, 2011. https://www.phnompenhpost.com/lifestyle/kr-soldiers-voice-views-film.

Meierhenrich, Jens. "Varieties of Reconciliation." *Law and Social Inquiry* 33, no. 1 (2008): 195–231.

Mérigard, Dominique. *Témoin S-21: Face au génocide des Cambodgiens*. Manosque: Le Bec en l'air, 2008.

Merigeau, Pascal. "Rithy Panh passe 'Duch' à la question." *L'Obs*, October 23, 2014. https://www.nouvelobs.com/cinema/20120104.CIN0404/rithy-panh-passe-duch-a-la-question.html.

Mesguich, Félix. *Tours de manivelle: Souvenirs d'un chasseur d'images*. Paris: Editions Bernard Grasset, 1933.

Morag, Raya. *Perpetrator Cinema: Confronting Genocide in Cambodian Documentary*. New York: Columbia University Press, 2020.

Morin, Florence. "L'image manquante, le chef d'oeuvre de Rithy Panh." *Le Petit Journal*, August 28, 2014. https://lepetitjournal.com/sortie-cinema-limage-manquante-le-chef-doeuvre-de-rithy-panh-208607.

Mydans, Seth. "In a Cambodian Friendship, a Secret Quest." *New York Times*, August 6, 2010. https://www.nytimes.com/2010/08/07/world/asia/07cambo.html.

Myers, David G. "Jean Améry: A Biographical Introduction." In *Holocaust Literature: An Encyclopedia of Writers and Their Work*, edited by S. Lillian Kremer, 20–24. New York: Routledge, 2002.

Najmi, Samina. "Naomi Shihab Nye's Aesthetic Smallness and the Military Sublime." *MELUS* 35, no. 2 (2010): 151–171.

Nguyen, Viet Thanh. "On True War Stories." In "(Re)Collecting the Vietnam War," edited by Cathy J. Schlund-Vials and Sylvia Shin Huey Chong. Special issue, *Asian American Literary Review* 6, no. 2 (2015): 140–145.

Nhem En, and Dara Duong. *Nhem En: The Khmer Rouge's Photographer at S-21: Under the Khmer Rouge Genocide: Personal Memoir.* Cambodia: self-published, 2014.

Nichols, Bill. "Documentary Reenactment and the Fantasmatic Subject." *Critical Inquiry* 35, no. 1 (Autumn 2008): 72–89.

Nietzsche, Friedrich Wilhelm. *On the Genealogy of Morals*. Translated by Douglas Smith. New York: Oxford University Press, 2009.

Niven, Douglas, and Chris Riley. *The Killing Fields*. Santa Fe, NM: Twin Palms, 1996.

Norindr, Panivong. *Phantasmatic Indochina: French Colonial Ideology in Architecture, Film, and Literature*. Durham, NC: Duke University Press, 1996.

———. "The Sounds of Everyday Life in Rithy Panh's Documentaries." *French Forum* 35, no. 2–3 (2010): 181–190.

Ōe, Kenzaburō. "Prize Stock." In *Teach Us How to Outgrow Our Madness*, translated by John Nathan, 117–170. New York: Publisher's Group West, 1977.

Olick, Jeffrey K. *The Politics of Regret: On Collective Memory and Historical Responsibility*. New York: Routledge, 2007.

———. "Time for Forgiveness: A Historical Perspective." In *Considering Forgiveness*, edited by Aleksandra Wagner with Carin Kuoni and Matthew Buckingham, 85–92. New York: Vera List Center for Art and Politics, 2009.

Ong, Aihwa. *Flexible Citizenship: The Cultural Logics of Transnationality*. Durham, NC: Duke University Press, 1999.

Oppenheimer, Joshua. "Perpetrators' Testimony and the Restoration of Humanity: S.21, Rithy Panh." In *Killer Images: Documentary Film, Memory and the Performance of Violence*, edited by Joram ten Brink and Joshua Oppenheimer, 243–255. New York: Columbia University Press, 2012.

Osborne, Milton. *Phnom Penh: A Cultural History*. Oxford: Oxford University Press, 2008.

———. *Sihanouk: Prince of Light, Prince of Darkness*. Honolulu: University of Hawaii Press, 1994.

Owen, Taylor, and Ben Kiernan. "Bombs over Cambodia." *The Walrus*, October 2006, 67.

Panh, Rithy. "Au Cambodge, le cinema est une medicine." Interview by Antoine Baecque, *Libération*, October 5, 2005. https://www.liberation.fr/cahier-special/2005/10/05/au-cambodge-le-cinema-est-une medecine_534510.

———. "Avec les Tombeaux sans noms, Rithy Panh rend leur dignité aux victimes des Khmers rouges." Interview by François Ekchajzer. *Télérama*, June 27, 2019. https://www.telerama.fr/television/avec-les-tombeaux-sans-noms,-rithy-panh-rend-leur-dignite-aux-victimes-des-khmers-rouges,n6299078.php.

———. "Cambodia: A Wound That Will Not Heal." *UNESCO Courier* 52 (December 12, 1999): 30–32.

———. "Ce sont les petits gestes qui éclairent les grandes causes." Interview by Marie Ingouf. *Les Ecrans Terribles*, November 28, 2017. http://www.lesecransterribles.com/petits-gestes-eclairent-grandes-causes-rencontre-rithy-panh/46720.

———. "Confronting Images of Ideology: An Interview with Rithy Panh." Interview by Deirdre Boyle. *Cineaste* 39, no. 3 (2014): 33–35.

———. "Epilogue." In *Bringing the Khmer Rouge to Justice*, edited by Jaya Ramji and Beth Van Schaack, 425–438. Lewiston, NY: Edwin Mellen Press, 2005.

———. "Interview." *Cinémoi*. Included as a special feature on the DVD release, 2008.

———. "On a Morality of Filming: A Conversation between Rithy Panh and Deirdre Boyle." *CineAction* 97 (2016): 39–44.

———. "La parole filmée: Pour vaincre la terreur." *Communications* 71 (2001): 373–394.

———. "Rithy Panh on Exile and Dignity." Interview by Alessandro Marazzi Sassoon. *Phnom Penh Post*, March 4, 2017. https://www.phnompenhpost.com/post-weekend/qa-rithy-panh-exile-and-dignity.

———. "Rithy Panh on Film Preservation and the Importance of Memory." Interview by Frako Loden. International Documentary Association, November 19, 2014. https://www.documentary.org/feature/rithy-panh-film-preservation-and-importance-memory.

———. "Rithy Panh on the Remembrance of Times Past." *Phnom Penh Post*, December 15, 2006. https://www.phnompenhpost.com/national/rithy-panh-remembrance-times-past.

———. "Rithy Panh Revisits the Horrors of the Khmer Rouge." Interview by Frédéric Burnand. *Swissinfo*, March 16, 2019. https://www.swissinfo.ch/eng/graves-without-a-name_rithy-panh-revisits-the-horrors-of-the-khmer-rouge/44827132.

———. "Rithy Panh: 'Comment parler de cette mort en nous?'" Interview by Jean-Claude Raspiengeas. *La Croix*, October 8, 2013. https://www.la-croix.com/Culture/Cinema/Rithy-Panh-Comment-parler-de-cette-mort-en-nous-2013-10-08-1036456.

———. "Rithy Panh: 'Une fois qu'on est exilé, apatride ou réfugié, on le porte toute sa vie.'" Interview by Elisabeth Cardon. *Le Temps*, March 10, 2017. https://www.letemps.ch/culture/rithy-panh-une-quon-exile-apatride-refugie-on-porte-toute-vie.

———. "Rithy Panh: J'entre dans l'histoire par les images." Interview by Marie-Noelle Tranchant. *Le Figaro*, November 19, 2018. https://www.lefigaro.fr/cinema/2018/11/19/03002-20181119ARTFIG00251-rithy-panh-j-entre-dans-l-histoire-par-les-images.php.

———."Rithy Panh: 'Je n'ai pas envie d'arriver à la conclusion que l'homme est mauvais.'" Interview by Arnaud Vaulerin. *Libération*, January 4, 2019. https://www.liberation.fr/debats/2019/01/04/rithy-panh-je-n-ai-pas-envie-d-arriver-a-la-conclusion-que-l-homme-est-mauvais_1701054.

———. "Rithy Panh: 'Je travaille comme un archéologue.'" Interview by Marcos Uzal. *Libération*, June 20, 2019. https://next.liberation.fr/cinema/2019/06/20/rithy-panh-je-travaille-comme-un-archeologue_1735109.

———. "Rithy Panh: Living the Experience of Genocide in Body and Soul." Interview by Thierry Cruvellier. *JusticeInfo.net*, November 27, 2018. https://www.justiceinfo.net/en/justiceinfo-comment-and-debate/in-depth-interviews/39596-rithy-panh-living-the-experience-of-genocide-in-body-and-soul.html.

———. "7 Questions with Rithy Panh." *Phnom Penh Post*, May 30, 2013. https://www.youtube.com/watch?v=QOzBvOtvtys.

———. "Un barrage contre le Pacifique (The Sea Wall)—Interview with Rithy Panh." Interview by Michael Guillen. *ScreenAnarchy*, September 25, 2008. https://screenanarchy.com/2008/09/tiff08-un-barrage-contre-le-pacifique-the-sea-wallinterview-with-rithy-panh.html.

Panh, Rithy, with Christophe Bataille. *L'élimination*. Paris: Grasset, 2012. *The Elimination: A Survivor of the Khmer Rouge Confronts His Past and the Commandant of the Killing Fields*. Translated by John Cullen. New York: Other Press, 2013.

———. *L'image manquante*. Paris: Grasset, 2013.

Panh, Rithy, with Christine Chaumeau. *La machine Khmère Rouge: Monti Santésok S-21*. Paris: Flammarion, 2003.

Panh, Rithy, with Louise Lorentz. *Le papier ne peut pas envelopper la braise*. Paris: Grasset, 2007.

Papazian, Elizabeth A., and Caroline Eades, eds. *The Essay Film: Dialogue, Politics, Utopia*. New York: Columbia University Press, 2016.

Peschoux, Christophe, and Haing Kheng Heng. *Itinerary of an Ordinary Torturer: Interview with Duch, Former Khmer Rouge Commander of S-21*. Chiang Mai: Silkwood Books, 2016.

Peterson, Jennifer Lynn. *Education in the School of Dreams: Travelogues and Early Nonfiction Films*. Durham, NC: Duke University Press, 2013.

Phay, Soko. "Fictions mortifères et esthétisation de la mort." *NAQD*, no. 33–34 (December 2016): 41–52.

———. "Les archives manquantes du génocide cambodgien." In *Archives au présent*, edited by Patrick Nardin, Catherine Perret, Soko Phay, and Anna Seiderer, 159–177. Saint-Denis: Presses Universitaires de Vincennes, 2017.

Picq, Laurence. *Le piège Khmer Rouge*. Paris: Buchet Castel, 2013.

Ponchaud, François. *Cambodge année zéro*. Paris: Julliard, 1977.

Quinn, Kenneth. "The Origins and Development of Radical Cambodian Communism." PhD diss., University of Maryland, 1982.

Rancière, Jacques. *The Emancipated Spectator*. Translated by Gregory Elliot. London: Verso, 2009.

———. *The Future of the Image*. Translated by Gregory Elliott. London: Verso, 2007.

———. *Mute Speech*. Translated by James Swenson. New York: Columbia University Press, 2011.

Rascaroli, Laura. *How the Essay Film Thinks*. Oxford: Oxford University Press, 2017.

———. *The Personal Camera: Subjective Cinema and the Essay Film*. New York: Columbia University Press, 2009.

Rechtman, Richard. "L'empreinte des morts: Remarques sur l'intentionnalité génocidaire." In *Cambodge, l'atelier de la mémoire*, edited by Soko Phay-Vakalis, 133–137. Battambang: Sonleuk Thmey, 2010.

Rich, Adrienne. *Of Woman Born: Motherhood as Experience and Institution*. New York: W. W. Norton, 1995.

Rigney, Ann. "Reconciliation and Remembering: (How) Does It Work?" *Memory Studies* 5, no. 3 (2012): 251–258.

Rivette, Jacques. "On Abjection." Translated by David Phelps and Jeremi Szaniakwi. http://www.dvdbeaver.com/rivette/ok/abjection.html.

Rony, Fatimah Tobing. *The Third Eye: Race, Cinema, and Ethnographic Spectacle*. Durham, NC: Duke University Press, 1996.

Ross, Corey. *Ecology and Power in the Age of Empire: Europe and the Transformation of the Tropical World*. Oxford: Oxford University Press, 2017.

Said, Edward. "Reflections on Exile." *Granta* 13 (1984): 158–172.

———. *Reflections on Exile and Other Essays*. Cambridge, MA: Harvard University Press, 2000.

Sambath, Thet. "The Truth about the Khmer Rouge Is Too Big for One Court Case." *The Guardian*, June 27, 2011. https://www.theguardian.com/law/2011/jun/27/truth-khmer-rouge-court-case.

Sánchez-Biosca, Vicente. "Challenging Old and New Images Representing the Cambodian Genocide: *The Missing Picture* (Rithy Panh, 2013)." *Genocide Studies and Prevention: An International Journal* 12, no. 2 (2018): 140–164.

———. "Perpetrator Images: Quel destin pour les images prises par les criminels?" *Mémoires en Jeu/Memories at Stake*, no. 8 (2018–2019): 131–134.

———. "The Perpetrator's *Mise-en-scène*: Language, Body, and Memory in the Cambodian Genocide." *Journal of Perpetrator Research* 2, no. 1 (2018): 65–94.

Schaack, Beth Van, Daryn Reicherter, and Youk Chhang, eds. *Cambodia's Hidden Scars: Trauma Psychology in the Wake of the Khmer Rouge*. Phnom Penh: DC-Cam, 2011.

Schaap, Andrew. "Reconciliation as Ideology and Politics." *Constellations* 15, no. 3 (2008): 249–264.

Schaffer, Kay, and Sidonie Smith. *Human Rights and Narrated Lives*. New York: Palgrave, 2004.

Scheler, Max. *Ressentiment*. Translated by Lewis B. Coser and William W. Holdheim. Milwaukee, WI: Marquette University Press, 2010.

Scherrer, Amandine. "Filmer pour voir: Ombre et lumières sur le genocide Khmer." *Cultures & Conflits* 97 (Spring 2015): 145–155.

Schlund-Vials, Cathy J. "Evincing Cambodia's Genocide: Juridical Belatedness, Historical Indictment, and Rithy Panh's *The Missing Picture*." *Contemporary French and Francophone Studies* 20, no. 2 (2016): 287–296.

———. *War, Genocide, and Justice: Cambodian American Memory Work*. Minneapolis: University of Minnesota Press, 2012.

Shahnon Ahmad. *No Harvest but a Thorn*. London: Oxford University Press, 1972.

Short, Damien. "Reconciliation and the Problem of Internal Colonialism." *Journal of Intercultural Studies* 26, no. 3 (2005): 267–282.

Slavin, David Henry. *Colonial Cinema and Imperial France, 1919–1939: White Blind Spots, Male Fantasies, Settler Myths*. Baltimore: Johns Hopkins University Press, 2001.

Staub, Ervin. "Genocide and Mass Killing: Origins, Prevention, Healing and Reconciliation." *Political Psychology* 21, no. 2 (2000): 367–382.

Stoler, Ann. *Carnal Knowledge and Imperial Power: Race and the Intimate in Colonial Rule*. Berkeley: University of California Press, 2002.

Strangio, Sebastian. *Hun Sen's Cambodia*. New Haven, CT: Yale University Press, 2014.

Suong Sikoeun. *Itinéraire d'un intellectuel Khmer Rouge*. Paris: Les Editions du Cerf, 2013.

Tagg, John. *The Disciplinary Frame: Photographic Truths and the Capture of Meaning*. Minneapolis: University of Minnesota Press, 2009.

Taing, Rinith. "Young Artists Explore Lasting Suffering of Forced Marriages." *Phnom Penh Post*, January 11, 2018. https://www.phnompenhpost.com/post-life-arts-culture/young-artists-explore-lasting-suffering-forced-marriages.

Thion, Serge. *Un témoignage occidental: Dans les maquis cambodgiens*. N.p.: Editions F.U.N.C., 1972.

Thompson, Ashley. "Mnemotechnical Politics: Rithy Panh's Cinematic Archive and the Return of Cambodia's Past." In *Modern and Contemporary Southeast Asian Art: An Anthology*, edited by Nora A. Taylor and Boreth Ly, 225–240. Ithaca, NY: Cornell University Press, 2012.

———. "Preface." In Vann Molyvann, *Modern Khmer Cities*, iii–viii. Phnom Penh: Reyum, 2003.

Thompson, James W. *A History of Historical Writing*. Vol. 2. New York: Macmillan, 1942.

Torchin, Leshu. "Mediation and Remediation: La parole filmée in Rithy Panh's *The Missing Picture (L'image manquante)*." *Film Quarterly* 68, no. 1 (2014): 32–41.

"Travelling." In *Le Robert: Dictionnaire historique de la langue française*, edited by Alain Rey, 3: 3901. Paris: Dictionnaires Le Robert, 2000.

Tsang, Hing. *Semiotics and Documentary Film: The Living Sign in the Cinema*. Berlin: De Gruyter, 2013.

Tumarkin, Maria. *Traumascapes: The Power and Fate of Places Transformed by Tragedy*. Melbourne: Melbourne University Publishing, 2005.

Turnbull, Robert. "A Burned-Out Theater: The State of Cambodia's Performing Arts." In *Expressions of Cambodia: The Politics of Tradition, Identity and Change*, edited by Leakthina Chau-Pech Ollier and Tim Winter, 133–149. New York: Routledge, 2006.

Um, Khatharya. *From the Land of Shadows: War, Revolution and the Making of the Cambodian Diaspora*. New York: New York University Press, 2015.

———. *Re/Membering: Meditation on War, Hope, and Home*. An exhibit curated in commemoration of the fortieth anniversary of the Cambodian diaspora, Berkeley, 2015.

"Un barrage contre le Pacifique." *Allociné*. Accessed December 9, 2020. http://www.allocine.fr/film/fichefilm125109/secrets-tournage/.

USAID Counter Trafficking-in-Persons Program. *Internal Migration for Low-Skilled or Unskilled Work in Cambodia: Preliminary Qualitative Results*. Open Institute, June 2016. https://www.open.org.kh/research/Internal_Migration-Qualitative_Results-June2016.pdf.

Vann Molyvann. *Modern Khmer Cities*. Phnom Penh: Reyum, 2003.

Vann Nath. *A Cambodian Prison Portrait: One Year in the Khmer Rouge's S-21*. Translated by Moeun Chhean Nariddh. Bangkok: White Lotus, 1998.

Verdeja, Ernesto. "Derrida and the Impossibility of Forgiveness." *Contemporary Political Theory* 3, no. 1 (2004): 23–47.

Vergès, Françoise. *Monsters and Revolutionaries: Colonial Family Romance and Metissage*. Durham, NC: Duke University Press, 1999.

Vetlesen, Arne Johan. "A Case for Resentment: Jean Améry versus Primo Levi." *Journal of Human Rights* 5 (2006): 27–44.

Vircondelet, Alain. *Duras*. Paris: Editions François Bourin, 1991.

Warren, Charles, ed. *Beyond Document: Essays on Nonfiction Film*. Middletown, CT: Wesleyan University Press, 1996.

Winston, Jane Bradley. *Postcolonial Duras: Cultural Memory in Postwar France*. New York: Palgrave, 2001.

Zolkos, Magdalena. "Jean Améry's Concept of Resentment at the Crossroads of Ethics and Politics." *European Legacy* 12, no. 1 (2007): 23–38.

Zucker, Eve Monique. "Trauma and Its Aftermath: Local Configurations of Reconciliation in Cambodia and the Khmer Rouge Tribunal." *Journal of Asian Studies* 72, no. 4 (2013): 793–800.

NOTES ON CONTRIBUTORS

LESLIE BARNES is senior lecturer of French studies at the Australian National University. Her first book, *Vietnam and the Colonial Condition of French Literature* (2014), offers a literary history of twentieth-century and twenty-first-century France that figures border crossings and contact with the colonial other as constitutive elements of metropolitan literary production. Her current project is focused on literary and cinematic narratives that engage with questions of sex work, mobility, and human rights in Southeast Asia.

STÉPHANIE BENZAQUEN-GAUTIER is an art historian and European Research Council Postdoctoral Research Fellow on the project Cultures of Occupation in Twentieth-Century Asia at the University of Nottingham. She has published on issues of images, remembrance, and political violence in journals such as *Dapim*; *Media, Culture and Society*; and the *Journal of Perpetrator Research*. She is currently working on her first monograph, "Beyond Skulls: Western Visual Culture and the Memory of the Cambodian Genocide."

JENNIFER CAZENAVE is assistant professor of French and film at Boston University. She is the author of *An Archive of the Catastrophe: The Unused Footage of Claude Lanzmann's "Shoah,"* which received an Honorable Mention for the 2020 Best First Book Award from the Society of Cinema and Media Studies. Her work has appeared in several edited volumes and journals, including *Memory Studies* and *Cinema Journal*.

LINDSAY FRENCH is associate professor of anthropology at the Rhode Island School of Design, and current chair of the Department of History, Philosophy, and the Social Sciences. In publications in edited volumes and in *Ethnos*, the *International Journal of Politics, Culture and Society*, and the *Oral History Review*, among others, she has addressed the traffic in antiquities from Angkor Wat; the ethics of exhibiting photographs from S-21, the Khmer Rouge detention and torture center; and the importance of attending to silences in the oral histories of survivors of trauma and genocide.

RACHEL HARRISON is professor of Thai cultural studies at School of Oriental and African Studies, University of London. She has published widely on modern literature, cinema, gender, and sexuality in Thailand, as well as on the comparative literature of Southeast Asia. She is currently conducting research on culture, well-being and public health in relation to diet and disease in Northeast Thailand, Laos, and Cambodia. She is editor of the quarterly journal *South East Asia Research*.

JOHN KLEINEN is a retired associate professor of anthropology, specializing in Vietnam, at the University of Amsterdam. He is the author or coauthor of a number of books and articles in international journals. Along with photography and filmmaking, his research interests include visual anthropology and history. Currently he chairs the board of Spaarnestad Photo-National Archives in the Netherlands.

DAVID LAROCCA is the author, editor, or coeditor of eleven books, including *The Philosophy of Documentary Film: Image, Sound, Fiction, Truth* (2017); *The Philosophy of War Films* (2015); and *The Thought of Stanley Cavell and Cinema* (2020). He participated in a National Institute of the Humanities Institute, a workshop with Abbas Kiarostami, Werner Herzog's Rogue Film School, and the School of Criticism and Theory at Cornell. He has held visiting research and teaching positions at Binghamton, Cornell, Cortland, Harvard, Ithaca College, and Vanderbilt.

BORETH LY is associate professor of Southeast Asian art history and visual culture at the University of California, Santa Cruz. She coedited, with Nora A. Taylor, *Modern and Contemporary Art of Southeast Asia* (2012). In addition, she authored *Traces of Trauma: Cambodian Visual Culture and National Identity in the Aftermath of Genocide* (2020), as well numerous articles and essays on the arts and films of Southeast Asia and its diaspora.

JOSEPH MAI is associate professor of French and a world cinema affiliate at Clemson University. He has published widely on the ethics, politics, and aesthetics of contemporary French cinema and literature. He is the author of *Jean-Pierre and Luc Dardenne* (2010) and *Robert Guédiguian: A Cinema of Friendship* (2017).

RAYA MORAG is associate professor of cinema studies in the Department of Communication and Journalism at the Hebrew University, Jerusalem. Her publications deal with post-traumatic cinema; perpetratorhood and ethics; cinema, war, and masculinity; perpetrator trauma; documentary cinema; and corporeal-feminist film critique. She is the author of *Defeated Masculinity: Post-traumatic Cinema in the Aftermath of War* (2009), *Waltzing with Bashir: Perpetrator Trauma and Cinema* (2013), and *Perpetrator Cinema: Confronting Genocide in Cambodian Documentary* (2020).

SOKO PHAY is full professor in art history and theory at Université Paris 8. She heads the EA 4010 Lab, "Arts des images et art contemporain," and cofounded, with Pierre Bayard, the International Centre of Research and Education on Mass Murders (CIREMM). She has also curated several exhibitions and has devoted several books and edited multiauthor volumes to the links between art and mass crimes. She is the coeditor of *Cambodge, le génocide effacé* (2013), *Cambodge cartographie de la mémoire* (2017), *Archives au présent* (2017), and *Les génocides oubliés?* (2020).

DONALD REID is professor of history at the University of North Carolina at Chapel Hill. He writes widely on the culture and politics of modern France. He is the author of *The Miners of Decazeville: A Genealogy of Deindustrialization* (1985); *Paris Sewers and Sewermen: Realities and Representations* (1991); *Germaine Tillion, Lucie Aubrac, and the Politics of Memories of the French Resistance* (2007); and *Opening the Gates: The Lip Affair, 1968–1981* (2018).

VICENTE SÁNCHEZ-BIOSCA is professor of film studies and visual culture at the University of Valencia. Among his books are *Cine y Guerra Civil Española: Del mito a la memoria* (2006) and *Miradas criminales, ojos de víctima: Imágenes de la aflicción en Camboya* (2017). He currently leads a research project on perpetrators of mass murder and public spaces (museums, memorials) including Buchenwald (Germany), Villa Grimaldi (Chile), Escuela Mecánica de la Armada (Argentina), Valley of the Fallen (Spain) and Tuol Sleng (Cambodia). See the project's site at www.repercri.com.

CATHY J. SCHLUND-VIALS is professor of English and Asian American studies at the University of Texas at Austin; prior to this appointment, she was Board of Trustees Distinguished Professor of English and Asian/Asian American Studies at the University of Connecticut. In addition to numerous articles, book chapters, essays, and edited collections, Schlund-Vials is the author of two monographs: *Modeling Citizenship: Jewish and Asian American Writing* (2011) and *War, Genocide, and Justice: Cambodian American Memory Work* (2012).

KHATHARYA UM is associate professor of Asian American and Asian diaspora studies at the University of California (UC), Berkeley. She has published extensively on Southeast Asia and Southeast Asian diaspora. She is the author of *From the Land of Shadows: War, Revolution and the Making of the Cambodian Diaspora* (2015), and coeditor of *Southeast Asian Migration: People on the Move in Search of Work, Refuge and Belonging* (2015). She is coeditor of the UC Press Critical Refugee Studies Book series.

JACK A. YEAGER is professor of French studies and of women's, gender, and sexuality studies at Louisiana State University in Baton Rouge. His research focuses primarily on Vietnamese Francophone narrative. Among his publications are *The Vietnamese Novel in French: A Literary Response to Colonialism* (1987) and his English translation of Kim Lefèvre's autobiography, *Métisse blanche*, as *White Métisse* (2018).

INDEX

Page numbers in italics refer to photographs.